# Global Human
# Rights Institutions

# GLOBAL HUMAN RIGHTS INSTITUTIONS

## BETWEEN REMEDY AND RITUAL

---

# GERD OBERLEITNER

*with a foreword by Conor Gearty*

polity

First published in 2007 by Polity Press

Polity Press
65 Bridge Street
Cambridge CB2 1UR, UK

Polity Press
350 Main Street
Malden, MA 02148, USA

ISBN-13: 978-07456-3438-8
ISBN-13: 978-07456-3439-5 (pb)

A catalogue record for this book is available from the British Library.

Typeset in 10.5 on 12pt Times
by SNP Best-set Typesetter Ltd., Hong Kong
Printed and bound in Great Britain by Biddles Ltd., King's Lynn, Norfolk

The publisher has used its best endeavours to ensure that the URLs for external websites referred to in this book are correct and active at the time of going to press. However, the publisher has no responsibility for the websites and can make no guarantee that a site will remain live or that the content is or will remain appropriate.

For further information on Polity, visit our website: www.polity.co.uk

# CONTENTS

# DETAILED CONTENTS

# FOREWORD

The idea of universal human rights needs more than ethics on its side if it is to survive in these turbulent times. Fortunately it has that something extra: a range of global human rights institutions with which to drive home its perspective while guarding against its evisceration by the countervailing forces of nationalism, extremism, ethnic particularism, politicized religion, or from wherever it is that the latest challenge has sprung. Global human rights institutions need to see these enemies off while protecting their own core from the dangers of bureaucratization, legalization and systematic hypocrisy. They must do all this while also developing and maturing as the world around them changes, finding new ways to help people both to avoid cruelty and to flourish through the assertion of their dignity. It is a tough task and of course these are failures along the way. But the trajectory is broadly upward, with the idea of human rights having been embedded in the public mind much more effectively for the existence of these institutions than would have been the case had they never been established.

Now global human rights institutions have their biographer. True, Gerd Oberleitner's book contains much that is rightly critical of the bodies that he surveys; his is not only a descriptive account of the origins and development of global human rights institutions, but one which engages also with the darker side, the contact with political reality from which not even the purest of international institutions is immune. But Oberleitner's support for his subject matter also shines through, his commitment to the cause of the institutionalization of human rights evident not only in the devotion that has produced this comprehensive account but also in the argument that he develops for the improvement and reform of the various organs that he has brought under his careful scrutiny. It is clear that 'global human rights institutions matter as the best presently available format for realizing human rights', with 'their proliferation [being] more a benefit than a danger' (p. 182). This diversity 'offers multiple channels of influence: where once individuals stood alone in facing governmental oppression, today there are a multitude of formalized avenues for redress and assistance in global human rights institutions' (p. 179). Dr Oberleitner sees global human rights institutions as particularly important because they 'reflect the move from vision to reality. . . . They allow the move from the acknowledgment of values to their realization on the international level: agreeing on community norms, casting them in legal form, and inventing tools, mechanisms and instruments' (p. 189). Their output 'may often be scant and their power may rest solely on persuasion', despite which 'they realize, in a practical manner, what would otherwise remain a philosophical, moral, religious or political discourse, and as such would be even more remote from meeting the demands of those whose dignity is being trampled upon' (p. 190).

It is clear that Gerd Oberleitner is right when he suggests that 'much would be lost if international institutions were to disappear from the global institutional landscape' (p. 179). Consider as a case study in their indispensability the current crisis generated by the inauguration by the United States and some of its allies of a 'war on terror' in the immediate aftermath of the attacks on New York and Washington on 11 September 2001. Initially human rights took a back seat while the Security Council and other international bodies sought to steer a course between the threat of serious international criminality on the one hand and the urge to sanction extreme state action in the name of counter-terrorism on the other. Gradually, however, as time has gone on, the language of human rights has reasserted itself, quietly at first and then with increased confidence and assurance. This could not have been done without the work of human rights functionaries such as high commissioner Louise Arbour, the special rapporteur on terrorism and human rights Kalliopi Koufa and, more recently, Martin Scheinin, with his report in December 2005 to the old Commission on Human Rights on 'the promotion and protection of human rights and fundamental freedoms while countering terrorism'. At the time of writing, human rights-based pressures are growing to rein in the tendency of Security Council resolutions to disregard due process and fundamental rights in their rush to take strong but non-military action in trouble spots across the world. How would basic rules of fair play, of equity and of respect for human dignity have fared in the first decade of the twenty-first century had they not had their ethical advocate embedded in institutional form within the United Nations and other global bodies?

Gerd Oberleitner has performed an important service in providing an account of global human rights institutions which manages to combine an authoritative descriptive style with a critical scholarly eye. His definition of terms frees him to roam widely across global institutions, assessing those that are obviously central, of course, and also unafraid to delve down pathways that might have been missed by a more hurried writer, but at the end of which are important issues so far as human rights are concerned: the World Bank and IMF, for example (pp. 129–35) and the World Trade Organization (pp. 135–9). Even the role of NGOs, very important is this field, is not missed, securing a chapter all to themselves (chapter 7). The overall effect is one of concise authoritativeness; the interested reader need look no further than Oberleitner for a definitive introductory account of the milieu of global human rights institutions and organs with a brief including human rights that are now to be found scattered across the global stage.

What of the future? In his moving final paragraphs Oberleitner says this:

> Administering and managing human rights, dispersing them into diverse institutional formats and diffusing them in an ever wider array of governmental and human activities may be unexciting and uninspiring and be accompanied by deficiencies and failures common to bureaucracies. This, however, is what it means to pursue a utopian aspiration in a tight political and normative framework, and this is what global human rights institutions do. After all, the road from vision to reality is called pragmatism. (p. 191)

Do we still as a community of nations want to pursue this 'utopian aspiration' or human rights? If we do not, then global human rights institutions will not save us from ourselves; they will drift into one of those nooks into which we manoeuvre ideas whose days have come and gone, an appendix on the international body politic, waiting its turn to be removed. But this is not an inevitable or even a probable future. The idea of human rights has demonstrated its flexible robustness in the past and gives no impression today of not continuing to capture the essence of the ethical life to which many of the worlds' citizens aspire. As long as dreams of justice and fairness and equality remain, there will always be a utopian language of human rights to help put their hopes into words. And with those words comes via global human rights institutions the possibility of concrete action, slow maybe, tedious often, but as essential in its way as the dreams that made such progress conceivable in the first place.

Conor Gearty

# ACKNOWLEDGEMENTS

A book is never just the product of a certain time of researching and writing. This one is the result of encountering human rights, over many years, in different international institutions. It draws on experiences made, as a researcher, in human rights bodies in the UN and in the European and African human rights systems; on being involved with local and international human rights NGOs; on repeated secondments to the human rights department in the office of the legal adviser of the Austrian Ministry for Foreign Affairs and the ensuing participation as a governmental delegate in international human rights bodies; and even on having been an intern, way back in the early 1990s, in the (then) UN Centre for Human Rights in Geneva. In each of these situations I saw human rights institutions with different eyes. The hopes which their work could raise and (more often) the frustrations which their shortcomings could provoke made me want to understand better what those institutions are for, what they do, and why they do it. More specifically, I became interested in what they do *with* human rights and *to* human rights.

When Polity Press expressed an interest in producing a textbook on global human rights institutions, I felt that mapping the field with a critical eye would allow me to wrestle with some of my assumptions, questions and doubts. The original plan of the book was laid out together with Conor Gearty, when I was a lecturer at the Centre for the Study of Human Rights at the London School of Economics and Political Science. I am indebted to Conor not only for working out the original proposal with me and for agreeing to write the preface, but for his encouragement throughout, for many comments on the draft, and for constantly reminding me to be guided by the kind of critical inter-disciplinary human rights scholarship which the centre has come to stand for under his leadership. While most of the book was written at my home institution, the Institute of International Law and International Relations at the University of Graz, I benefited greatly from having been accepted (back) so warmly as a Visiting Fellow at the Centre for the Study of Human Rights. I am grateful to colleagues at both institutions for their continuing support.

Louise Knight and Emma Hutchinson at Polity Press have been supportive and patient in equal measure, and I owe them my warm thanks for kicking off the whole project, putting their trust in me, and agreeing to the inter-disciplinary approach I have taken. I am indebted to many friends and colleagues who provided ideas and commented on various drafts. My particular thanks go to Wolfgang Benedek, Christine Chinkin, Frank Elbers, Francesca Klug, Renate Kicker, Zdzislaw Kedzia, Jan Klabbers, Manfred Nowak, Catrin Pekari, Christian Pippan, Kirsten Schmalenbach, Andrea Shemberg and Bert Theuermann, as well as to the two anonymous reviewers. The book also benefited greatly from many stimulating thoughts and questions from the students I have had the privilege to teach over the years in my human rights classes in the MSc human rights programme at the LSE, at the University of Graz, on the web, and in summer schools and courses in many places. The support of my wife throughout the writing has been essential – thanks, Carla! The book is dedicated to Felix, who makes such a difference.

# ABBREVIATIONS

| | |
|---|---|
| CAT | Convention against Torture and Other Cruel, Inhuman or Degrading Treatment |
| CEDAW | Convention on the Elimination of All Forms of Discrimination against Women |
| CERD | Convention on the Elimination of All Forms of Racial Discrimination |
| CMW | Convention on the Protection of the Rights of All Migrant Workers and Members of Their Families |
| CRC | Convention on the Rights of the Child |
| CSW | Commission on the Status of Women |
| doc. | document |
| DPKO | Department of Peacekeeping Operations |
| DSB | Dispute Settlement Body |
| ECOSOC | Economic and Social Council |
| FAO | Food and Agricultural Organization |
| FIFA | Fédération Internationale de Football Association |
| GATS | General Agreement on Trade in Services |
| GATT | General Agreement on Tariffs and Trade |
| GRULAC | Group of Latin American and Caribbean Countries |
| HABITAT | United Nations Human Settlements Programme |
| HIV/AIDS | Human Immuno-Deficiency Virus/Acquired Immuno-Deficiency Syndrome |
| HURIST | Global Programme on Human Rights Strengthening |
| IBRD | International Bank for Reconstruction and Development |
| ICC | International Criminal Court |

| | |
|---|---|
| ICCPR | International Covenant on Civil and Political Rights |
| ICESCR | International Covenant on Economic, Social and Cultural Rights |
| ICISS | International Commission on Intervention and State Sovereignty |
| ICJ | International Court of Justice |
| ICRC | International Committee of the Red Cross |
| ICSID | International Centre for the Settlement of Investment Disputes |
| ICTR | International Criminal Tribunal for Rwanda |
| ICTY | International Criminal Tribunal for the Former Yugoslavia |
| IDA | International Development Association |
| IFC | International Finance Corporation |
| ILO | International Labour Organization |
| IMF | International Monetary Fund |
| ITU | International Telecommunication Union |
| MDGs | Millennium Development Goals |
| MIGA | Multilateral Investment Guarantee Agency |
| NGO | non-governmental organization |
| OCHA | Office for Humanitarian Affairs |
| OHCHR | Office of the High Commissioner for Human Rights |
| para. | paragraph |
| PCIJ | Permanent Court of International Justice |
| PMC | Permanent Mandates Commission |
| PRSP | Poverty Reduction Strategy Paper |
| TPRM | Trade Policy Review Mechanism |
| TRIPS | Trade-related Aspects of Intellectual Property Rights |
| UN | United Nations |
| UNDP | United Nations Development Programme |
| UNESCO | United Nations Educational, Scientific and Cultural Organization |
| UNHCR | United Nations High Commissioner for Refugees |
| UNICEF | United Nations Children's Fund |
| UNIFEM | United Nations Development Fund for Women |
| UPR | Universal Periodic Review |
| VDPA | Vienna Declaration and Programme of Action |
| WEOG | Western European and Others Group |
| WHO | World Health Organization |
| WIPO | World Intellectual Property Organization |
| WSIS | World Summit on the Information Society |
| WTO | World Trade Organization |

# 1 INTRODUCTION

The establishment of a breadth and range of global human rights institutions over the past half century seems a remarkable achievement. Today, a complex web of institutions is entrusted with protecting and promoting human rights and with preventing and remedying human rights violations. They fulfil a variety of functions that would have been inconceivable a few years, let alone decades, ago. What is often described as a system, though, is a multitude of entities which vary greatly in their range, remit and composition. Established *ad hoc* in response to concrete needs rather than as part of any master plan, such institutions have experienced sustained, yet mostly unplanned and uncoordinated, growth and internal development. In addition to the proliferation of institutions specifically entrusted with human rights matters, the idea of mainstreaming human rights is increasingly leading institutions charged with humanitarian, development, health-related, economic and other issues to perceive human rights as part of their mandate or to develop policies and activities on human rights.

The sustained development and growth of global human rights institutions pose considerable challenges to international politics, international legal and international relations scholarship and reveal a series of questions: Why do states create human rights institutions in the first place, knowing that all they will do is nag about states' preparedness to respect human rights? What do states seek to achieve through such cooperation, and is it different from what the institutions themselves seek to accomplish? Questions as to the practical consequences and the effectiveness of establishing and expanding an ever tighter institutional web composed of bodies, councils and commissions, with their professional human rights bureaucrats, monitors, judges and experts, flow from these queries: Are multilateral forums suitable venues for protecting human rights, or do they provide a fig leaf for governmental inaction in the face of massive human suffering? What happens to human rights when they are being encased in global institutions? What are the benefits, consequences and drawbacks of institutionalizing human rights? Does the latter turn human rights, this powerful force for social change, into a stale bureaucratic routine? Or does it give practical meaning to otherwise lofty goals? How does the design of a global human rights 'infrastructure' impede the implementation of human rights, and how does their continuing institutionalization affect our understanding of human rights? Many of these questions have never been systematically examined (Steiner, 2003: 760).

Like states, individuals, too, have long since joined forces and established voluntary associations on a global scale. The likes of Amnesty International, Human Rights Watch and the International Commission of Jurists have over time acquired a strong position towards both states and inter-governmental organizations. In fact, those non-governmental organizations (NGOs) have become indispensable to the successful development and implementation of human rights, and their impact on the work of inter-governmental organizations can be considerable. As with inter-governmental organizations, their spread and rising influence deserves critical appraisal: What is their role and legal standing in international affairs and international law? Who do they represent? Are they the antithesis of inter-governmental organizations or merely another component in a proliferating global 'bureaucratic' web?

This book is an introduction both to the world of global human rights institutions and to the challenges and paradoxes of 'institutionalizing' human rights. It provides a comprehensive treatment of such institutions, both governmental and non-governmental. It examines institutions established within the United Nations (UN) which are explicitly mandated with the promotion and protection of human rights; the process of mainstreaming human rights into formerly 'non-political' or 'technical' institutions; international courts which adjudicate human rights; and human rights NGOs. In mapping the ever more complex network of such global human rights institutions it asks, in essence, what these institutions *are* and what they *are for*, and whether this 'hardware' of the global human rights system is fit for today's demands.

This book does not describe or analyse human rights norms, standards and principles, nor is it a handbook on how to use international procedures and mechanisms. Such questions of substance (What are human rights?) and procedure (How are they realized?) find answers in a number of other textbooks. The analysis of institutional aspects of the global human rights system and the relationship between form and function has attracted less attention. What is of interest here are the expectations for and consequences of institutionalizing human rights, as well as the advantages and drawbacks of this process. By critically assessing and appraising the increased 'institutionalization' or 'bureaucratization' of human rights through an ever expanding range of global institutions, the following chapters reflect on how this process may change our perception of human rights. Given the approach and scope of the book as an introductory text, this will amount neither to an empirical assessment of how international human rights regimes lead to domestic change (such as the one undertaken by, e.g., Risse, Ropp and Sikkink, 1999) nor to the formulation of a comprehensive theory on the behaviour of international organizations (as carried out by, e.g., Barnett and Finnemore, 2004). What this book seeks to achieve is to bring together, in an accessible way, the multitude of global institutions which are concerned with human rights, and to acknowledge and analyse the manifold legal questions and theoretical concerns associated with the institutionalization of international relations in the field of human rights.

In examining these questions, the book draws on international legal scholarship and international relations literature alike. It goes without saying that such an approach may leave scholars in both fields unsatisfied, as it will not do justice to the particular theoretical depths which each discipline has reached in discussing human rights. This has to be weighed against the hope that the book will contribute to a growing literature that sees human rights as an inter-disciplinary concept. The need to understand the competences and constraints of human rights institutions necessitates, first and foremost, a dissection of international human rights law. As a consequence the predominance of legal discourse in matters of human rights will become visible in the following chapters. Yet, the book rests on the assumption that 'excessive attention to human-rights law distorts our understanding of human rights' (Freeman, 2002: 12). International law alone is insufficient to understand why human rights institutions are being formed, what they do and why they do it, what they seek to achieve and where they fail, and what sort of human rights infrastructure we are effectively creating.

For the purpose of this analysis, the term 'global human rights institutions' brings together a range of entities of diverse legal character, internal organization and appearance. The vagueness of the term 'global human rights institution' is one of deliberate choice: this is not a treatise of the law of international organizations, nor does it fan out theories on institutions and regimes as elements of international relations. It simply allows the examination of formally established institutions which have, or are perceived to have, a profound impact on the way in which human rights are developed, implemented, supervised, enforced or promoted on a global scale. The focus is on formally established institutions and not on 'the human rights movement' or networks and coalitions concerned with the promotion and protection of human rights, or on UN conferences or initiatives, such as the UN Global Compact (which brings together business, inter-governmental agencies and civil society groups in support of social and human rights principles). This is not to deny the importance of such networks and initiatives for the development of human rights; in fact some of those initiatives may have a more profound impact than the work of inter-governmental bodies. Likewise, the discussion of regional human rights institutions in Europe, the Americas and Africa is beyond the remit of this book, notwithstanding that some of these systems have more sophisticated and sustainable institutions, including human rights courts, for the protection and promotion of human rights.

The approach of the book is both descriptive in a functional sense, mapping the field of global human rights institutions and their activities, and analytical and critical in its exposure of the advantages and dangers of organizing human rights in institutional formats. Chapter 2 raises some theoretical questions and discusses the process of institutionalizing human rights, the (self-)perception of global human rights institutions and the paradoxes encountered in casting human rights in formal structures. Chapter 3 traces the development of global human rights institutions, from first attempts of social movements to promote humanitarian issues via the League of Nations and the International Labour Organization (ILO) to the UN. Chapters 4 to 6 present, discuss and critically assess global human rights institutions, thus demonstrating the practical consequences of the theoretical and conceptual concerns raised before. More specifically, chapter 4 introduces UN human rights institutions with an explicit mandate to promote and protect human rights, commonly referred to as the 'UN human rights system', including the UN Human Rights Council as the most recent innovation. Chapter 5 discusses the progress and challenges of mainstreaming human rights into institutions entrusted with global humanitarian, social, economic and financial concerns. In doing so, it takes stock of a decade of mainstreaming human rights since the

UN Secretary-General's proposal on this in 1997 and also highlights the Security Council's position towards human rights. Chapter 6 is devoted to international tribunals, which play an increasingly important role for the adjudication of human rights violations. It examines the International Court of Justice (ICJ) and the International Criminal Court (ICC) and discusses the prospects for a world court on human rights. Chapter 7 turns to global non-governmental institutions, the rise of which not only accompanies but exceeds the growth of inter-governmental institutions. It focuses less on the role of NGOs vis-à-vis governments, or the emergence of a global civil society, and more on the nexus between inter-governmental and non-governmental institutions as two structural frameworks for human rights.

# 2 INSTITUTIONALIZING HUMAN RIGHTS: EXPECTATIONS, PARADOXES AND CONSEQUENCES

The term 'institution' is charged with a specific meaning in various academic disciplines and their schools. As a matter of fact, in both international law and international relations the respective terminology is disputed. While international law clearly sets apart inter-governmental from non-governmental organizations as two types of organization rooted in different legal grounds (the former in international law, the latter in national law), the difference between an international 'organization' and an 'organ' is less clear. At times a sharp distinction is made between the two, at others both terms are used interchangeably, or the notion 'international institution' is used as a synonym (Klabbers, 2002: 10). International relations theory applies the term institution differently from international law (Lang, 1994), and the move in the 1970s away from the study of formally established international organizations to that of 'regimes' has altered the discipline's understanding of what an 'institution' is. Today, a range of usages of the notion 'institution' exist (Simmons and Martin, 2002: 192–4), and often institutions are equated with international regimes, that is 'sets of implicit or explicit principles, norms, rules and decision-making procedures around which actors' expectations converge in a given area of international relations', to use Krasner's standard definition (Krasner, 1983: 2). In human rights scholarship, the term 'human rights regime' is, in a similar way, often used to describe the totality of relevant standards, procedures and institutions in the field of human rights (Donnelly, 1984; Nowak, 2003; Donnelly, 2003: 127–54).

For the purpose of this analysis, the term 'institution' refers to formally established international organizations and their organs, international courts and international non-governmental organizations. The following chapters approach global human rights institutions neither from a realist perspective (which would assert that such institutions are nothing but states in disguise) nor with an idealist assumption that their existence and output is necessarily beneficial for all parties concerned. What is said here is based on the premise that such institutions matter, but that we still find it difficult to explain why and how they matter. This analysis presents a range of such institutions, based on a more constructivist approach, which asks if, why, and how they are able to assert themselves as autonomous actors for 'managing' global human rights norms and what consequences this may entail.

The question why states set up global institutions continues to puzzle international relations scholars and drives international lawyers in their ongoing search for a legal theory of international organizations. With idealists and neoliberals pointing out their significance and necessity, functionalists invoking their usefulness, institutionalists and constructivists asserting their influence, realists being sceptical about all that, and normative theories dissecting their foundations, there is no shortage of analytical engagement with international organizations. Yet, as Abbott and Snidal have remarked, neither of these theories 'adequately explains why states use formal international organizations; each holds key insights' (Abbott and Snidal, 2001: 12–15). Once set up, international institutions confront us with another set of questions, which interestingly has found less resonance in international relations scholarship (Barnett and Finnemore, 2004: 2): What are such institutions: autonomous actors or puppets on governments' strings? What makes them behave the way that they do? Is it their masters, the states, that set them up, or are they endowed with a will of their own? And where would such a will come from? International lawyers consider such questions in the form of legal theories. They award or deny international institutions different degrees of legal 'personality' or 'subjectivity', and they attribute or withdraw powers on the basis of such theories (e.g., Klabbers, 2002: 42–81).

Human rights institutions seem to be a particularly fertile ground for analysing such questions. The matter they manage – human rights – makes the existence and proliferation of such institutions even more enigmatic than the spread of international institutions in other fields. Unlike many global institutions devoted to cooperation in 'technical' areas (say, the Universal Postal Union), international cooperation in human rights is politically sensitive, and the activities of human rights institutions are more likely to be a constant provocation to governments, a conceptual challenge for international law and an irritation for (realist) international relations scholarship. The idea of human rights continuously tests the established concepts of sovereignty, territoriality and non-interference in domestic affairs, allows individuals to stand up against states in ways unimaginable in other fields of international law, questions the primacy of states in international affairs, and thus forecasts a more participatory and inclusive international legal order. Why would states support all this by setting up human rights institutions? Surprisingly, and in contrast to discussing the existence of international institutions as a general phenomenon, the evolution of international institutions specifically devoted to human rights has attracted less attention in international relations scholarship (Schmitz and Sikkink, 2002: 528), and so has their performance. Likewise, international legal scholarship, while engaging with human rights institutions, has largely been content to describe such institutions rather than to debate the conditions for and consequences of their establishment and proliferation. While this book does not aim to put forward a comprehensive theory to settle such questions, some assumptions and paradoxes with regard to the establishment and behaviour of such institutions will be discerned in the following, as they have a profound impact on the way in which these institutions approach human rights.

## Efficiency, legitimacy, power

One main assumption as to why states set up international institutions is that such bodies are useful because they provide a means of cooperation in areas in which such cooperation is to the advantage of all participants. Bennett and Oliver, for example, argue that their creation is not only logical for states, but indispensable, because they provide channels for communication; they allow for decisions on such cooperation to be reached; they offer an administrative machinery for supporting this process and putting the decision into action; and they offer a way of settling differences and finding compromises, thus minimizing the effects of conflicts (Bennett and Oliver, 2002). The same is said to be true of the ability of international institutions to guarantee a higher level of stability, durability and predictability than can be achieved by purely inter-state relations (Abbott and Snidal, 2001). States may be interested in setting up and acceding to human rights institutions to achieve results they would find difficult or impossible to realize in bilateral encounters: adopting a treaty on the rights of children, defining the scope of the right to housing, or settling disputes over what constitutes a violation of freedom of expression.

The reduction of transaction costs in deciding on and implementing community norms is, however, only part of the answer as to why states set up human rights institutions. To the rationality and stability which international institutions may offer, other (sociological) considerations may be added which link international institutions with legitimacy and power (Barnett and Finnemore, 1999: 702). Wielding power, i.e., influencing decisions, is an important, if not the most important, incentive which makes states participate in human rights institutions. Such participation allows them to shape the outcome of the work of these institutions in line with their national interest, to defend their position, to avert scrutiny, to confront other states with accusations, or, at the very minimum, to be kept informed on developments and trends in the field of human rights. Still, states' attitudes towards and expectations for human rights institutions differ. In the Commission on Human Rights, for example, China has repeatedly undertaken considerable efforts to avert, through procedural means, the adoption of a critical resolution on its own human rights situation, while other countries, such as Burma/Myanmar, largely ignore whatever resolution the Commission may consider passing. There are also differences in what, e.g., Cuba may seek to achieve by membership in the UN Human Rights Council compared to, e.g., Sweden. Yet, while there is some scholarly engagement with the factors affecting states' desire to wield influence in international organizations (Smith, 2006: 27–8), there is comparably little (empirical) research to analyse and explain such different attitudes and expectations in the field of human rights (with a few exceptions, e.g., Kent, 1999).

Concerns over legitimacy, coupled with an interest in a state's credibility and international reputation, is the third element in explaining why states participate in human rights institutions (Barnett and Finnemore, 1999: 703). Both the creation of an international human rights institution and the participation therein may be considered as endowing governments with legitimacy, credibility and reputation. Moreover, it is worth noting that sometimes institutions are not only set up for what they do, but also for what they are and what they symbolize (ibid.). Human rights institutions may be particularly prone to conveying the doubtful message that participation in such an institution would, in itself, raise a state's reputation in matters of human rights or be a contribution to their advancement. Was this, for example, the reason why Libya sought to chair the UN Commission on Human Rights in 2003 (and succeeded in doing so)? Or was it the result of group dynamics in the African regional bloc in the commission which put its trust in Libya to best represent its concerns? Or was it other considerations that guided Libya's decision? Again, in the absence of studies into these questions, speculations have to fill in where research is lacking. All three considerations together – efficiency, legitimacy and power – may, however, help to explain why international human rights institutions are set up, and why states compete for membership in human rights bodies.

## Arena, instrument, actor

This description of international institutions as arenas, instruments and actors is also helpful for understanding why states set up human rights institutions and explaining their role, potential and limits (Archer, 2001: 68–92; White, 2005: 47–59). As instruments, international institutions are used by member states for their purposes and act as mere transmissions for participating governments, executing their decisions and projecting national policies to the international level. As an arena, they provide an (allegedly neutral) space in which inter-governmental action takes place, facilitating meetings, discussions, negotiations and decision-making. As actors, inter-governmental organizations assume independence above and beyond the wishes of member states. Such independence does not mean the elevation to actors *on a par* with states, but rather that the institutions may respond in ways that differ from states' expectations and requests (Archer, 2001: 79). After all, institutions do not always develop as expected: 'use confers power and power unused diminishes' (O'Donovan, 1992: 105).

Those three functions are usually interwoven, with sometimes one function being foregrounded, then the other. And indeed no single function alone sufficiently explains what international institutions are and what they do. The view that they are mere instruments is proven wrong by many practical instances of institutions acting in their own capacity or simply misbehaving (Barnett and Finnemore, 1999: 715). The view that institutions are mere arenas is naïve, as it assumes that form and procedure of such institutions, and decisions over such form and procedure, are 'apolitical', which they most certainly are not (as will be shown below). And the view that institutions are independent has the utopian touch of institutions as global human rights guardians which are able to curtail states as they see fit, which is not the case in reality.

In the Commission on Human Rights, the arena/instrument dichotomy was usually expressed in terms of a 'cooperative' versus a 'confrontational' approach. Whenever a group of states (usually Western) pushed for the adoption of a country resolution, they were accused of instrumentalizing this allegedly neutral forum for political purposes – to which Western states responded that their counterparts would prevent the Commission from acting in an effective manner. At times, human rights institutions free themselves from the constraints of being mere instruments or arenas, and go about their business in a more autonomous way. The UN Human Rights Committee (the expert committee set up to monitor implementation of the International Covenant on Civil and Political Rights) is an independent body and arguably the closest the UN has come to a human rights 'tribunal' (notwithstanding it lacks any enforcement capacity). And the UN High Commissioner for Human Rights provides perhaps a striking example of the tensions arising from being an actor and an instrument, as the holder of this post is both secretary to the UN and its member states and mandated to speak out on human rights violations in those very states.

Ignoring that all human rights institutions, to varying degrees, may simultaneously be arena, instrument and actor leads to a misunderstanding as to their potential and limits. To put it in other words: the mistaken perception that global human rights institutions are always and only autonomous actors is at the heart of much of the frustration over their performance. On the other hand, the view that they do not matter at all because they are nothing other than a reflection of the will of some powerful states is equally short-sighted and does not properly reflect the reality of human rights institutions.

# Autonomy and dependence

The last of the three functions mentioned above – institutions as autonomous actors – deserves closer analysis, as it lies at the heart of the often heard outcry that 'the UN must do something!'. Is there such a thing as 'the UN' (or 'the Human Rights Council') as an autonomous entity, or is the organization (or the organ, in the case of the Council) merely the sum of its members? Different strands of international relations and legal scholarship argue that international institutions can be autonomous and powerful actors in global politics (Barnett and Finnemore, 1999: 700, with an overview of the respective authors). In much the same vein, Abbott and Snidal speak of the two main functions of international organizations, centralization – i.e., managing 'collective activities through a concrete and stable structure and a supportive administrative apparatus' – and independence, which is 'the ability to act with a degree of autonomy within defined spheres' (Abbott and Snidal, 2001: 10–11). Similarly, principal-agent analysis understands international institutions as 'agents' of states ('principals'), and asks whether agents are simple delegates of their principles or whether they pursue their own preferences (authors quoted in Barnett and Finnemore, 1999: 705).

International legal theory is plagued by the same problem: is an international organization an autonomous legal personality, distinct from the assembled member states and endowed with a will of its own, or does it depend entirely on its member states to function? The view that international organizations are mere arenas for international cooperation, empty shells to be filled with states' demands, is now viewed largely as simplistic and outdated (White, 1997: 1–2). To explain the dichotomy of dependence and independence, different solutions have been put forward (Klabbers, 2002: 34–41; Alvarez, 2006: 336–9). The theory of functional necessity is based on the premise that an organization can claim all those rights and privileges which enable it to function effectively. The implied powers doctrine considers all those powers which an organization needs to function effectively as inferred in its founding documents. The doctrine of attributed powers leaves member states in control over their creation by negating all powers which have not expressly been attributed to it. An objective theory of the personality of international organizations was suggested by Seyersted in the 1960s, the effect of which would be to grant them inherent powers and allow them everything that is not expressly prohibited in their constituent documents (Klabbers, 2002: 75). Still, as in international relations scholarship, no overall or universally accepted theory has yet solved the dichotomy of the independence and at the same time dependence of international institutions.

This dichotomy affects human rights institutions, whether they are governmental councils, independent expert bodies, hybrid institutions composed of governmental and non-governmental representatives, secretariat units of international organizations, specialized agencies or international tribunals. As mentioned above, the position of UN High Commissioner for Human Rights, created by UN member states in a General Assembly resolution, is placed in a delicate situation. The High Commissioner is called upon to serve governments as part of the UN secretariat, but is at the same time entrusted with a mandate to protect and promote human rights as if acting as an independent entity, when in fact she or he remains answerable to the UN Human

Rights Council, a governmental body. Despite the High Commissioner being entangled in this matrix of dependence and accountability, many perceive the post as a partner in – and even leader of – the global human rights movement. The shaky legal foundations of the special procedures of the Human Rights Council, to give yet another example, entitle mandate holders to work completely independently, yet they are unable to visit states without prior consent. Furthermore, they depend on the services of the UN secretariat, the resources and mandate of which are controlled by exactly the same governments that the mandate holders are meant to scrutinize. Nor are international courts exempt from this dichotomy. They are not only dependent on support from states, but the ICJ, for example, despite being part and parcel of the UN's machinery, can only be accessed once states have specifically accepted its jurisdiction. The criminal tribunals for the former Yugoslavia and for Rwanda were set up by the Security Council and remain dependent on the Council, while the ICC is based on an international treaty, of which state parties remain the masters. The autonomy of international courts can, furthermore, be curtailed by legal manoeuvres such as the successful move of the USA to make states approve bilateral agreements requiring them not to surrender American nationals to the ICC (the so-called Article 98 agreements). International courts also remain dependent on states' support in enforcing their decisions. Even the European Court of Human Rights, arguably the most advanced judicial mechanism for remedying human rights violations, has to rely on the Committee of Ministers (the Council of Europe's inter-governmental body) to supervise the execution of its judgments.

All of this is a reflection of what may be termed 'Frankenstein's dilemma'. At some point in Mary Shelley's novel, Frankenstein's creature, trying to break free from his miserable life, hurls into Frankenstein's face: 'You are my creator, but I am your master; – obey!' It is a dilemma all international institutions face (Klabbers, 2002: 28–81), but institutions mandated with upholding individual rights against the very states that have created them are exceptionally prone to suffer from it. In setting up human rights institutions, states seem to express a dual expectation: on the one hand they wish such institutions to remain at their disposal to increase efficiency in cooperation, enhance their legitimacy and power, and serve as their arenas and instruments. On the other hand, they want such institutions to reach a degree of autonomy from states which would allow them to confront their creators with their deviant behaviour. To fulfil the latter expectation, however, they would have to 'develop along their human rights mandate rather than state preferences' (Schmitz and Sikkink, 2002: 526).

## Form and function

Unlike human rights activists, movements or initiatives, global human rights institutions work in a strictly institutional, bureaucratic and legal framework. They seek to translate the concerns of human rights – upholding human dignity, protecting the vulnerable, empowering the powerless, remedying wrongdoing – into processes and procedures. In order to gain access to global human rights institutions, victims have to be turned into 'parties' submitting a 'communication', or else they go unheard; perpetrators have to be labelled as 'agents of the state', or else they cannot be held accountable; and NGOs have to seek 'consultative status' with inter-governmental bodies, or else they will not gain access to the conference hall. Form and procedure begin to matter, and function may be moulded to fit the form. In the choice of the appropriate body, the proper procedure and the suitable mechanism lie the chances for success and failure for those who seek redress, assistance or guidance. The novice in matters of human rights is confronted with an astounding array of questions: in the case of, say, torture, what is the appropriate forum, and why – the UN Human Rights Committee, the UN Committee on the Prevention of Torture, the UN Special Rapporteur on Torture, or the ICC? And what difference does it make that in 2004 the UN Commission on Human Rights appointed an Independent Expert on Sudan under its agenda item 3 ('organization of work') rather than item 9 ('violation of human rights in any part of the world')?

The choice of forum and procedure is crucial, but the exuberance of human rights bodies, committees, councils, working groups and commissions, with their different rules of procedures and working methods, makes access for victims and their advocates difficult. For the uninitiated, navigation through this jumble is challenging. Excluding unrepresented groups on procedural grounds is common, and even those groups and individuals who gain access to the meeting rooms of international institutions must transform their concerns in response to formal requirements. It is not so much the preamble of the UN Charter ('We, the peoples') that matters in UN conferences, but formal and informal codes of behaviour which regulate issues such as accreditation, speaking times, lobbying, or the circulation of documents. How to convey the plight of your fellow sufferers to a human rights body in only three minutes? How best to approach the ambassador of Pakistan? How to submit a document formally? For those wishing to participate or seeking redress and assistance, the rules of procedure are as important as the rules of personal networking (Smith, 2006: 223–45).

Form matters not only for individuals and groups seeking to access global human rights institutions, but for states, too, when they set up or participate in such institutions. In the architecture, structure and form of human rights institutions lies just as great a challenge for human rights as in interpreting their content and scope. Indeed, 'in states' decisions about architecture lie some of the most acerbic fights and deepest divisions in the human rights movement' (Steiner and Alston, 2000: 562). One need not recall the struggle over setting up the ICC, as a more unassuming example may suffice: the composition of the Office of the High Commissioner in terms of the geographic distribution of staff is a recurring contentious issue in inter-governmental debates in the UN, as reflected in the Office's most recent report in this respect (UN doc. E/CN.4/2006/103). Similarly, whenever human rights bodies have to resort to voluntary contributions to make up for what is lacking in an organization's regular budget, discussions follow suit over the influence donors gain by offering such contributions. The struggle over design and modalities, procedure and membership, voting rules and methods of work is a fight not only over influence and power but often also over the place and role of human rights in international affairs.

## Bureaucracy: authority and alienation

Let us take further the argument that form matters as much as substance: would we then have to conclude that the establishment of ever more institutions for the protection and promotion of human rights turns human rights, the rallying-cry of the subjugated against their oppressive governments, into a bureaucratic affair? And is this a development we should wish for or dread? Philip Allott has offered perhaps the most scathing critique of institutionalizing human rights:

> But, as so often in human social experience, the installation of human rights in the international constitution after 1945 has been paradoxical. The idea of human rights quickly became perverted by the self-misconceiving of international society. Human rights were quickly appropriated by governments, embodied in treaties, made part of the stuff of primitive international relations, swept up into the maw of an

international bureaucracy. The reality of the idea of human rights has been degraded. From being a source of ultimate anxiety for usurping holders of public social power, they were turned into bureaucratic small-change. Human rights, a reservoir of unlimited power in all the self-creating of society, became a plaything of governments and lawyers. The game of human rights has been played in international statal organizations by diplomats and bureaucrats, and their appointees, in the setting and ethos of traditional international relations. The result has been that the potential and energy of the idea has been dissipated. Alienation, corruption, tyranny, and oppression have continued wholesale in many societies all over the world. And in all societies governments have been reassured in their arrogance by the idea that, if they are not proved actually to be violating the substance of particularized human rights, if they can bring their willing and acting within the wording of this or that formula with its lawyerly qualifications and exceptions, then they are doing well enough. The idea of human rights should intimidate governments or it is worth nothing. If the idea of human rights reassures governments it is worse than nothing. (Allott, 1990: 287–8)

The development of international bureaucracies as embodied in international institutions follows the same pattern as described for domestic bureaucracies by various strands of sociological theory beginning with Max Weber (Barnett and Finnemore, 1999: 706). International bureaucracies, like all bureaucracies, control knowledge and information, and therein lies much of their strength and authority. It allows them to classify information, actors and actions; define problems; articulate norms; fix meanings; and enforce values and norms. Barnett and Finnemore have recently shown how the fact that international organizations are bureaucracies helps explain their status and behaviour as autonomous entities (Barnett and Finnemore, 2004: 16–44). Their argument rests on the idea that, in international relations, authority may not be derived only from state sovereignty. Consequently, the authority which international organizations possess may not come solely from being set up by states, but may be a rational-legal authority (stemming from the regulatory framework in which bureaucracies operate), a moral authority (which comes from a bureaucracy's perceived neutrality, impartiality and objectivity) or an expert authority (which reflects the bureaucracy's control over knowledge). International organizations, Barnett and Finnemore say,

> can have authority both because of the missions they pursue and because of the ways they pursue them. International organizations act to promote socially valued goals, such as human rights, providing development assistance, and brokering peace agreements. International organizations

use their credibility as promoters of 'progress' toward these valued goals to command deference, that is, exercise authority, in these arenas of action. In addition, because they are bureaucracies, international organizations carry out their missions by means that are mostly rational, technocratic, impartial, and non-violent. This often makes international organizations appear more legitimate to more actors than self-serving states that employ coercive tactics in pursuit of their particularistic goals. Their means, like their missions, give international organizations authority to act where individual states may not. (Barnett and Finnemore, 2004: 5)

While their bureaucratic nature is a prominent reason why states set up global human rights institutions in the first place and – based on the assumption that their legal, rational, and technocratic approach makes them legitimate – allow them to 'take charge of a problem and sort it out' (Barnett and Finnemore, 2004: 22), the consequences of their exercise of power and authority may be less positive. Like others, Barnett and Finnemore, too, have described in detail the 'pathologies' of international organizations that derive from their bureaucratic nature: inflexible rules and procedures, insensitivity to particular situations for the sake of 'bureaucratic universalism', and insulation as a result of professionalism, to name but a few (ibid.: 31–4).

Indeed, authoritative control over information on and expertise in human rights creates a human rights bureaucracy which runs the danger of being increasingly remote from the realities on the ground. Henry Steiner once asked, much in the same vein as Philip Allott, 'has the human rights movement then constructed a paper paradise for its advocates and bureaucrats that fails to touch the world's victims?' (Steiner, 1998). Given that human rights not only form a protective shield against governmental repression but are also tools for individual empowerment, such a critique is particularly alarming. It not only covers the allegation that the enforcement mechanisms for international human rights norms are ineffective, but means, more fundamentally, that, even where there is room for translating international norms into domestic change, global human rights institutions hinder rather than enhance this process. Decisions which affect local communities are taken in faraway places, or in commissions and councils often hardly known outside expert circles. Must it be feared that the more efficiently this international human rights machinery runs, the more alienated and disempowered the victims feel? David Kennedy has described this process of disempowering and demobilizing individuals by the international human rights bureaucracy as 'attention turning like sunflowers to Geneva, New York, to the Centre, to the Commission. To the work of resolutions and reports' (Kennedy, 2002: 120). This is why the move from headquarters to the field, as undertaken by the UN High Commissioner for Human Rights over the past years, is so important as a corrective.

The tendency of bureaucracies to be self-referential is particularly dangerous for institutions that are in need of reform. This is the case with global human rights institutions, given that they have mostly been established *ad hoc* in response to needs and with little long-term planning, and are based on compromises among negotiating governments. Indeed, many of them are permanent building sites rather than stable frameworks, seeking to make ends meet with scarce resources, striving for outside support, and constantly adjusting their work so as to enhance coordination and cooperation. Necessary as such perpetual improvements are, their effect may be to turn institutions into dysfunctional entities fluttering around each other in disregard for events in the outside world and entirely absorbed with reforming alleged and existing shortcomings. David Kennedy once remarked that 'reform of the human rights movement is not reform of the world' (Kennedy, 2002: 118), thus referring to the trap into which bureaucracies tend to fall, namely a self-referential attitude which is entirely concerned with internal processes. One should, however, not forget that, as with quarrels over budgets and posts, the reform of human rights institutions is, in addition, the place where not only diverging interests but also different positions as to the role and relevance of human rights collide. In reforming the (then) UN Commission on Human Rights (now the Human Rights Council), euphemisms such as 'streamlining' or 'rationalizing' covered up attempts by states to cut back existing monitoring mechanisms rather than making them more efficient.

# Predominance of law

Professionalizing, formalizing, institutionalizing and bureaucratizing human rights are largely processes of legalization. Lawyers might feel comfortable with this, but there is a growing stream of critique on the predominance of law in human rights (e.g., Freeman, 2002). The advantages and shortcomings of expressing human rights in terms of (international) law have to be weighed carefully. After all, law puts human rights on firmer ground than debates on values, traditions, attitudes and morality can offer. Law offers definitions, and it subjects human rights to accepted rules of legal reasoning and interpretation. It puts human rights in an established and tested framework and makes practical tools available, including judicial means. It turns human rights from demands to entitlements and from needs to rights which correspond with duties. It assures consistency in legal practice and discourse and inserts means of control and coercion into human rights.

On the other hand, institutionalizing human rights also means squeezing values and ideas that were meant to empower individuals into the straitjacket of international institutional law. This particular field of international law is both overly narrow and surprisingly fragmentary (Klabbers, 2002: 5–6). It is exclusionist in its focus on states and its neglect of social realities, and insecure in attributing entitlements and responsibilities to the actors it seeks to cover. In swerving between the contradictory poles of sovereignty and community, it provides little certainty in which human rights could be placed as a global good. Furthermore, the predominance of law in human rights ensures that any possible gains come at the expense of excluding other views – sociological, anthropological, religious, etc. It creates a system caught in its own doctrinal borders and rituals, inaccessible to the outsider and unresponsive to innovation. It has empowered lawyers and created elites of human rights experts, and it often seems to 'denaturate' the human rights discourse. Global human rights institutions are expressions and bulwarks of such a legal approach to human rights, with all its advantages and drawbacks.

## Exclusion and inclusion

The more activities human rights institutions take on, and the further they reach, the more important will stakeholders consider it to gain access to them and be represented in their deliberations. Yet, given that global human rights institutions are covered by international law, they tend to exclude non-state actors as a matter of principle. While a range of NGOs has – albeit limited – participation rights in some institutions (this will be discussed in more detail in chapter 6), it is particularly the most marginalized, vulnerable, and non-dominant groups that find it hardest to gain access to human rights institutions. Obstacles to both formal participation and informal influence abound (Smith, 2006: 137–8). Indigenous populations, to give but one example, were excluded from decision-making processes in the UN from the very beginning. In the field of human rights, the UN had, at least, set up two institutions, a Working Group on Indigenous Populations and a Special Rapporteur of the Commission on Human Rights. Yet, both institutions talked *about* indigenous populations, rather than giving them the chance to speak for themselves. Only since the year 2000, when the Permanent Forum on Indigenous Issues was set up (in which eight out of the sixteen members are nominated by indigenous organizations rather than governments), can voices of representatives of indigenous populations be heard in the UN.

When it comes to the participation of women in global human rights institutions, feminist critique has repeatedly pointed out the obstacles to their accessing and participating in international institutions bodies, including human rights institutions. Charlesworth and Chinkin have described these obstacles in detail (Charlesworth and Chinkin, 2000: 174–95). In UN treaty bodies, to give just one example, women make up only around 20 per cent of the overall number of experts, with most of them monitoring women's and children's rights (Bayefsky, 2001: 104–5; the situation has not changed since). Likewise, the adequacy of women's access to mechanisms for the enforcement and implementation of human rights remains questionable (Charlesworth and Chinkin, 2000: 220). This is particularly disturbing in a field such as human rights, which is based on the premise of equality and non-discrimination.

## Guarding the guards

Some human rights institutions are explicitly entrusted with holding human rights violators to account for violations of international norms. Welcome as this is, it leads to the question if and how human rights institutions themselves can be held accountable for failures. The somewhat puzzling answer is: they cannot. The critique that global human rights institutions, like other international institutions, lack accountability for their failures and wrongdoing is encapsulated in the question '*quis custodiet ipsos custodes?*' (who will guard the guardians?). The increasing involvement of peacekeeping forces in reconstruction programmes, training, police reform, rebuilding infrastructure, humanitarian assistance, and the administration of war-torn territories, for example, makes the UN often act like a government in all but name. Alleged failures of UNMIK (the UN Mission in Kosovo) and KFOR (the Kosovo Stabilization Force) to uphold human rights standards and guarantee respect for human rights in Kosovo have repeatedly led to fierce criticism and calls for introducing mechanisms to ensure greater accountability (e.g., Council of Europe, Parliamentary Assembly resolution 1417 of 2005).

Strange as it may seem to the outsider, it is questionable whether international institutions, including human rights institutions, are themselves bound by international human rights law. Obstacles to holding the UN and its organs accountable abound: the organization is not a party to any human rights treaty, and cannot be, as those treaties are open only to states. The UN is also usually granted privileges and immunities laid down in specific agreements which exempt UN staff and peacekeeping personnel from prosecution by national courts. Scholarly discussion and practitioners suggest several options to remedy this situation and to see international institutions, which are, after all, the subjects of international law, bound by general principles or customary international law and made accountable on the basis of their 'internal', 'constitutional' requirements (Mégret and Hoffmann, 2003). Others consider the UN in some situations as the functional equivalent of a state, with the same standards applicable (Mertus, 2005: 130–2). As yet, however, there is no comprehensive and universally agreed legal framework to hold those institutions accountable. This is one of the challenges ahead which human rights scholarship has begun to tackle (most recently Clapham, 2006), namely to better understand and define the human rights obligations of actors other than states, including international institutions.

## Remedy and ritual

Let us frame all the challenges referred to in this chapter again as the accusations they are: global human rights are bureaucracies, with all their benefits, but also deficiencies; in their reflection of the present international legal order they are exclusive rather than inclusive; they have the potential to alienate stakeholders; they put law before reality and form before function; they have become absorbed with remedying their own dysfunctions; and they attempt to hold others to account while themselves failing to respect their own standards. Has the creation of global human rights institutions turned human rights, once a tool of resistance against oppression and a remedy against injustice, into shallow rituals to be performed in ineffective, unaccountable, elitist and remote bureaucratic institutions?

David Kennedy has furthermore rightly remarked that the creation of an institution is an act, but not necessarily a response, and has formulated the critique that the attachment of the human rights movement to establishing institutions based on law 'makes the achievement of these forms an end in itself. Elites in a political system –

international, national – which has adopted the rules and set up the institutions will often themselves have the impression and insist persuasively to others that they have addressed the problem of violations with an elaborate, internationally respected and "state of the art" response' (Kennedy, 2002: 110). Are global human rights institutions such fig leaves in the face of continuous human suffering, more absorbed with themselves than with the matter they are supposed to handle – human rights? In the following chapters, in which we present global human rights institutions, we will not only refer to the assumptions and challenges we have just outlined, but also consider the design of global human rights institutions as a factor which can both constrain and encourage success.

# 3 THE RISE OF GLOBAL HUMAN RIGHTS INSTITUTIONS

## A timeline

Today's global human rights architecture bears the imprint of historic events and reflects various shifts in the global political landscape. No carefully crafted master plan for designing human rights institutions was ever at hand. Rather, they were devised in response to concrete needs, pushed by dramatic events and limited by specific political circumstances. It is through various stages that the rise, and sometimes fall, of global human rights institutions took place. While the beginning of the human rights 'story' is usually set in 1945, human rights have been a matter of international concern since well before this time. Yet, that year clearly separates the United Nations' bold vision of setting up a universal and durable system for the protection of human rights from previous scattered transnational attempts to uphold human dignity through various movements and international organizations, such as the League of Nations and the ILO.

Slavery and the slave trade, the atrocities of war, the fate of minorities, abysmal working conditions, refugee flows, religious freedom, racial inequality and the struggle of colonized peoples for self-determination were the issues which drove the creation of human rights institutions from the mid-nineteenth century to 1945. The attempts to guarantee human rights, or whatever notion was used in legal and political parlance to designate the quest to uphold human dignity, led to legal and organizational structures, some of which survived and are still significant today, while others were 'more important as historical stepping stones than as durable solutions in and of themselves' (Weiss,

Forsythe and Coate, 1997: 134). The International Committee of the Red Cross (ICRC) and the ILO are the most prominent institutions created in response to such violations of human dignity. Not only were they able to demonstrate their necessity over many decades, but they remain active to this day, unlike other institutions created under the auspices of the League of Nations to solve the plight of refugees, minorities and inhabitants of dependent territories, which vanished and left their activities to be taken up by the UN in 1945.

Among the first institutions created to fight violations of human dignity were, however, pressure groups set up in the quest to abolish slavery and the slave trade. The anti-slavery movement was spearheaded by private advocacy groups, most prominently the British and Foreign Anti-Slavery Society, founded in 1839, with earlier attempts to organize for the abolition of slavery stretching back to the 1780s. The society was instrumental in abolishing slavery and the slave trade in Britain and in the colonies, continued its work throughout the nineteenth and twentieth centuries to combat slavery-like practices, and was influential in adopting the 1926 Convention on the Abolition of Slavery and the 1956 Supplementary Convention on the Abolition of Slavery, the Slave Trade and Institutions and Practices Similar to Slavery. Such civil society organizations were the forerunners of today's human rights NGOs, and the Anti-Slavery Society is still in existence, making it arguably the oldest human rights NGO in the world. It changed its name to Anti-Slavery International in 1990 and is active today in areas such as forced and bonded labour, child labour and trafficking in human beings (http://www.antislavery.org), thus bridging the pre-1945 attempts of civil society organizations to give structure and format to the struggle for human dignity with more recent efforts to protect human rights.

Transnational moralism and international human rights began to shape the international institutional order in an even more profound way when, in the 1860s, Henri Dunant started what later came to be known as the Red Cross and Red Crescent Movement. Appalled by what he had witnessed in the battle of Solferino in 1859, Dunant worked towards the establishment of private agencies to care for wounded and sick soldiers. This finally led to the adoption of the first Geneva Convention in 1864 and subsequently to a comprehensive legal and institutional framework for the protection of soldiers and civilians in conflict. The establishment of the International Committee of the Red Cross in 1863 institutionalized these attempts to protect the lives and ensure the dignity of war victims. Today, the International Red Cross and Red Crescent Movement consists of 179 National Red

Cross and Red Crescent societies, the International Committee of the Red Cross and the International Federation of Red Cross and Red Crescent Societies. For long, international humanitarian law, which guides the activities of the ICRC, was seen as a field separate from human rights law. While both are based on the belief that human dignity must be upheld in all circumstances, one was considered applicable in times of war, the other in times of peace. More recently, however, the close nexus between the two fields of law as well as the quest to apply human rights norms in conflict situations has led to an increased convergence of human rights and humanitarian law. While this development gives rise to legal and practical questions aplenty (Provost, 2002; Heintze, 2004; Lubell, 2005), it opens up new possibilities for the stronger protection of civilians in armed conflict, as reflected in the most recent practice of the Security Council, which will be discussed in chapter 5. The continuing importance of the ICRC makes it a centre-piece in this discussion.

Different from civil society organizations, intergovernmental institutions all but ignored human rights well into the twentieth century, when the League of Nations and the ILO finally took on the challenge of protecting individuals and groups. The League was founded in the wake of the Paris Peace Conference of 1919, to prevent further wars through collective security, dispute settlement and disarmament, and to promote social welfare. Two subsidiary organs of the League were specifically entrusted with what today would qualify as human rights matters (Weiss, Forsythe and Coate, 1997: 134–5). The Commission for Refugees, headed by Fridtjof Nansen, oversaw the repatriation and resettlement of refugees spread over Europe as a consequence of World War I and tried to come to terms with the phenomenon of stateless persons. The 'Nansen passport' for stateless persons, widely used in the inter-war period, was one of the few successes of the League. The second commission, the Slavery Commission, assisted in the fight which the anti-slavery movement had initiated, and also aimed to combat forced prostitution and drug trafficking. Efforts to include religious freedom and racial equality in the League's Covenant remained unsuccessful, as did the attempt to adopt a general international agreement on human rights in the 1930s. The League was also concerned with and partly successful in the protection of minorities and the welfare of the inhabitants of dependent territories. The latter task was laid down in the Covenant (Article 23 (b)), which obliged the League to 'secure just treatment of the native inhabitants of territories' under the control of its member states. To this end, a mandate system was established, putting former colonies into three categories, A, B and C, depending on their states of 'development'. Mandatory powers were assigned to guide them towards independence. In 1922, a Permanent Mandates Commission (PMC) was set up, composed of independent experts elected in their personal capacity. It was entitled to consider state reports as well as individual complaints on shortcomings in the policies of mandatory powers, making it a 'remarkably successful' tool (Bennett and Oliver, 2002: 385) to supervise state behaviour and safeguard fundamental human rights. In effect, the PMC was a forerunner of the supervisory mechanisms established later under UN human rights treaties (Oberleitner, 1998: 31–4).

In the wake of World War I, several treaties were concluded which were indentured to solve the plight of minorities in about a dozen European states. This system did not survive the inter-war period. It was insufficient to protect minorities and discredited the issue to such an extent that for half a century the UN did not dare touch upon it. Only in 1992, with the adoption of the UN Declaration on the Rights of Persons Belonging to National or Ethnic, Religious and Linguistic Minorities, did a renewed attempt come to secure the protection of minorities on an international level. Under the League of Nations, a Minority Committee was appointed to ensure that these states would grant the rights enshrined in the respective treaties to the minorities on their territory. Like the PMC, the Minority Committee was entitled to receive complaints, and by 1938 it had dealt with approximately 650 such complaints (Nowak, 2003: 21). The League was dissolved in 1946, transferring many of its mandates to the newly founded United Nations.

The ILO, established alongside the League of Nations in the Peace Treaty of Versailles, was a response to what was originally meant to be the League's obligation to 'secure and maintain fair and humane conditions of labour for men, women, and children' (Article 23, League of Nations Covenant). The first annual International Labour Conference was convened in Washington in 1919 and succeeded in adopting the first six International Labour Conventions on hours of work in industry, unemployment, maternity protection, night work for women, and minimum age and night work for young persons in industry, with these then paving the way for the substantial range of treaties that followed. The ILO itself was set up in 1920. Its conventions and recommendations, together with the supervisory system set up in 1926, make the ILO effectively the first human rights institution.

It is clear therefore that neither transnational concern for safeguarding individual human dignity and guaranteeing group rights nor the institutionalization of this concern is an exclusive phenomenon of the post-1945 world or an invention of the United Nations. On the contrary, it is 150 years (and even longer in the case of the abolition of slavery) since the first steps were taken to build institutional frameworks for the protection of war victims, refugees, minorities and inhabitants of dependent territories, and for safeguarding labour rights. Some of these efforts succeeded and lasted, such as the ICRC and the ILO, while others failed, such as the inter-war minority treaties. Some were of temporary importance, such as the League of Nations mandate system, and some paved the way for subsequent developments, such as the League's refugee protection system.

In 1945, European fascism, the Holocaust, Asian militarism and the atrocities of World War II were the driving forces behind the establishment of the United Nations and the entrusting of it with a mandate and a range of mechanisms to guarantee international peace and security which were superior to those enjoyed by the League of Nations. The events of 1939–45 also reinforced the belief in many quarters that the protection and promotion of universal human rights must be part and parcel of any endeavour to build a safer world. The San Francisco conference in 1945, which adopted the UN Charter, replaced the piecemeal approach of the inter-war period with a comprehensive universal human rights system. While there are different accounts of how human rights eventually found their way into the UN Charter, much must be attributed to Franklin D. Roosevelt's 'four freedoms' (freedom of speech and expression, freedom of religion, freedom from want and freedom from fear), to Eleanor Roosevelt's campaigning for human and women's rights, to the efforts of Latin American countries in particular, and to the acceptance of these efforts by the then Soviet Union (Weiss, Forsythe and Coate, 1997: 137–8).

The development of the international institutional framework for human rights since 1945 is also not linear but comes in waves, with the focus changing and approaches and trends ebbing and flowing. All of them have left their traces in the UN human rights system as we know it today: the establishment of universal human rights standards, with the Universal Declaration of Human Rights in 1948, in reaction to atrocities on an unimaginable scale; the focus on decolonization and the impact of new UN member states in the 1960s and the introduction of the UN development agenda; the move away from a bipolar world order in the 1990s, together with the renaissance of the UN and its subsequent decline in the face of Rwanda and Kosovo; and the terrorist attacks of 11 September 2001, with the subsequent and ongoing quest to balance human rights with security.

The human rights provisions of the UN Charter are the foundations on which the UN human rights regime is built and on which it continues to develop. In the preamble, the Charter affirms the UN's 'faith in fundamental human rights, in the dignity and worth of the human person, in the equal rights of men and women'. Article 1 makes it a 'purpose' of the UN to 'achieve international cooperation [. . .] in promoting and encouraging respect for human rights and for fundamental freedoms for all without distinction as to race, sex, language, or religion' (Article 1(3)). Article 55 spells out this purpose, albeit in cautious language and framed by a number of conditions: 'with a view to the creation of conditions of stability and well-being which are necessary for peaceful and friendly relations among nations based on respect for the principle of equal rights and self-determination of peoples', the UN shall 'promote [. . .] universal respect for, and observance of, human rights and fundamental freedoms for all without distinction as to race, sex, language, or religion' (Article 55(c)). This language left open how precisely the UN should go about promoting and encouraging respect for human rights.

The adoption of the Universal Declaration of Human Rights in 1948 (with no votes against but eight abstentions, including the Soviet Union, Saudi Arabia and South Africa) clarified the scope and content of human rights as referred to in the Charter. While the declaration, adopted by the General Assembly, is a non-binding document, it has, at least in part, gained normative force through subsequent events (Nowak, 2003: 76). UN human rights treaties followed, which together with previous treaties and various declarations and resolutions of UN bodies now constitute the UN human rights standards, norms and principles. Altogether some 120 documents (conventions, protocols, declarations, resolutions, codes of conduct and statements of standards and principles) form the basis on which UN human rights institutions operate today. What is commonly referred to as the UN human rights system rests on three pillars. Under each of the core UN human rights treaties a body composed of independent experts ('treaty body') was established with the task of monitoring the implementation of treaty provisions. This 'treaty-based' system brings together those states which have signed the respective treaties. Under the second pillar, the 'charter-based' system, a range of institutions have been created which all derive their mandate from the UN Charter, and whose decisions reach out to all UN member states regardless of their adherence to human rights treaties. The General Assembly, the Economic and Social Council (ECOSOC), the Commission on Human Rights (dissolved in 2006) and its successor, the Human Rights

Council, together with the Sub-Commission on the Promotion and Protection of Human Rights and a number of other subsidiary bodies, as well as the Commission on the Status of Women, strive to translate the Charter's commitment to human rights into action. Charter-based bodies are sometimes also referred to as 'non-conventional', i.e., not based on human rights treaties. The third pillar was added in 1993, when the post of the UN High Commissioner for Human Rights was created.

Convenient as it is, the term 'UN human rights system' is not accurate – just as the very existence of a coherent 'UN system' is questionable (White, 2002: 3–11). While it brings together institutions entrusted with a specific human rights mandate, it fails to acknowledge human rights as a cross-cutting issue for the UN, just as it omits taking on board other UN institutions (specialized agencies, programmes and funds) with a human rights, or human rights-related, mandate, and institutions into which human rights are gradually being mainstreamed. UNESCO, the United Nations Educational, Scientific and Cultural Organization, for example, has a specific mandate to promote certain human rights. The UN Children's Fund (UNICEF) and the UN Development Programme (UNDP) have successfully mainstreamed human rights into their activities, and the World Health Organization (WHO) and the Food and Agricultural Organization (FAO) manage core social rights, even though their mandates refrain from using human rights language.

The UN never created a global human rights court. Still, the possibility of judicial protection of human rights has existed since 1922, when the Permanent Court of International Justice (PCIJ) was created by the League of Nations. This court and its successor, the ICJ, which took up its work in 1946, have on occasion spoken out on human rights. While they were precluded from delivering judgments on individual cases of human rights violations, they have contributed to clarifying the place of human rights in international law. With the creation of the ICC in 1998, individual human rights violators can now be brought to court for a range of crimes, giving new impetus to the fight against impunity for human rights violations and adding an important judicial institution to the array of global human rights institutions.

The continuing proliferation of human rights institutions in the UN since 1945, the process of mainstreaming human rights into UN specialized agencies, programmes and funds, and the establishment of the ICC, together with the survival of century-old institutions such as the ILO or the ICRC, have woven a net of inter-governmental human rights institutions over the globe. Regional systems make this net even tighter in Europe, the Americas and Africa, and the spread of civil society organizations in virtually all countries of the world helps to fill the gaps in this fabric. As a consequence, human rights are no longer merely the concern of a few idealists or lofty ideas awaiting their reality check. They have become part and parcel of international relations and international law, developed in accordance with rules and procedures, interpreted by special organs, monitored by elected bodies and adjudicated by courts. What specific functions do such global human rights institutions serve, and is there a typology which, together with our exploration of the reasons behind their establishment, allows us to better appreciate their performance? These are the questions to which we are now turning.

# A typology

The *Yearbook of International Organizations* gives a total number of between 246 and 7,350 inter-governmental and between 7,306 and 51,509 international non-governmental organizations (Yearbook of International Organizations, 2004). The varying numbers are due to different ways of grouping international organizations, and the vast range proves that there is neither a universally accepted definition of their make-up nor an agreed typology. Indeed, it seems that 'the proliferation of [international organizations] has overtaken the international lawyers' ability to classify them' (Alvarez, 2006: 334). For the purpose of this book a functional approach has been chosen, and global human rights institutions are presented in four groups: international institutions which deal with human rights; international institutions which *also* deal with human rights; international courts; and non-governmental organizations. Scholarly literature has developed a number of other criteria by which such institutions can be categorized. Usually, this is done by pitting ideal types of institutions against each other in terms of their composition (governmental bodies contrast with expert bodies) or function (judicial versus non-judicial bodies, such as governmental or expert bodies). Often, (allegedly) 'political' bodies are confronted with (allegedly) 'legal' bodies. It seems useful to examine briefly the validity of postulating such ideal types of global human rights institutions, because what will emerge from this examination is not so much a neat grid pattern but rather a set of contradictory results, adding to the paradoxes of global human rights institutions which we began to describe in the previous chapter.

*Governmental* institutions such as the UN Commission on Human Rights are composed of representatives of governments (usually ambassadors and staff of diplomatic missions). Representatives serving on such bodies are supposed to put forward their government's views. They contrast with *expert* bodies (such as the UN Sub-Commission on the Promotion and Protection of Human Rights or the UN treaty bodies), on which independent individuals serve. Their independence is often expressed as a combination of incorruptibility and wisdom (e.g., 'high moral standing and recognized competence', as required in Article 17(1) of the UN Convention on the Rights of the Child for members of the Committee on the Rights of the Child). This allows for critical voices to be raised and academic rigour to be applied without the constraints of political considerations. The frequent appointment to expert bodies of ambassadors or other high-ranking government officials as 'independent experts', however, distorts such a classification. A study on the UN Sub-Commission on the Promotion and Protection of Human Rights (or Sub-Commission on Prevention of Discrimination and Protection of Minorities, as it was then called) showed that, for decades, many of its members had been in full-time employment in the administration or diplomatic service of their states – up to as many as 90 per cent in the (then) Eastern European group (Eide, 1992: 254). This reveals already one of the tensions inherent in human rights institutions: even where independence is a legal requirement for the composition of such bodies, the choice of experts to serve on these bodies rests with states, and even the most independent of experts must ultimately be presented by governments. Yet, affiliation to a government says little about how the mandate holder will perform his or her function or what degree of independence he or she will eventually demonstrate. On the other hand, the governmental character of the UN Commission on Human Rights never precluded countries from appointing independent experts as part of their governmental delegations which, in the ambit of the delegations' mandates, were asked to bring their expertise and independent views to bear within both the delegation and the respective institution.

*Judicial* institutions, composed of independent judges who serve in their personal capacity, can be distinguished from *non-judicial* bodies, whether they are composed of governmental representatives or independent experts. Judicial institutions, such as the ICC, guarantee the independence of judges and provide for rules and procedures akin to those of domestic courts, while business in non-judicial bodies is conducted in accordance with the rules of procedure of international organizations. Yet again, a closer look reveals inconsistencies: while the *ad hoc* criminal tribunals on ex-Yugoslavia and Rwanda guarantee the independence of judges, the existence and continuance of the tribunals themselves depend on (political) decisions taken by the Security Council, the body which, after all, created those tribunals. On the other hand, the Special Rapporteurs of the Human Rights Council operate with great independence, go out to collect evidence and, like prosecutors, 'accuse' governments of human rights violations. They do all this despite being subsidiary organs of a governmental body. The UN Human Rights Committee, which decides on individual complaints under the International Covenant on Civil and Political Rights, is composed of independent experts, but conducts quasi-judicial proceedings in the absence of a proper procedural framework on, e.g., assessing evidence presented to it. Again, neither the judicial nor the non-judicial set of institutions lives up to the promises which its label offers: international courts may conduct business impartially, but depend on the cooperation and support of states; and expert bodies transcending their recommendatory role and posing as judges to fill the void of a non-existent international human rights court perform a doubtful role, too.

The most problematic differentiation is between *'legal'* and *'political'* bodies (e.g., White, 2002: 222–32). Whereas, e.g., the UN Human Rights Council (formerly the Commission on Human Rights) is said to be a 'political' body (on account of its being composed of governmental representatives), the UN treaty bodies are considered as 'legal' bodies. Pitting political against legal human rights bodies, however, leads to a discourse which creates more confusion than bringing clarity. Sometimes this dichotomy seeks to describe the composition of human rights bodies (do ambassadors or academic experts serve?), sometimes the output of institutions (do they produce legal texts or policy statements?) and sometimes the legitimacy of their work (political bodies represent their governments, while legal bodies are 'independent'), but sometimes the distinction is simply applied to separate allegedly 'good' human rights law from 'bad' politics. In reality, all these lines of argument are blurred. While the composition and conduct of business of the UN Human Rights Council (just like the Commission before it) is indeed political, in the sense that governments bring their domestic political considerations and weight into the conference room, the resolutions adopted are legal texts, albeit of a recommendatory character. The Special Rapporteurs originally created by the (political) Commission on Human Rights are independent ('apolitical') experts. On the other hand, treaty bodies are based on treaty law and apply treaty law, but they issue recommendations which are policy-oriented suggestions (van Boven, 2003: 541). All that the distinction between 'legal' and 'political' bodies seems to do is to reveal the tension between 'law' and 'politics' in human rights, a matter to which we will turn later.

In the UN human rights system, the distinction between *'charter-based'* and *'treaty-based'* bodies has become commonplace. The treaty-based system comprises the bodies set up under the UN human rights treaties, while the charter-based system includes bodies such as, first and foremost, the UN Human Rights Council and the Sub-Commission on the Promotion and Protection of Human Rights. This categorization highlights one important aspect, namely the outstanding position of the UN Charter as a document which binds all states – different from the UN human rights treaties, to which states are free to accede. More precisely, one would have to distinguish between institutions provided for in the UN Charter (such as the case of the UN Commission on Human Rights, the creation of which was provided for in Article 68), and institutions set up by their parent bodies in accordance with the Charter (the Human Rights Council, e.g., was created by a General Assembly resolution). Unlike charter-based bodies, the reach of treaty-based bodies (i.e., the seven committees established under the major UN human rights treaties) extends only to state parties to the respective treaty.

Hierarchy is another feature of international institutions, and, like other characteristics of global human rights institutions, it can affect human rights. Before the establishment of the UN Human Rights Council, to take one example, human rights issues were considered in the following hierarchical sequence: from the Sub-Commission on the Promotion and Protection of Human Rights, to the Commission on Human Rights, to ECOSOC, to the Third Committee of the General Assembly, to the plenary of the General Assembly. The Sub-Commission put forward independent expert considerations. States in the Commission moulded this into a text which met governmental concerns, but, as a kind of counterweight, allowed NGO input. In ECOSOC a different group of states decided on the basis of broader considerations. The Third Committee, with a different group of states again, but excluding NGOs, changed or added to the text. And finally, the General Assembly gave its imprimatur. Like a crushing mill, the different hierarchical stages processed a human rights concern into a legal text. While the final result may have been both questionable in terms of substance and remote from the original idea, which was floated by concerned individuals perhaps years before the onset of this process, the institution, at least, has succeeded in satisfying the demands of the fluctuating membership of its different layers of bodies, has done justice to their diverging rules of procedure and has duly considered their different bureaucratic practices. What such institutions deem a success, however, is likely to be seen by outsiders as an aberration.

## Functions, activities and expectations

With what functions are global human rights institutions entrusted, and with what expectations are they created? These questions are intertwined with the reasons why states set up global institutions, and both international legal and international relations scholarship offer some insights. Constructivist theorists, in particular, have long argued that international society is based on social and political processes of which international institutions are part: 'international institutions define who the players are in a particular situation and how they define their roles, and thus place constraints on behaviour [. . .] international institutions can alter the identities and interests of states' (Simmons and Martin, 2002: 198). Others have argued that the articulation and aggregation of interests, norm-creation, socialization and rule-making, rule-application and -adjudication, information, and operative activities are domains of international institutions (Archer, 2001: 91–108). Abbott and Snidal conclude that states use international organizations 'to reduce transaction costs in the narrow sense and, more broadly, to create information, ideas, norms, and expectations; to carry out and encourage specific activities; to legitimate or delegitimate particular ideas and practices; and to enhance their capacities and power' (Abbott and Snidal, 2001: 14–15). Powerless as international organizations often are in terms of financial resources, political backing, operational abilities or enforcement capacity, their ability to 'constitute and construct the social world' has been highlighted (Barnett and Finnemore, 1999: 700).

Assuming that global human rights institutions fulfil some of these functions between reducing transaction costs and constructing the social world, how do they go about their business? What do states wish global human rights institutions to do, and what are their concrete activities? Not all of the possible functions, activities and expectations which we will consider in the following apply to all human rights institutions. Their (increasing) specialization does not allow all of them to perform all functions at all times. Furthermore, NGOs serve different functions from inter-governmental organizations (which will be discussed in chapter 6). Yet, the brief survey which follows will demonstrate the great range of functions and activities which global human rights institutions have taken over in 'managing' the global good human rights: they are 'agoras' for dialogue and venues of agenda-setting and decision-making; they set standards and create, interpret and adjudicate rules; they accompany the domestic implementation of rules and decisions; they prevent and remedy human rights violations; they undertake operational activities; they substitute domestic processes; and they are agents of social change. All of these functions are of importance for developing and guaranteeing human rights, but most of them also carry the potential for negative effects. This seems in line with what we have considered as the downsides of international bureaucracies in chapter 2.

## Agoras

Global human rights institutions provide a space for discussion and dialogue on human rights issues and allow for the finding of a consensus and for establishing differences on the scope, content and implementation of human rights. Even where such a dialogue remains without consequences, the agora function ensures that the global discourse on human rights is at least conducted as a consistent and continuous process and that international public attention remains focused on human rights issues. Relying on procedural rules and practices, different stakeholders – governments, inter-governmental institutions, NGOs, individuals and transnational networks of experts, the so-called epistemic communities – can place their statements on public record. With dusty UN archives largely having been replaced by the world wide web, an accessible panel for sharing information is at their disposal. The aggregation of information may lead to debate and give birth to ideas and expectations that would otherwise be unavailable. The fact that in reality global human rights institutions are never simply neutral blackboards on which human rights news are posted does not take away from this function as a debating hall (but it should of course be borne in mind when evaluating and appraising this function).

## Agenda-setting and decision-making

Global human rights institutions are venues for decision-making based on consultations and negotiations, and allow states, NGOs and inter-governmental organizations to put issues of concern on the agenda in a formalized way. Procedural rules on the presentation and adoption of resolutions and on voting processes give stability and predictability to decision-making processes on norm-creation, implementation, supervision, enforcement and sanction. Sporadic bilateral encounters are replaced by more consistent multilateral diplomatic processes. These processes give direction and speed to dialogue and confrontation on human rights. At the same time it cannot be denied that they also remove much of the debate and decision-making on human rights out of domestically legitimized decision-making bodies such as parliaments and into a system largely devoid of checks and balances. Furthermore, human rights diplomacy has become a skill with which UN diplomats, NGO activists and international civil servants must be endowed in order safely to navigate through the corridors of global institutions. Not being acquainted with such abilities leaves individuals and groups out.

## Standard-setting, interpretation and adjudication

What today is commonly referred to as 'human rights' is in fact international human rights law, created by global human rights institutions. In fact, the field of human rights has proven to be a particularly fertile ground for norm-making, outdoing many other fields of international law (Alvarez, 2005: 156–68). Human rights institutions develop human rights norms, principles and standards, from binding treaties to voluntary codes of conduct. In a step which precedes the production of rules, expert bodies such as the UN Sub-Commission on the Promotion and Protection of Human Rights identify and conceptualize human rights issues and translate them into legal obligations. Subsequent to norm-production, institutions such as UN treaty bodies interpret norms and apply them to specific circumstances. They produce conclusions, recommendations and standards which refine international human rights law. Courts add jurisprudence and establish precedence, while NGOs contribute amicus curiae briefs, background papers, documents for litigation and academic studies.

As a consequence of the increased legalization of human rights through global human rights institutions the coverage of human rights extends to ever more areas. At the same time, the discourse on human rights has superimposed upon it a form of expert language which often baffles the observer: why, exactly, is it of interest that the Guiding Principles on Internally Displaced Persons were not formally adopted but merely 'appreciated' by the Commission on Human Rights (Commission on Human Rights resolution 2004/55: para. 6)? What, exactly, is the value of a resolution in the Human Rights Council which is adopted by a close majority rather than one passed by an overwhelming vote? We have discussed the consequences of such professionalization in the previous chapter. Concern is also voiced over the development of international human rights into a highly specialized field of international law. While it may raise the status of human rights law, it makes international law an ever more fragmented system and leads to inconsistencies and conflicts within a disjointed legal order (Mosoti, 2005).

## Implementation, scrutiny and assistance

Global human rights institutions not only articulate and interpret human rights standards, but seek to influence states to uphold these standards and attempt to hold them accountable if they fail to do so (Flood, 1998). Human rights institutions accompany the implementation of international obligations in domestic law and practice. 'Monitoring' has become the catchword for the way in which global institutions critically review domestic developments. Monitoring is, *a priori*, intended to discover violations (and violators) of human rights commitments and to make assistance or sanctions possible. Yet, in reality, monitoring is a process of great subtlety and is not based on a crime/punishment model. Rather, it is a socializing and educational process in equal measure (Szasz, 2001: 78). Human rights institutions scrutinize the performance of states (and increasingly also non-state actors), appraise legal and factual development and investigate specific situations. They use international human rights law as a benchmark and indicator and put forward conclusions, assessments, observations and recommendations. They have few, if any, means available to sanction deviant behaviour, so that persuasion or relying on public pressure have to stand in and expose the frailty of global human rights institutions. Human rights institutions increasingly offer assistance, education, training and advice to governments on matters such as legal reform, good governance, development, and setting up national human rights institutions. In short, global human rights institutions are in equal measure 'sources of pressure, providers of assistance, partners in change' (Steiner, 2003: 785).

## Operational activities

The move from headquarters to the field in many human rights bodies, first and foremost in the Office of the High Commissioner for Human Rights since the 1990s, allows for ever more operational roles of human rights bodies. The integration of human rights into operational activities of institutions such as the UN High Commissioner for Refugees (UNHCR) or the UN Office for Humanitarian Affairs (OCHA) and into UN peace missions ensures that they become operational tools for 'hands-on' organizations. Trial observation or election monitoring are other examples of such operational activities. Notwithstanding repeated disagreements among governments on the precise mandate within which such activities should be undertaken, this move from headquarters to the field is perhaps the most striking and most promising development of the past years.

## Remedy and prevention

Where human rights violations occur, human rights institutions can step in *ex post facto* to remedy violations, mitigate the consequences, compensate victims, and hold perpetrators accountable. UN institutions, however, have a rather sad record in these activities. Neither is there a global human rights court which would speak out on human rights violations and, like the European Court of Human Rights, award financial damages to victims, nor are the treaty bodies, in considering individual complaints, able to provide financial compensation or the like. The adoption of a recommendation to the respective states by the treaty body will, for the victim, often be a remedy which comes too little and too late. With the establishment of the ICC, the fight against impunity for human rights violators has been taken a decisive step further, yet the hundreds of thousands of individuals who every year write to the UN in search for a remedy for injustice they have suffered still get little in return.

In preventing human rights violations, the UN did not fare much better either, and the genocide in Rwanda will remain a lasting legacy of the organization's inability in that respect. If, and to what extent, the existence of human rights institutions themselves has an effect which might prevent human rights violations is an open question, and even the ICC, with its threat of judicial procedure and prison sentences, has yet to prove its ability to deter potential perpetrators.

## Substituting domestic processes

International institutions may 'change international outcomes [. . .] by substituting for domestic practices' (Simmons and Martin, 2002: 202). This also holds true for global human rights institutions. The idea that as a matter of principle international bodies should be subsidiary to the application of domestic means (expressed, for example, in the

demand for the exhaustion of domestic legal remedies before com-
plaining to international human rights bodies) is not in question. Yet,
occasionally global institutions are established in order to substitute
the dysfunctional or missing national structures, procedures and
means. The tribunals for the former Yugoslavia and for Rwanda carry
out criminal investigation and adjudication in place of national courts;
international experts draft constitutions, and in UN territorial administrations, such as in Kosovo, entire parts of domestic political and
administrative processes, including those relating to human rights
matters, are taken over by inter-governmental organizations and international civil servants. Remarkable as this function is, it raises questions as to the role and responsibility of governments to guarantee a
domestic human rights infrastructure, the alienation of the domestic
constituency, and the possible drawbacks inherent in replacing the
local with the global.

## Social change

The socializing influences of international institutions have been
described, together with their agency and agenda-setting effects, by
Simmons and Martin (2002: 193). More specific inquiries into global
human rights institutions, based on empirical evidence, seem to be
missing. The socializing and educational processes to which the various
participants of the global human rights discourse, as conducted in
human rights institutions, are exposed have yet to be analysed in detail.
Four assumptions, however, may be made. First, some global human
rights institutions, such as the UN High Commissioner for Human
Rights, are specifically entrusted with a mandate to promote human
rights and to undertake awareness-raising and educational activities.
Dispersing standards, knowledge and skills is the core task of such
institutions. Second, social change is also achieved as a 'by-product'
of human rights institutions. It is worth remembering that they are not
abstract entities, but social constructs in which human beings work
and interact. Individual members of human rights bodies are most
often members of epistemic communities, thus ensuring the transfer of
ideas between international institutions and academic, social or political arenas (Abbott and Snidal, 2001: 24). Third, debating, adopting
and interpreting human rights is, again according to Abbott and Snidal
(ibid.: 14–15), a process of constantly legitimizing and delegitimizing
ideas and practices. Fourth, there is evidence in the mandates of many
global human rights institutions, including 'legal' ones such as treaty
bodies, that what they seek to achieve is not legal but societal change.

The challenge is to find ways of enabling technocratic, legalistic and formal institutions to foster cultural change. While they may contribute more to societal change than is often anticipated, high hopes that the activities of global human rights institutions alone will bring about a global culture of human rights seem misplaced. Such hopes, which seek to locate the world's moral conscience in UN conference rooms, disregard the limitations of global human rights institutions. After all, they are not so much a glimpse into utopia as real institutions, firmly anchored in contemporary legal and power structures.

# 4 UNITED NATIONS HUMAN RIGHTS INSTITUTIONS

## Commission on Human Rights

In some ways, the UN Commission on Human Rights was, from its establishment in 1946, a permanent building-site on which transformations took place not as a steady process of change according to plan, but as 'spasmodic reforms, which seem to befall the Commission ever couple of years [. . .] fuelled more by confrontation than by rational debate' (Alston, 1992: 197). The latest of these reforms started in 2000, when the Commission set up a working group on reform, the deliberations of which dragged on for a number of years and yielded modest results. Given this history, it came as something of a surprise to many when, in 2006, the Commission was dissolved and replaced by a new body, the Human Rights Council. To understand this significant step, we need to look back to 1946 when the Commission was constituted.

The establishment of the Commission was provided for in the UN Charter (Article 68: 'the Economic and Social Council shall set up commissions in economic and social fields and for the protection of human rights'). The mandate, functions and composition of the Commission were decided in lengthy discussions and negotiations (Tolley, 1987: 4–13) before it could formally be established by ECOSOC resolution 5(1) of 1946. Building on the Charter, the original idea in late 1945 was to entrust the Commission with the following tasks: formulating an international bill of rights and recommendations for an international declaration or convention on civil liberties; discussing the status of women, freedom of information, the protection of minorities and the prevention of discrimination; and considering any matter in human rights which would be likely to impair the general welfare or friendly relations among nations (Alston, 1992: 127). This last competence was not acceptable to governments, much to the disappointment of key figures in the establishment of the Commission such as Eleanor Roosevelt. She wanted it to be given a clear role not only to set standards and promote respect for and observance of human rights, but also to be able to assist the Security Council in deciding when a human rights violation amounted to a breach or threat to the peace (ibid.: 127–8). This was precisely what the 'nuclear' Commission, meeting in 1946, put as a proposal to ECOSOC, but ECOSOC would have none of it. At least it granted the Commission the right to consider, in addition to standard-setting activities, 'any other matter concerning human rights' (ECOSOC resolution 5(1) of 1946). With this decision, close ties between the Commission and the Security Council were prevented, but despite this the Commission secured a sufficiently broad and open mandate to allow for considerable development. In 1979, this mandate was further broadened with ECOSOC resolution 1979/36, which entitled the Commission also to coordinate the UN's human rights activities.

Membership was enlarged several times after the 'nuclear' Commission, with nine members, met for the first time in 1946. When it was finally dissolved, the Commission was composed of no fewer than fifty-three member states, elected by ECOSOC for a period of three years with the possibility of unlimited re-election. Membership was based on geographical distribution, allowing for fifteen seats for the African group, twelve for the Asian group, five for Eastern Europe, eleven for Latin American and Caribbean countries (GRULAC) and ten for the 'Western European and Others Group' (WEOG). In addition to members, other states and inter-governmental organizations participated as observers with the right to speak. NGOs participated as observers, too, with the right to be present in public meetings and deliver statements. Despite being excluded from voting, observer governments and NGOs played an active role in the deliberations of the Commission. Like the members themselves, they delivered statements, lobbied, formed alliances and drafted joint statements and resolutions. In addition, observer governments supported initiatives by Commission members and 'co-sponsored' resolutions.

While formal and informal negotiations, plenary speeches and voting procedures made up the Commission's work for the greater part of its existence, two innovations, both introduced in 2003, gave the sessions more prominence and fervour. A High-Level Segment (HLS), scheduled in the first week of the Commission's session, provided space

for heads of states, prime ministers, foreign ministers and other digni-
taries to deliver key policy speeches on human rights. The Commission
also institutionalized the practice of discussing the reports of its 'special
procedures' (Special Rapporteurs and other investigative mandates) in
an Inter-Active Dialogue (IAD), allowing governments and NGOs to
discuss the findings of special procedures. The Human Rights Council
is expected to continue to conduct business along these lines.

The Commission used to hold annual six-week long sessions in
March–April at UN headquarters in Geneva, where the attendance of
member states, observer governments and organizations and international NGOs brought the total number of participants up to 3,000 or
more. The Commission's agenda was overwhelming in relation to the
time allocated, and in retrospect the idea that a 53-member body with
meagre support from the UN secretariat was supposed to discuss,
decide and act upon all human rights violations worldwide in only
thirty working days, let alone draft new standards and discuss thematic
issues, seems somewhat preposterous. Overloading the Commission
with tasks, not giving it the space and time to work, and not allocating
adequate resources are, of course, examples of allegedly 'procedural'
decisions the fight over which is in reality a fight over the effective
protection of human rights.

Like other inter-governmental bodies, the Commission concluded
its deliberations with the adoption of resolutions (or decisions on
organizational matters); in some cases, mostly to resolve a crisis situation in negotiations, conclusions were reached as chairperson's statements. In its last (61st) 'substantive' session in 2005 (the 62nd and last
ever session in 2006 was devoted to concluding business and making
the transition to the Council) the Commission adopted eighty-five
resolutions and eighteen decisions. The text of a draft resolution was
presented by an interested government (not necessarily a member of
the Commission), and then negotiated and sponsored by other governments. The majority of resolutions were adopted by consensus, though
a few were voted on. In effect, the Commission's sessions were processes of intense and constant formal and informal negotiations among
governmental representatives, strongly influenced by the lobbying
activities of hundreds of NGOs, with the plenary meetings largely
reduced to reading out prepared speeches. In each Commission session
roughly one hundred substantial issues as diverse as the rights of
persons with disabilities, human rights assistance for Nepal, the abduc-
tion of children in Africa or violence against women were dealt with.
Whether these decisions were remedies which effectively assisted
victims and enhanced human rights remains doubtful, not least because

the precise or immediate effect of such recommendatory texts is hard to ascertain. Many of those resolutions, however, were more rituals than remedies, as the Commission had long since developed the damaging practice of repeating many of its resolutions over and over again, changing little more than the date of adoption and marginally amending the text.

While concerns about the Commission's overloaded agenda, procedural lacunae, and scarce meeting time and resources were addressed, if not remedied, by the reform that was a constant throughout its existence, two fundamental problems finally led to its dissolution: membership and selectivity. Both gave rise to the ever more resounding critique that the Commission was 'politicized'.

## 'Politicization': membership and selectivity

As mentioned, membership in the Commission was restricted to governments. Its history shows, however, that what was always perceived as the central characteristic of the Commission, namely its governmental nature, is actually a deviation from the original concept – a deviation which continues in the Human Rights Council, which is equally governmental in nature. It could all have been different: the 'nuclear' Commission, meeting in 1947, was made up of individual experts (eighteen at that time) and suggested that the Commission-to-be should likewise be composed of individuals acting in their personal capacity. This idea was rejected and replaced by a compromise according to which members should be representatives of states while at the same time selected 'with a view to securing a balanced representation in the various fields covered by the Commission' (Humphrey, 1984: 17.). No attempt, however, was ever made to find such balance, and ECOSOC always confirmed governments' nominees without further ado (ibid.). Hence, a Commission which was intended to bring together individual expertise was turned into an inter-governmental body right from the start. It retained this structure throughout its life. No doubt this was a realistic approach. After all, it made sense for governments themselves to prepare and adopt the human rights standards by which they would be bound. Yet, the governmental nature became an obstacle once the Commission started monitoring human rights violations committed by governments (ibid.: 18), and it has remained an obstacle ever since.

Furthermore, the Commission never had a membership criterion other than the geographical distribution of seats. In particular, there was no link between the human rights situation in a given country and its membership in the Commission. The question of membership criteria is central to understanding both the work of the Commission and the reform process which led to the creation of the Council. The 2004 Report of the UN High-Level Panel on Threats, Challenges and Change succinctly identified the problem: 'in recent years, the issue of which States are elected to the Commission has become a source of heated international tensions, with no positive impact on human rights and a negative impact on the work of the Commission' (UN, 2004: para. 285). Kenneth Roth, the Executive Director of Human Rights Watch, put it more bluntly when he called the Commission an 'Abusers' Defence Society' (Roth, 2005: 135). The situation escalated in 2002, when the USA did not win the vote in ECOSOC and was denied a seat in the Commission, while at the same time Syria joined as a member. The following year, Libya was elected to chair the Commission's session, which led to concerns among governments and NGOs alike. Jeanne Kirkpatrick, head of the US delegation to the Commission in 2003, asked in an op-ed in the *International Herald Tribune*, entitled 'a scandal in Geneva', whether it is 'so ludicrous to require that those sitting in judgment of the human rights practices of others must first themselves respect human rights?' (Kirkpatrick, 2003) – a valid and timeless question indeed.

Subsequently, different options were considered to resolve this dilemma, all of which met with considerable challenges in practice (Amnesty International, 2002; Kälin and Jimenez, 2003). The simple requirement that candidate countries should 'respect human rights' seemed in any case overly vague. The suggestions to introduce formal and measurable criteria, such as issuing a standing invitation to the Commission's special procedures, would have excluded all but the fifty-five states which had extended such invitations. The proposal to make membership dependent on the implementation of the recommendations of special procedures might have been difficult to measure and would, in effect, have turned compliance with non-binding recommendations into a prerequisite for enjoying the sovereign right to participate in a UN body. Suggestions that the ratification of all or a certain number of human rights treaties, the acceptance of individual complaints procedures of human rights treaties, or the implementation of treaty body recommendations would have made participation in a charter-based body dependent on fulfilling treaty obligations. The same can be said for the proposed criteria of having ratified the ICC statute: for a number of states, first and foremost the USA, accepting the Commission on Human Rights (and now the Council) must not be equated with accepting international criminal jurisdiction.

Negative criteria to exclude countries, such as being scrutinized under the 1235 or 1503 procedure (both introduced in the late 1960s to examine gross and systematic violations of human rights) or explicit refusal to cooperate with special procedures, would also have met with practical as well as political problems: practical because of the confusion, had such a procedure been initiated during a state's membership in the Commission, and political because it is precisely these procedures which were under attack for being biased (Kälin and Jimenez, 2003: 8–9).

More importantly, the crux of the matter is that any criterion would have led to the exclusion of important parts of the international community, and this would have gravely affected the standing of the Commission or turned it into an exclusive club of 'idealists' trying to lecture all other states about their duties, and would thus have been in some way comparable to excluding countries which have not disarmed from UN bodies concerned with disarmament (Kälin and Jimenez, 2003: 8–9). The UN High-Level Panel on Threats, Challenges and Change suggested enlarging the Commission to universal membership to put an end to such discussions (UN, 2004: para. 285). While procedural debates may then indeed have subsided, so too would have speediness in decision-making and effective response to human rights emergencies – not to mention that, instead of a handful of the worst human rights violators, all of them would have gained entrance to the club. It remains debatable as to whether the added suggestion to entrust a panel of fifteen experts to advise the Commission on country-specific and thematic procedures, and to carry out research, standard-setting and definitions (ibid.: para. 287), would have helped.

The other fundamental reason for replacing the Commission with a new body was the accusation of double standards and selectivity, levelled mostly by 'non-Western' (or 'non-Northern') countries. In essence, it was claimed that the Commission was biased in favour of powerful (Western) countries and would let their human rights abuses go unchecked, but would relentlessly go after powerless countries instead. This claim was often intertwined with the allegation that the Commission was also biased in favour of civil and political rights to the detriment of economic, social and cultural rights, the former allegedly the main concern of the West, the latter allegedly of the South.

These concerns – governmental membership, no entrance criteria and a selective approach – were lumped together in the accusation of 'politicization' made against the Commission. But what does it mean to speak about 'politicization' of human rights? Is a 'political' body bad for human rights? And what is a 'political' body? It seems that such an accusation can be put forward mainly on two levels: human rights institutions can be political for both their participants and their approach. The Commission's composition of ambassadors and diplomatic staff meant that it was driven by diplomats. Neither proven expertise in human rights law nor personal commitment to human rights is a necessary prerequisite for joining a governmental delegation to Geneva, a fact which was usually overlooked when presenting the Commission as the UN's centre of competence for human rights. As a footnote, it seems interesting that the influence of delegates' personal attitudes, values, commitment to, motivation for, and knowledge in human rights on the performance of human rights institutions is a field still largely neglected by research (Smith, 2006: 41–51). More important is the fact that diplomats are, as a seasoned participant has observed, 'often less concerned about achieving a balanced overall view and clear expression of opinion on effective protection and promotion of human rights in all parts of the world, and in individual countries with a record of human rights violations, than they are in reaching a consensus or conducting bilateral feuds in multilateral surroundings' (Strohal, 1993: 352).

Secondly, in a political body, 'decisions are taken on political lines, albeit in the light of appropriate international legal standards' (Alston, 1992: 193). In such an environment, human rights are not a free-floating humanitarian concern, nor are decisions always based on expertise, academic rigour or regard for the systematic and consistent development of the human rights regime. Human rights issues are linked with political considerations, such as national and international security or economic demands, and the different political weight of member states comes to bear in the negotiations.

Accusing a governmental body of being composed of governmental delegates or acting along political lines seems thus a somewhat empty accusation; all it says is that a political body will act like a political body. If the result of the push for 'depoliticization' is meant to make governments act apolitically in such an institution, it is not only unrealistic but also unhelpful. In a puzzling way, the political nature of human rights institutions such as the Commission seems to be the source of both their failure and their success. It is true, as many observers find, that the political games played in the Commission have damaged its credibility, effectiveness and efficiency throughout much of its existence (e.g. Humphrey, 1984: 18). Yet, it is equally true that the governmental nature of the Commission in effect contributed to its success (Strohal, 1999: 161), because it meant that governments were forced to be active in human rights issues, to take interest, to engage, to formulate an opinion, and to defend themselves in a formal, repetitive multilateral setting under the eyes of the public.

Utopian projects of a global legislating body aside, the political acts of deciding on and spelling out human rights as community norms in international law will remain the domain of governments. They may, as happened in the Commission, accept non-governmental input. Seeking to depoliticize human rights standard-setting, though, is like removing politics from national parliaments. Certainly, the Commission and all other inter-governmental human rights bodies lack essential elements of, say, national parliaments. Yet, the false division between human rights in its legal form and the political community from which they come, as criticized by Conor Gearty in the domestic arena (Gearty, 2006: 70), holds true also on the international level.

Over time, and notwithstanding political manoeuvring often slowing down its development, the Commission has acquired a variety of functions which stretched its original mandate. It has become the main global forum for human rights 'standard-setting', a place for dialogue and discussion, a space for civil society participation, a body to monitor the observance of human rights worldwide, a tool to respond to human rights violations, and a provider of technical assistance and advice to governments. All of these functions have been taken over by the Human Rights Council, which will have to continue and accommodate them within its new and somewhat broader mandate. Let us examine the achievements on which the Council can base its future activities.

## Standard-setting

Standard-setting was the first, and for long the only, task of the Commission. Drafting the Universal Declaration of Human Rights, the cornerstone of the universal human rights framework, in 1947–8 was the first accomplishment of the newly created Commission, followed by the Covenant on Civil and Political Rights and the Covenant on Economic, Social and Cultural Rights, both adopted in 1966. A range of other conventions elaborated during this period, however, most notably the Genocide Convention of 1948, did not see any input by the Commission (Alston, 1992: 132), and a closer look at its standard-setting activities after the elaboration of the two covenants also shows a mixed record. A number of human rights declarations and treaties were prepared with little input from the Commission, such as the Apartheid Convention 1973 (ibid.: 134–5). It was often the General Assembly or the Sub-Commission which performed the tasks that might have been expected to have fallen to the Commission. In the late

1970s, the tide turned, and the Commission was able to take on more responsibility for standard-setting, and this resulted in documents such as the Torture Convention in 1984, the Declaration on the Right to Development in 1986, and the Convention on the Rights of the Child in 1989 (ibid.: 136). In this period, the drafting of conventions also shifted from the plenary to subsidiary bodies within the Commission. Even then, however, the Commission had no monopoly on standard-setting. The drafting of the Convention on Migrant Workers and the Second Optional Protocol to the International Covenant on Civil and Political Rights on the death penalty saw the major involvement of the General Assembly (ibid.: 136). Despite standard-setting being the Commission's primary role for decades, its achievements should not be overestimated, as it shared this task with other UN bodies and specialized agencies such as UNESCO and ILO. The Commission was also criticized for the quality of its standard-setting, with commentators pointing out its failure to prioritize human rights concerns, the neglect of human rights standards drafted by other bodies, the lack of efficiency and expertise in the drafting process, and a weak and unsystematic quality control before the final adoption of a text (ibid.: 138; Strohal, 1999: 164).

## Advisory services and technical cooperation

As early as 1955 the Commission adopted a US-sponsored 'Action Plan' on educational and promotional activities, which included advisory services, studies, fellowships, the publication of an annual *Yearbook of Human Rights*, other promotional activities and even the submission of annual country reports (Tolley, 1987: 32–54). With this, it became clear that the Commission's activities were not limited to standard-setting and would also include assistance to governments. The advisory programme of the 1950s was reactivated in 1987, when a UN Voluntary Fund for Advisory Services and Technical Assistance in the Field of Human Rights was established (Strohal, 1993: 356–7). Technical cooperation, the term used today to describe advisory services and technical assistance, is the domain of the Office of the High Commissioner for Human Rights. Advisory services were not only used to offer assistance to states willing to improve a range of their domestic activities, from primary school education to court systems, and bring them into line with their human rights obligations. They also allowed the Commission to scrutinize countries' human rights performance outside the 1503 and 1235 procedures. Providing assistance to governments in the form of human rights education and learning, advisory services, technical assistance and capacity-building will continue to be a task of the Human Rights Council.

## Response to human rights violations: 1235 and 1503

The Commission was not set up primarily as a body to respond to human rights violations, and indeed the first two decades of its work were characterized by refraining from such activities. Nevertheless, it later turned into the principal global forum for scrutinizing and criticizing states' performance in the field of human rights. What led to this dramatic change in the Commission's role? Three phases of development can be distinguished (Alston, 1992: 139–45): a phase in which the Commission insisted that it had no power to act in response to human rights violations, followed by the development of the so-called 1235 and 1503 procedures, and finally the increased use of the so-called special procedures.

Historically, the Commission did not make much use during the first twenty years of its existence of its broad mandate to consider 'any other matter concerning human rights'. Standard-setting remained the preferred and only task, as the Commission made clear in 1947 when it stated that it 'had no power to take any action in regard to any complaints concerning human rights' (Commission on Human Rights, UN doc. E/259 of 1947: paras. 21–2). It is interesting to note that the decision could well have been a different one. Confronted with a similar situation, the Commission on the Status of Women decided at the same time that it did in fact have the power to consider complaints on violations of women's rights, and only ECOSOC decided that it would be granted no such powers (Kedzia, 2003: 65).

The 'no-power' doctrine of the Commission on Human Rights prevailed from 1946 to 1967. It was not so much the Cold War which prevented it from condemning human rights violations. Rather, the Commission itself took on a 'technical' rather than a 'political' role (Alston, 1992: 130). It perceived itself as a quasi-legislative body, for reasons Humphrey explains as follows: 'too much name-calling would have diverted us from work in hand, and there were other forums in the United Nations for the purpose' (Humphrey, 1984: 24). One may argue that in the 1940s the 'no-power' doctrine was well in line with the strict reading of Article 2(7) of the UN Charter as it prevailed at that time, and which bars the UN from intervening in matters 'essentially within the domestic jurisdiction of any State'.

The wisdom of this decision, however, was called into question not only by the victims of human rights violations, activists and observers, but even by the UN itself. A secretariat report warned that the 'no-power' doctrine would lower the prestige and authority not only of the Commission, but of the UN as a whole (Alston, 1992: 139). It is not that the Commission did not receive complaints and information on human rights violations – more than 25,000 communications in a thirteen-month period in 1951–2 alone (ibid.: 140) – but the Commission did not react. The lack of political will to respond must be attributed to Western states, as they formed the majority of UN member states at the time. There can be little doubt that they were fearful of petitions relating to their human rights performance in a time of widespread racial discrimination in parts of the Western world and colonialism in much of the rest. Back then it was developing countries which pushed for the establishment of a complaints system (ibid.: 141).

Only from 1967 onwards, in the second phase of its development, did the Commission shoulder the responsibility of striving for more effective protection against human rights violations. Having been the powerhouse for the making of human rights law, it now developed mechanisms to react to serious and gross human rights violations. South Africa provided the incentive (Pace, 1998: 501). With membership in the UN on the rise and the Convention on the Elimination of All Forms of Racial Discrimination adopted, developing countries, with the support of Eastern European countries, put the fight against apartheid in South Africa on the Commission's agenda as a priority, until it reached a point where the General Assembly called upon the Commission to put an end to apartheid and similar gross human rights violations, using the phrase 'wherever they occur' (General Assembly resolution 2144 A (XXI) 1966). This led to the establishment of the 1235 and 1503 procedures in the Commission, both based on ECOSOC resolutions (ECOSOC resolution 1235 (XLII) of 1967 and ECOSOC resolution 1503 (XLVIII) of 1970).

With resolution 1235, ECOSOC authorized the Commission and its (then) Sub-Commission on the Prevention of Discrimination and the Protection of Minorities to 'examine information relevant to gross violations of human rights and fundamental freedoms, as exemplified by the policy of apartheid as practised in the Republic of South Africa and in the Territory of South West Africa' (para. 2) and decided 'that the Commission on Human Rights may, in appropriate cases, and after careful consideration of the information thus made available to it, [. . .] make a thorough study of situations which reveal a consistent pattern of violations of human rights [. . .] and report, with recommendations thereon, to the Economic and Social Council' (para. 3). This resolution was a breakthrough, because it allowed a public debate on the human rights situation in states. This developed later into the Commission's famous agenda item 9 ('Question of the violation of human rights and fundamental freedom in any part of the world'). It also paved the way for the establishment of the Commission's special procedures, which we will consider further below.

While a considerable number of human rights violations were brought to the attention of the Commission in the years following the adoption of resolution 1235, it was not before the late 1970s that it acted in any useful manner with regard to such allegations. In condemning human rights violations in Kampuchea, Nicaragua and Equatorial Guinea, it made the first steps towards publicly discussing and condemning human rights violations (Alston, 1992: 159). Since then, a substantial number of countries have been subjected to scrutiny under the 1235 procedure, albeit in an unbalanced and haphazard manner (ibid.: 162). Indeed, the way in which the Commission singled out countries to be subjected to the 1235 procedure made up the core of the criticism levelled against it (e.g., Franck, 1984; Boekle, 1995).

With resolution 1503, ECOSOC allowed the Commission (or rather a specific body set up within the Commission's (then) Sub-Commission on the Prevention of Discrimination and the Protection of Minorities) 'to consider all communications, including replies of Governments thereon, received by the Secretary-General under Council resolution 728F (XXVIII) of 30 July 1959 with a view to bringing to the attention of the Sub-Commission those communications, together with replies of Governments, if any, which appear to reveal a consistent pattern of gross and reliably attested violations of human rights and fundamental freedoms.' As can be seen, the 1503 procedure developed gradually (Ize-Charrin, 2001: 293–6): in resolution 75(V) of 1947, ECOSOC – while still accepting its 'no-power' doctrine – asked the Commission to summarize communications on human rights violations received by the UN in a confidential list. In ECOSOC resolution 728 F (XXVIII) of 1959 the Commission was asked to compile two lists, a non-confidential one with communications on general human rights principles and a confidential one on other relevant communications, which, in the absence of any further action, was obviously an exercise in futility (Alston, 1992: 140; Kedzia, 2003: 65–6). It is hardly surprising that observers referred to this procedure as 'the most elaborate wastepaper basket ever invented' (Humphrey, 1984: 28). Finally, resolution 1503 introduced a three-step procedure, with a working group of the Sub-Commission, the Sub-Commission itself and the Commission, to examine the cases under its remit. The procedure evolved further and was revised in 2000 to 'reinforce the value of

1503' and to ensure 'objectivity, impartiality and confidentiality' (ECOSOC resolution 2000/3). The number of cases rose from around 20,000 a year to 300,000 in the late 1980s (Alston, 1992: 146). There were nearly 100,000 communications in 2000, around 30,000 in 2002 and around 18,000 in 2003 (Kedzia, 2003: 69). Impressive as these figures seem, the rigorous filtering process ensured that each year only a handful of states were considered by the Commission under the 1503 procedure.

Furthermore, unlike the public 1235 procedure, 1503 was (and still is) a confidential procedure. The resolution left no doubt about that: 'the committee's procedure shall be confidential, its proceedings shall be conducted in private meetings and its communications shall not be publicized in any way' (para. 7(c)). The Commission has become more lenient along the way, and since 1978 the names of the countries under scrutiny are made public (Nowak, 1991: 48); today they can be found on the UN's website (http://www.unhchr.ch/html/menu2/8/stat1.htm).

The objective of both the 1235 and the 1503 procedure has always been to identify situations of consistent patterns of gross human rights violations. The 1503 procedure, in particular, is an 'information-petition system' (Rehman, 2003: 42), as it uses petition-like submissions to the UN in order to ascertain information on systematic human rights violations. The two procedures were never intended to provide solace or remedy for individual acts of wrongdoing, but rather to see the victim as a 'piece of evidence' (Alston, 1992: 146). While 1235 has become synonymous with the public scrutiny of countries which violate human rights and as such was, notwithstanding its shortcomings, a major step forward, the value of 1503 remains disputed.

Historically it is of great importance, as, together with 1235, it paved the way for the understanding that massive human rights violations are no longer within the domestic jurisdiction of states. Scholars and NGO activists agree, however, that otherwise the 1503 procedure has shown limited results (Nowak, 1991: 53–6; Bossuyt, 1985: 184–5; Cook, 1993: 41–4; Rodley, 2002: 188–90). Out of the vast numbers of complaints received, very few countries made it to the final stage of the procedure, and a 'thorough study', as requested by resolution 1503, was hardly ever commissioned; nor have other serious follow-up measures been reported which would lend credence to the procedure. Also, being applied only once a year, it was not a tool for urgent action. Due to its confidentiality and the exclusion of non-governmental organizations, it lacked the strongest, perhaps the only, effective pressure: the mobilization of public opinion. For decades, calls for changing the procedures went unheard. Some have called for the abolition of 1503 (Ermacora, 1993: 141), others for drastic reform because 'the short-comings of the procedure are so considerable, its tangible achievements so scarce, the justifications offered in its favour so modest, and the need for an effective and universally applicable petitions procedure so great' (Alston, 1992: 154). True, 1503 provided a fall-back procedure which allowed the Commission to take up country situations in relation to which it could not find support for either a public discussion under 1235 or the establishment of a special procedures. By the time the Commission came to an end, however, it had become an outdated reminder of a time when human rights protection meant inter-governmental action based on the secret exchanges of diplomatic formulas in sealed conference rooms.

The future of both the 1235 and 1503 procedure is now in the hands of the Human Rights Council, which is obliged (under General Assembly resolution 60/251 of 2006, which established the Human Rights Council), 'to maintain a complaints procedure' (para. 6). The Council has to review all mandates, mechanisms, functions and responsibilities within one year of its first session, and this includes the 1235 and 1503 procedures. The future scope of the procedure and the criteria to be applied to complaints as well as the logistical framework could (at least one may hope) lead to the establishment of new subsidiary bodies or introduce entirely new avenues for victims of human rights violations to address the Council and file complaints to the UN.

## Special procedures

In a third phase of the development of the Commission on Human Rights, which commenced in the 1960s, a new tool was invented to remedy the weaknesses of its monitoring mechanisms. The Commission began to resort to so-called special procedures for investigative purposes. Over the years, special procedures became the backbone of its activities. They deal either with selected human rights issues ('thematic procedures') or with the human rights situation in a given country ('country procedures'). The term 'special procedures' covers in fact four types of mandate: Special Rapporteurs, Independent Experts, Working Groups, and Special Representatives of the Secretary-General. While initially this terminology was meant to demonstrate hierarchy among the mechanisms, the different denominations are today used more imprecisely (Kedzia, 2003: 51). The Human Rights Council has taken over these special procedures, so what is said in the following in a retrospective view will be of future relevance, too.

The development of country procedures can be traced back to 1963, when for the first time the Commission planned a mission to investigate human rights violations in the Buddhist community in Vietnam, which never materialized as a result of changed circumstances on the ground (Sunga, 2001: 236). In 1967 the Special Working Group of Experts on Southern Africa was created, followed in 1975 by an Ad Hoc Working Group to Inquire into the Human Rights Situation in Chile (Bossuyt, 1985: 185–6; Sunga, 2001: 236–41). Thematic procedures were created as a response to human rights violations in Latin America in the 1970s and 1980s (Alston, 1992: 173–4; Rudolf, 2000: 292–6). The first such procedure was the Working Group on Enforced Involuntary Disappearances, established in 1980 (Flood, 1998: 49–70). Others followed, such as the Special Rapporteur on Summary or Arbitrary Executions (1982) and the Special Rapporteur on Torture (1985). To date, forty-one special procedures exist, thirteen of which deal with country situations (Belarus, Burundi, Cambodia, Cuba, the Democratic People's Republic of Korea, the Democratic Republic of Congo, Haiti, Liberia, Myanmar, the occupied Palestinian Territories, Somalia, Sudan and Uzbekistan). Twenty-eight thematic mandates span issues as diverse as torture, housing, education, extrajudicial executions, child pornography, freedom of expression and religion, health, indigenous peoples, mercenaries, migrants, people of African descent, terrorism, racism, the dumping of toxic waste, trafficking in persons, economic reform policies and foreign debt, minorities, the independence of judges and lawyers, extreme poverty, violence against women, internally displaced persons and the human rights responsibilities of transnational corporations.

Bearing in mind the number of massive human rights violations worldwide and the number of possible thematic concerns, it seems astounding that the Commission has not created more mandates. Yet the establishment of a special procedure, in particular a country procedure, was a political process which allowed for selectivity, and this remains the case (Flinterman, 1999: 148; Ricca, 2002: 166–8). Commission members were free to decide on which countries and issues to focus their attention, as long as majorities among Commission members were found. No wonder that the reasons for establishing special procedures varied (Cook, 1993: 33–4). Some were created in response to prior studies or recommendations, others in reaction to public pressure or lobbying by NGOs. Some were strongly requested by governments (often themselves driven by domestic pressure groups), either in pursuit of specific interests in human rights issues or to exert political pressure on other governments. As a consequence, the list of special procedures remains an inchoate assemblage of serious human rights concerns, governmental pet projects, and compromise decisions and, once again, opened up the Commission to critique for being biased, selective and guided by double standards.

Legally, Special Rapporteurs, Independent Experts, Working Groups, and Special Representatives of the Secretary-General reside in two worlds: they are subsidiary bodies of the Commission (Rudolf, 2000: 296), but the mandate holders and working group members are independent experts. As such, they decide independently (within their overall mandate) on their focus, priorities and work schedule. They are covered by the 1946 Convention on the Privileges and Immunities of the United Nations (Lempinen, 2001: 60–80). Country procedures are established for a renewable period of one year (with the exception of the Special Rapporteur on the occupied Palestinian Territories, whose mandate lasts 'until the end of occupation'), thematic procedures for three years. The actual appointment of the mandate holder(s) was the obligation of the Commission's chairperson (or, in the case of a Special Representative, of the UN Secretary-General), who had considerable freedom in his choice and was only bound by political consideration in negotiating with interested parties. The choice of mandate holders was, and remains, crucial because much rested on their personality. Balancing independence and objectivity with authority and political skills, research qualities, and a charismatic and eloquent appearance on stage makes for the ideal candidate, provided he or she has a solid income, as the position is unpaid and little assistance is provided by the Office of the High Commissioner of Human Rights. In the two years 2002–3, for example, the regular UN budget allowed for only fifteen posts in the office to assist thirty-seven special procedures (Kedzia, 2003: 57).

Special procedures serve a range of functions. The mandate holders themselves have put it like this:

> Our task is clear: what we do is render the international norms that have been developed more operative. We do not merely deal with theoretical questions, but strive to enter into constructive dialogues with governments and to seek their cooperation as regards concrete situations, incidents and cases. The core of our work is to study and investigate in an objective manner with a view to understanding the situations and recommending to governments solutions to overcome the problem of securing respect for human rights. (Joint declaration of the independent experts responsible for the special procedures for the protection of human rights, UN doc. A/CONF.157/9, 1993)

Country procedures assess a given state, while thematic procedures examine specific, contemporary human rights concerns. Put simply, country procedures monitor the application of all human rights in one country, while thematic procedures monitor one human right in all countries. For both, a number of intertwined functions can be identified: study, 'prosecution', protection, promotion, good offices and publicity. Thematic procedures may be endowed with two additional functions, namely knowledge generation and standard-setting.

All country and thematic mandates presented reports to the Commission (now the Council), together with their recommendations, based on an investigation carried out in their capacity as independent experts. This main 'study' function of all special procedures can be traced back to ECOSOC resolution 1235 and its mandate of making 'a thorough study of situations which reveal a consistent pattern of violations of human rights', as discussed above. The process of studying, which in fact consists of three steps (investigation, reporting, recommendation), has been refined over time. Observation, fact-finding and documentation produce the necessary information. Such information is analysed and assessed in the light of human rights norms and standards, which in turn allows for the identification of shortcomings. 'Studies' are anything from simple factual reports, detailed country analysis, and databases to the engagement with an issue on an academic level. The outcome of studies is reported (previously to the Commission, now to the Council), and contains conclusions and recommendations for further action.

Field visits are a crucial element in this process, as they allow for visibility, reliability and first-hand information (Lempinen, 2001: 23–6). Constraints on such visits are twofold: limited financial resources often mean that necessary specialist medical, forensic and other expertise cannot be deployed, but more importantly special procedures depend on governments' cooperation for such visits. Refusal to cooperate is common and takes various forms, such as denying entry into the country or declining access to specific places. For some country procedures this makes the task of special procedures next to impossible, and they have to try and fill in information from other sources. In contrast, cooperative governments often complain that, once they open their doors to special procedures, what they get in return is a hive of excited experts descending on their prey, while countries with far worse human rights records continue to rest undisturbed. It is debatable whether there is in fact an obligation under international law to cooperate with special procedures, or whether such cooperation is a voluntary act (ibid.: 214–20).

Sometimes, the political cost of non-cooperation makes governments more open towards special procedures, but such costs are generally felt as 'not consistently prohibitive' (Alston, 1992: 171). Only fifty-five states have by now extended a standing invitation to all holders of thematic mandates (http://www.ohchr.org/english/bodies/chr/special/index.htm).

Special procedures assess a country's performance, whether or not they are explicitly mandated to do so. This is particularly true for country procedures, but may also be the case with thematic procedures, once they relate the human right under examination to the performance of a given country. Their assessment is based on international human rights law, and, however cautiously worded or academically paraphrased some of these assessments may be, they inevitably speak out on 'right' and 'wrong'. This comes close to the work of a prosecutor in national legal systems (Alston, 1992: 168) in the sense that special procedures compile sufficient evidence for the Commission (now the Council) to decide upon and respond to. It is this inherent 'prosecutorial' function to which states often object. They see it as incompatible with the cooperative and recommendatory approach to which special procedures should, in their view, resort.

Despite their primarily consultative and recommendatory role, special procedures can also be protective agents. This protective function becomes particularly apparent in 'urgent actions' or 'urgent appeals' undertaken by some mandate holders in reaction to individual cases of human rights violations. Urgent actions are usually based on information submitted by NGOs and are addressed directly to the foreign minister of the country in question in the hope of avoiding irreparable harm to the victim. Four mandates, namely the Working Group on Enforced or Involuntary Disappearances, and the Special Rapporteurs on Summary and Arbitrary Executions, for Torture, and for Religious Intolerance, are explicitly empowered to do so (Kedzia, 2003: 54–5). Unlike complaints procedures under human rights treaties, which are a response to allegations put forward by the victim, urgent actions are preventive 'humanitarian' measures and are not necessarily accusatory in character (Rodley, 2001: 282). The Special Representative on human rights defenders established in 2000, to name another example, is mandated to recommend effective strategies for the protection of human rights defenders. As states could only agree on a non-binding declaration on human rights defenders (UN doc. A/RES/53/144, 1999) rather than a legally binding treaty with its own supervisory means, the Special Representative is a kind of substitute for such a protective mechanism.

Special procedures may establish and continue a dialogue between the UN and governments, promote acceptance of human rights norms and standards, and generally engage governments in a multilateral environment (Lempinen, 2001: 27–30). In so doing, they have a promotional role, which is less specific and targeted than protective or prosecutorial functions, but not less important. The promotional function is closely associated with the publicity function, which enables special procedures, whatever their mandate, to 'inform the world' (Alston, 1992: 168). In their dual role as independent experts (usually with an academic and/or NGO background) and as subsidiary bodies of the UN which are established and mandated by governments, they often bridge the gap between governments, inter-governmental institutions, epistemic communities, civil society organizations and the public. The links to NGOs are usually close, and mandate holders rely heavily on cooperation with NGOs, engage in public debate, and work with national human rights and civil society institutions. In turn, their reports provide valuable tools for NGOs, not only because of the information they contain, but also because they carry with them the authority and reliability of the UN.

In addition, special procedures have an inherent diplomatic function, which may also be described as conciliatory function or as making use of 'good offices'. This is particularly apparent for Special Representatives of the Secretary-General. As a matter of fact, the very first thematic special procedure, the Working Group on Enforced or Involuntary Disappearances, was mandated to act as a channel for communication between families of disappeared persons and governments. More recently, the Special Rapporteur on the human rights situation in Somalia suddenly found himself, in Febuary 2005, entrusted with ensuring the safe passage home of a seventeen-year-old woman accused of espionage, who was released from prison by Somaliland authorities and given 'into his custody' (UN Press Release HR/4811, 4 February 2005), thereby combining the protective function with one of good offices.

Thematic procedures can fulfil an additional function, namely generating knowledge. It is often only through their work that the full implications of a certain human right or a range of rights surfaces and enters into the broader human rights discourse in the political or academic field and the public domain. Shedding light on new developments, linkages between different concerns, and obstacles for the implementation of human rights sometimes creates a new understanding of the scope and limits of human rights. In a few cases, this can in fact amount to standard-setting activities. The (then) Special

Representative on internally displaced persons, Francis Deng, may serve as an example. He, together with a team of legal experts of his choice, drafted a set of standards to be observed when dealing with internally displaced persons. The entire drafting process took place outside formal inter-governmental frameworks, and while the guiding principles were never formally adopted – as mentioned in chapter 3, they were 'appreciated' by the Commission (Commission on Human Rights resolution 2004/55: para. 6) – they exerted, and continue to exert, considerable influence (Cohen, 2005).

It seems remarkable that an accumulation of such *ad hoc* mandates, carried out by a handful of part-time, unpaid academics, constituted the core of the Commission's protective and promotional activities, and continues to do so in the Human Rights Council. The procedures developed in response to concrete needs, and there was never any overarching master plan in the creation of special procedures; nor was there any exhaustive accompanying normative framework to guide their development. The mandate holders themselves emphasized their unique position in a joint statement during the 1993 Vienna World Conference on Human Rights, when they said that

> [t]his broad range of procedures constitutes a unique and crucial element in the implementation of the body of specific standards that have been adopted by universal consensus through the United Nations General Assembly. While it may have never been conceived as a 'system', the evolving collection of these procedures and mechanisms now clearly constitutes and functions as a system of human rights protection. (Joint declaration of the independent experts responsible for the special procedures for the protection of human rights, A/CONF.157/9, 1993)

Special procedures differ in mandate, focus, style, resources and working methods, and the *ad hoc* nature of their establishment makes reform attempts difficult and unpredictable. The lack of planning, structure and financial support, the political element in the creation of mandates, their questionable legal status, and their inconsistent working methods have led to calls for reform throughout their existence. Enhanced coordination and cooperation between special procedures and other UN human rights bodies, a clear normative framework for the nomination and selection of mandate holders, rules and codes of conduct of their work, and improved follow-up to their reports have been identified as priorities for change (Cook, 1993: 50–2).

The mandate holders themselves have reacted to calls for reform by establishing closer links, and since 1994 they have met annually to discuss possible cooperation and reform of the system. Joint urgent appeals, joint visits and joint press releases are becoming more frequent, and more interaction between special procedures, treaty bodies and the Office of the High Commissioner can be observed (Kedzia, 2003: 58). Although some common standards in their work can be identified (Rudolf, 2000: 292), the quest is ongoing for the establishment of a common code of practice or guidelines for their work, including their work ethics, standards, methodology and benchmarks in documenting, fact-finding, assessing information and reporting, and conduct of on-site visits (Ramcharan, 2002a: 103–4). Once again, the struggle over formal arrangements is a contest over rival versions of human rights institutions between dependence and autonomy, and nowhere is this battle fought more fervently than in the debate over the future of special procedures. The attempts of a great number of states to exercise tighter control and curtail the work of special procedures in the name of 'streamlining' and 'rationalizing' them are but an acknowledgement that they are effective. Preserving their independence and, as a consequence, keeping the respective regulatory framework to the minimum is crucial for the functioning and credibility of the UN's human rights system.

Special procedures have long left their mere auxiliary character behind. Over time, the have acquired new functions and gained autonomy from their parent body (Kedzia, 2003: 49–59); indeed, they are the most autonomous bodies in our analysis of global human rights institutions. The praise they receive from human rights activists speaks for the credibility and success which such autonomy entails: they have been called the 'most innovative, responsive and flexible tools of the human rights machinery' (Amnesty International, 2005: 5). They are held in high esteem by human rights NGOs, as they 'have provided valuable conceptual analysis on key human rights themes; have served as a mechanism of last resort for victims; have sometimes prevented serious abuses, and even saved lives, through urgent appeals; have served as an early-warning mechanism to draw attention to human rights crises; and have frequently provided high-quality diagnosis of individual country situations, including by carrying out country missions' (International Commission of Jurists, 2005: 4). Because they are the most visible element of the Commission's protective work, they have been referred to as the 'front-line protection actors of the United Nations' (Ramcharan, 2002a: 81). Indeed, unlike other UN human rights institutions, they move around, go to places where human rights are violated and talk to victims. They link the domestic with the international and the global with the local. They have given operational capacity to the Commission and remain perhaps the most successful devices the UN has yet developed to protect and promote human rights, assist victims, suggest solutions, give visibility to human rights, expose states which routinely violate human rights, and bring human rights from the conference room to the field and to the public domain.

## The Commission 1946–2006: achievements and legacy

The Commission is a prime example of the three manifestations of global human rights institutions (arena, instrument and actor), and evaluating its overall achievements over the past sixty years depends on which of those manifestations is in the observer's mind (Alston, 1992: 205–9). As a forum, the Commission allowed for confrontations between states with different views while at the same time keeping tensions and conflicts within a formalized arena. It brought together the like-minded and forced consensus on many questions. It opened space for NGOs and civil society groups. As such, and taking into account the limited financial assistance human rights receive in the UN institutional structure, it was as successful as could be expected of any international forum. And it was as inclusive towards non-state actors as the international legal order would allow; in fact it has left other international institutions behind with regard to the participation of NGOs and has precluded any idea of ever returning to discussing human rights behind closed doors (historic remnants such as the 1503 procedure notwithstanding). It contributed to human rights standard-setting and gave some direction to the UN's human rights system. However, while it overcame its initial reluctance to scrutinize states and received and channelled complaints, its response to massive human rights violations was inadequate. On the other hand, its special procedures are remarkably autonomous actors which have overturned the perception of the Commission as a mere instrument of governments. They are also a case study for the ways in which, in the absence of a substantial regulatory framework, success can come about.

Measuring the Commission by its output, i.e., the effectiveness of protection offered, shows a mixed record with little success and many more failures. The sluggish response to crisis situations, the lack of fairness in procedure, waning moral authority, practical ineffectiveness, inconsistent approach, block voting and regional alliances undermined its credibility. Its design as a governmental body often precluded any sanctioning of states' misbehaviour. Too often, the Commission was more a ritual than a remedy, as too many of its repetitive statements and resolutions went unheard. Yet, for sixty years it was the main globally accepted forum in which governments fought their battles on human rights. Furthermore, the process mattered as much as the result, and what we witnessed over six decades was indeed 'an important socialization process by which competing conceptions [were] not just communicated but explained and justified' (Alston, 1992: 205).

# Human Rights Council

In March 2006, the General Assembly dissolved the Commission and replaced it with a Human Rights Council. The proposal to create such a council had been rather modestly tucked away in the final part of the UN Secretary-General's Report *In Larger Freedom* (UN, 2005: para. 183). The idea which was floated in the report was to elevate the new Council to become a principal organ of the UN (and thus to put it on the same level as the Security Council) or, alternatively, to make it a subsidiary body of the General Assembly. UN Secretary-General Kofi Annan was strongly in favour of the former option, so that the two UN councils on security and development (the Security Council and ECOSOC) would be complemented by a council on human rights, thus bringing more institutional clarity to the UN framework (Secretary-General's address to the 61st session of Commission on Human Rights, http://www.ohchr.org/english/bodies/chr/docs/61chr/sgchr.doc). Even before that, other suggestions were on the table, including enlarging the Commission to universal membership (UN, 2004: para. 285) or changing it back into its originally intended shape as an expert body to assist the new Human Rights Council (Kälin and Jimenez, 2003: 3–4).

At the 60th UN General Assembly, the 'World Summit', in 2005, UN member states decided to create a Human Rights Council as a subsidiary body of the General Assembly (General Assembly resolution A/RES/60/1, 2005: para. 157), but it took five more months of negotiations before the General Assembly could (in General Assembly resolution 60/251 of 15 March 2006) establish it. The text had to be put to a vote at the request of the USA. They had wished to exclude from membership in the Council states against which measures under Chapter VII of the UN Charter, related to human rights abuses or acts of terrorism, were in place (as explained by US Ambassador John Bolton after the vote, http://www.state.gov/p/io/rls/rm/63143.htm), but this proposal was not taken on board in the negotiations. Subsequently the USA (together with Israel, the Marshall Islands and

Palau) voted against the establishment of the Council. Three countries abstained (Belarus, Iran, Venezuela) and 170 states voted in favour of the resolution. As a subsidiary body of the General Assembly the Council is no longer subordinate to ECOSOC, as was the case with the Commission, but neither is it on a par with the Security Council, as wished for by Kofi Annan and others. The Commission ended its existence on 16 June 2006, at its 62nd session, and the new Council began its work on 19 June 2006.

## Membership

Whereas the Commission consisted of fifty-three members, the Council is composed of forty-seven members. The Council has assumed, by the said resolution, all the mandates, functions and responsibilities of the Commission and will maintain the system of special procedures and complaints, but it is under an obligation to review these mandates, mechanisms, functions and responsibilities so as to improve or rationalize them. It will also assume the role and responsibilities of the Commission with regard to the work of the Office of the High Commissioner. Within five years, the General Assembly is obliged to review the status of the Council.

Members of the Council are elected in secret ballot by a majority of the General Assembly. This is a positive development compared with the election of Commission members, the open process of which allowed for more horse-trading between candidates. More important, a set of membership criteria introduces hurdles for candidates wishing to join the Council. As with the Commission, membership remains open to all UN member states, but when electing members the General Assembly 'shall take into account the contribution of candidates to the promotion and protection of human rights and their voluntary pledges and commitments made thereto' (para. 8 of General Assembly resolution 60/251). Candidates for the first election have already given such voluntary and non-binding promises ('pledges') on how they will uphold human rights and what steps they will take during their time on the Council. Para. 9 of General Assembly resolution 60/251 stipulates three other duties of Council members, one general ('members elected to the Council shall uphold the highest standards in the promotion and protection of human rights'), one specific ('[members shall] be reviewed under the universal periodic review mechanism during their term of membership') and one covering general cooperation ('[members shall] fully cooperate with the Council'). These five new elements – members' contribution to human rights, voluntary pledges, the obligation to cooperate, the duty to uphold the highest standards of human rights and the universal periodic review procedure for members – are certainly not the qualitative criteria some states and observers wanted introduced. There are also no sanctions for failing to comply with the requirements.

General Assembly resolution 60/251 thus aims to raise the credibility of the Council by mixing voluntary self-commitments of members with a heightened responsibility of the General Assembly to look after its subsidiary body. Not only is the General Assembly meant to consider the possible contribution of candidates and consider their pledges, but it may also, by a two-thirds majority, suspend the right of membership in the Council. The proactive elements (the General Assembly's responsibility to choose candidates carefully, their pledges, their anticipated cooperation and their responsibility to uphold the highest human rights standards) lack binding force, and any non-fulfilment will remain without consequences. The obligatory application of the universal periodic review is merely a procedural requirement, and the General Assembly's power to suspend membership in the Council will in all likelihood be applied in only the most serious of cases, if at all. Tucked away in para. 7 of General Assembly resolution 60/251 (which stipulates that Council members shall be elected for a period of three years) is a provision with consequences for the permanent members of the Security Council, which, following an unwritten agreement, were able permanently to be present in the Commission on Human Rights. Now, only two consecutive terms of office are allowed for all Council members, after which they will not be immediately re-eligible.

The provision on equitable geographic distribution was kept and adapted to the new figures, allowing for the election of thirteen states from the African group, thirteen from the Asian group, six from the Eastern European group, eight from GRULAC and seven from WEOG. This leaves in place the group system which had contributed to the decline of the Commission. Regional groups have usually put forward as many candidates as seats available, thus leaving others no choice but to ratify the decision of the respective group. In addition, some groups, such as the African group, were never overly concerned with the human rights credentials of their candidates (Roth, 2005: 135). In general, the group system simply does not adequately reflect the realities of today's world (Kedzia, 2003: 11). As in all international institutions (Smith, 2006: 55–78), other groups have formed or gained influence in UN human rights bodies, such as the European Union, the Organization of the Islamic Conference, JUSCANZ (Japan, the USA, Canada, Australia and New Zealand, now expanded to include

Switzerland, Norway, Mexico and Iceland), the Like Minded Group (LMG), an informal network of developing countries, among them Algeria, China, Cuba, Egypt, India, Indonesia, Malaysia, Pakistan, Nigeria, Syria and Tunisia, and the Human Security Network (Austria, Canada, Chile, Costa Rica, Greece, Ireland, Jordan, Mali, the Netherlands, Norway, Slovenia, Switzerland and Thailand, with South Africa as observer). All these groups work in a landscape scarred by the fault-lines of the tension between 'the North' and 'the South', or between industrialized and less industrialized countries, making the group system appear largely anachronistic.

Can all these provisions ensure that countries which are grossly violating international human rights norms will not be able to sit on the Council? The reader may answer this question in light of the list of countries which the first elections to the Council on 9 May 2006 brought into office: Algeria, Cameroon, Djibouti, Gabon, Ghana, Mali, Mauritius, Morocco, Nigeria, Senegal, South Africa, Tunisia and Zambia from the African group; Argentina, Brazil, Cuba, Ecuador, Guatemala, Mexico, Peru and Uruguay from GRULAC; Bahrain, Bangladesh, China, India, Indonesia, Japan, Jordan, Malaysia, Pakistan, the Philippines, the Republic of Korea, Saudi Arabia and Sri Lanka from the Asian group; Canada, Finland, France, Germany, the Netherlands, Switzerland and the United Kingdom from WEOG (the USA did not choose to be a candidate for this first election); and Azerbaijan, the Czech Republic, Poland, Romania, the Russian Federation and Ukraine from the Eastern European group.

Obviously, countries with a troublesome human rights record still make it into the Council. As a footnote, it may also be interesting to note that the African and Asian group combined have strengthened their position compared with the other regional groups. This may have implications for setting up country mechanisms, towards which those two groups traditionally display a more hostile attitude. While in the Commission ten WEOG members (which as a group are most supportive of country procedures) faced twenty-seven African and Asian members in deciding on such procedures, the ratio in the Council is seven to twenty-six.

There is no reason to believe that, with this composition, the Council will be less 'politicized' than the Commission was. Set in larger context, however, the attempt to introduce criteria for states' participation in inter-governmental bodies which are no longer in line with traditional legal requirements based on sovereignty as an absolute right must be viewed as an inspiring innovation and a possible example for other institutions to follow.

## Mandate

General Assembly resolution 60/251 specifies a considerable range of tasks for the Council. By and large, the Council builds on the Commission's functions, thus ensuring continuity. In particular, it is required to:

- address situations of human rights violations, including gross and systematic violations, and make recommendations;
- undertake a universal periodic review of each and every state;
- contribute, through dialogue and cooperation, to the prevention of human rights violations;
- respond promptly to human rights emergencies;
- serve as a forum for dialogue on thematic issues;
- make recommendations on the promotion and protection of human rights and, more specifically, make recommendations to the General Assembly for the further development of international human rights law;
- cooperate closely with governments, regional organizations, national human rights institutions and civil society;
- promote universal respect for human rights;
- promote human rights education and learning, advisory services, technical assistance and capacity-building;
- promote the full implementation of human rights obligations undertaken by states and the follow-up of UN human rights conferences and summits; and
- promote the effective coordination and mainstreaming of human rights within the UN system.

This list weaves together a considerable range of the core tasks identified in chapter 3, making the remit of the Council an example of the breadth and scope of activities which human rights institutions have come to fulfil. The most innovative among them is the Universal Periodic Review (UPR), a procedure under which all UN member states are to be subjected to scrutiny on a regular basis. In the words of General Assembly resolution 60/251, the Council shall 'undertake a periodic review, based on objective and reliable information, of the fulfilment by each State of its human rights obligations and commitments in a manner which ensures universality of coverage and equal treatment with respect to all States; the review shall be a cooperative mechanism, based on an interactive dialogue, with the full involvement of the country concerned and with consideration given to its capacity-building needs; such a mechanism shall complement and not duplicate the work of the treaty bodies' (para. 5).

The hope is that this peer-review system will end the double standards applied in the Commission in deciding which countries are the subject of a resolution. The precise means by which the Council can ensure that the requirements of the UPR (universality, objectivity, cooperation and interactivity) are implemented will be crucial for its credibility. In particular, the new system must not duplicate the work of special procedures and treaty bodies (Nowak, 2006: 25). It is up to the Council to determine the modalities of the UPR within one year after holding its first session. The trade policy review mechanism under the World Trade Organization (WTO), the OECD peer review mechanism, or the African Peer Review Mechanism set up under NEPAD, the New Partnership for Africa's Development, provide elaborate examples of similar mechanisms. A simpler model, which has been proposed by Canada, is more likely to be realized. It would be easier to administer as it relies on information provided by the High Commissioner, the treaty bodies and special procedures, with NGOs submitting additional information, all of which would be discussed in interactive dialogue sessions with government representatives (Abraham, 2006: 79).

While the Council is free to decide on the format, some guidelines on conducting UPRs can be found in General Assembly resolution 60/251 (Abraham, 2006: 73–4): universal coverage and equal treatment of all countries, a cooperative approach, due consideration for a state's capacity-building needs, complementing rather than duplicating the work of treaty bodies, impartiality, objectivity and non-selectivity, and a general attitude towards enhancing the promotion and protection of human rights. The UPR must also reflect the Council's working methods, which are to be transparent, fair and impartial, be designed to enable genuine dialogue, be results oriented, allow for follow-up to recommendations and give space for interaction with special procedures.

Still, critical questions remain to be resolved. General Assembly resolution 60/251 refers only in a general way to the human rights standards of states which are to be scrutinized, leaving the precise nature of these standards open: is it treaty provisions, the Universal Declaration of Human Rights, customary law, resolutions of the Commission and the Council, or voluntary commitments that the Council will use as benchmarks? Furthermore, the logistics of the UPR should not be underestimated. Scrutinizing over 190 states in a process which reasonably should include some form of dialogue with governments will take considerable time and resources. Estimates indicate that, were the Council to follow the Canadian suggestion of interactive dialogue based on existing information, and hold three hours of dialogue with each government, this could still mean six weeks of review per year for approximately sixty states, meaning that after three years a first round of review of all states could be concluded (Canada, 2006: 4). In addition, states with a hostile attitude towards country-oriented special procedures will be encouraged to call for the abolition of this type of monitoring and replace it with the UPR, whose modalities are yet uncertain (Bossuyt, 2006: 553). Fine-tuning the interplay between the UPR, country resolutions and country-specific mandates, special sessions of the Council and the work of treaty bodies is not an easy task and shows that it is no longer the lack of adequate inter-governmental human rights procedures, bodies and institutions which is the crux, but rather their coordination and cooperation.

## First steps

The idea that, like the Security Council, the Human Rights Council should meet permanently was not taken on board by the General Assembly when it decided on its establishment. Still, the Council can meet with more continuity than the Commission, which was in session only once a year for six weeks. Now, sessions have to be scheduled no fewer than three times a year for a total period of no less than ten weeks, and special sessions may be convened as necessary. Any Council member is entitled to call for such a special session, which is held upon agreement by one-third of members. Soon after its inauguration, in July 2006, the Council held its first such session, on the occupied Palestinian Territories, and others followed. Increased meeting time, more evenly spread out over the year, and more special sessions are indeed a welcome and badly needed innovation.

The Council has to apply the rules of procedure established for committees of the General Assembly rather than the rules of procedure of ECOSOC functional commissions, as was the case with the Commission. The conduct of business is to be – in the words of the resolution establishing the Council – 'transparent, fair and impartial and shall enable genuine dialogue, be results oriented, allow for subsequent follow-up discussions to recommendations and their implementation and also allow for substantive interaction with special procedures and mechanisms' (General Assembly resolution 60/251: para. 12). There is no change in the way in which NGOs, inter-governmental organizations, national human rights institutions and UN specialized agencies participate in the sessions. In fact, the Council is called upon to work closely not only with governments and inter-governmental organizations but also with national human rights institutions and civil society (General Assembly resolution 60/251: para. 5(h)). The UN High Commissioner for Human Rights also retains its position vis-à-vis the Council.

As noted earlier, the Commission's mandates (i.e., the special procedures) are carried over. Within one year of establishment of the Council, a review has to be conducted so as to examine ways to rationalize and strengthen the special procedures. This review has to extend also to the Sub-Commission on the Promotion and Protection of Human Rights. In its inaugural session in June 2006, the Council decided – much as was to be expected – to extend the mandate of all special procedures of the Commission for one year and to establish working groups which would elaborate the modalities of the UPR and formulate concrete suggestions to rationalize and improve the special procedures (Human Rights Council decision 2006/102). It also adopted a draft programme of work for the first year (Human Rights Council decision 2006/105). With this, the Council has laid a foundation for its future work.

Has the reform succeeded in 'giving the emperor real clothes' (Rahmani-Ocora, 2006: 15)? Some innovative features provide reasons to be optimistic: longer and more frequent meetings and the Council's obvious readiness to hold emergency sessions may lead to a more consistent effort to protect human rights. The ability to report directly to the General Assembly may strengthen its position, and the UPR may initiate a time of more even-handed scrutinizing of governments. The new rules of procedure might allow the Council to move away from the rigid, overly broad and somewhat cryptic agenda of the Commission and towards more flexibility, focus, responsiveness and balance. The voluntary pledges and feebly worded duties of Council members, however, are weak compromise formulae. The Council will remain a 'political' body, and the new election process will not change much, if anything. Whether a two-thirds majority in the General Assembly will ever be found to kick countries out of the Council seems questionable. On the other hand, the new structure provides the chance of moving away from repetitive resolutions and inventing new decision-making methods (Abraham, 2006: 27–9) and opening the way for what General Assembly resolution 60/251 calls a more 'results-oriented' approach than that which prevailed in the Commission. So, somewhat ironically, the Council may not be more legitimate or credible than the Commission, but perhaps it will be more efficient.

# Sub-Commission on the Promotion and Protection of Human Rights

## Membership, mandate and activities

Initially, the Commission on Human Rights had several sub-commissions, of which only one survived, the Sub-Commission on the Prevention of Discrimination and the Protection of Minorities. In 1999, ECOSOC changed its name to Sub-Commission on the Promotion and Protection of Human Rights. The creation of the Sub-Commission was something of a 'retaliatory measure' rather than a planned step. When Eleanor Roosevelt, in 1946, proposed the creation of a sub-commission on freedom of information and the press, the delegate from the Soviet Union 'countered' by calling for a sub-commission on the protection of minorities and against discrimination (Humphrey, 1984: 20). ECOSOC liked neither idea, and in 1952 abolished the Sub-Commission on the Freedom of Information and the Press. It had sought to abolish the Sub-Commission on the Prevention of Discrimination and the Protection of Minorities the year before, which only the General Assembly prevented (ibid.: 21). The third sub-commission set up by ECOSOC – on the status of women – met only once and then became the Commission on the Status of Women (ibid.: 19). With the dissolution of the Commission on Human Rights in 2006, the Sub-Commission lost its parent body, but for the time being continues to function. Its relationship to the Human Rights Council has yet to be fixed.

The Sub-Commission on the Prevention of Discrimination and the Protection of Minorities came together for its first session in 1947, entrusted with the task

(a) in the first instance, to examine what provisions should be adopted in defining the principles to be applied in the field of the prevention of discrimination on grounds of race, sex, language or religion, and in the field of the protection of minorities, and to make recommendations to the Commission on urgent problems in these fields; (b) to perform any other functions which may be entrusted to it by the Economic and Social Council or the Commission on Human Rights. (Commission on Human Rights, UN doc. E/259, 1947: para. 19; Eide, 1992: 211–12)

Given that the Universal Declaration of Human Rights was adopted only a year later, the Sub-Commission had to begin its work in the absence of concrete UN human rights standards in both fields, the prevention of discrimination and the protection of minorities. With the adoption of the Declaration, the Commission amended the mandate accordingly in 1948 and the Sub-Commission, on the basis of the Declaration, undertook several studies on different aspects of discrimination (Eide, 1992: 212). The absence in the Declaration of minority rights, however, made their protection a much harder task (ibid.: 219–20). The UN was deeply divided over the question of minority rights, and many proposals by the Sub-Commission were ignored or rejected. Nevertheless, even in this inhospitable environment the Sub-Commission achieved some success: it was behind the inclusion of a provision on minority rights (Article 27) in the International Covenant on Civil and Political Rights in 1966, and in 1971 it appointed as its Special Rapporteur Francesco Capotorti, whose study on the protection of minorities, completed in 1977, is still a landmark document on the subject. The Sub-Commission saw another fruitful period in the 1990s: the Declaration on the Rights of Persons Belonging to National or Ethnic, Religious and Linguistic Minorities was adopted in 1992 and the Sub-Commission's Working Group on Minorities was set up in 1995 (Thompson, 2003: 532; Eide, 2001b).

When the Commission on Human Rights abandoned its 'no-power' doctrine on accepting complaints on human rights violations, the Sub-Commission was integrated into the 1235 and 1503 procedures. The initial intention was to have the Sub-Commission prepare a general report on human rights violations in the world and to bring consistent patterns of gross violations to the attention of the Commission, as provided for by ECOSOC resolution 1235. In fact, the Sub-Commission prepared only one such report, in 1967 on Southern Africa, creating unrest in the Commission because, by mentioning also Haiti and Greece, it went beyond apartheid and colonialism. The Sub-Commission played a pivotal role until it was eliminated altogether from the 1503 procedure (Commission on Human Rights decision 2000/109).

In addition to its activities under the 1235 and later the 1503 procedure, the Sub-Commission increasingly undertook studies outside the prevention of discrimination and the protection of minorities: surveying more than half a century of activities, one finds a remarkably diverse range of issues. Over recent years alone it has considered the human rights aspects of the administration of justice; states of emergency; the criminal justice system; military tribunals; women in prison; sexual violence; the right to development; drinking water and sanitation; extreme poverty; transnational corporations; housing and forced evictions; globalization; the rights of non-citizens; contemporary forms of slavery; and terrorism and counter-terrorism.

Like the Commission, the Sub-Commission has grown in terms of activities as well as in membership. Today it is composed of twenty-six members and the same number of alternates, who all serve in their individual capacity as independent experts. They are elected for a period of four years on the principle of geographic representation. Seven experts come from Africa, five from Asia, five from Latin America and the Caribbean, three from Eastern Europe and six from WEOG. Candidates are nominated by their respective governments, but criteria for membership are vague, and this has resulted in the repeated nomination and election of high-ranking government officials, including ambassadors, thereby damaging the Sub-Commission's credibility as independent think-tank. The Sub-Commission meets annually for a period of three weeks in August, in Geneva. Like the Commission's sessions, the meetings are attended by observer governments, UN agencies and programmes, other inter-governmental organizations and NGOs in consultative status with ECOSOC.

A number of pre- and in-sessional working groups support the Sub-Commission's work (Eide, 1992: 230–9): the above-mentioned working group on minorities as well as working groups on contemporary forms of slavery, transnational corporations, the administration of justice and human rights in combating terrorism. Setting up the Working Group of Indigenous Populations in 1982 has given an additional boost to civil society participation: what started as a working group comprised of five individuals is now attended by no fewer than 1,000 observers (Eide, 2001a: 27). This development has helped to pave the way for the participation of previously unrepresented sections of civil society in the UN.

At its request, in 2003 the Commission authorized the Sub-Commission to hold 'an annual inter-sessional forum on economic, social and cultural rights to be known as the Social Forum' (Commission on Human Rights decision 2003/107). The Forum is intended as a new mechanism within the UN system, one that allows broad participation, including from grassroots organizations which are not in consultative status with ECOSOC. As such it is meant to give a voice to vulnerable groups, an innovative approach transcending the rigid UN rules of participation of non-governmental actors. In stressing the interaction between economic, civil, cultural, social and political rights, the Forum examines issues such as poverty, international trade, finance and economic policies, and development cooperation. It is indentured to facilitate the exchange of information, to propose standards, guidelines and recommendations, and to follow up agreements reached at World Conferences (Sub-Commission on the Promotion and Protection of Human Rights resolution 2002/12). The first session of the Forum took place in 2002, and the session in 2006 was devoted to poverty and women's human rights.

## Hierarchy, expertise and politics

The relationship between the Commission on Human Rights and the Sub-Commission has always been a difficult one. At times the Sub-Commission has been seen to be lax, while at others it has been perceived as too independent and has been criticized by the Commission for transgressing its boundaries as an auxiliary body. Eide noted that, had it been any other way, this would have been 'a sure sign that the Sub-Commission was no longer playing an independent or expert role' (Eide, 1992: 256). The alleged dichotomy between 'legal' expert bodies and 'political' governmental bodies, discussed in chapter 3, is visible in the Sub-Commission. Likewise, the Sub-Commission is a case study for the implications of hierarchical structures of international organizations for human rights. And finally, it represents an example of one of the functions global human rights institutions may perform, detached from the will of its creators, namely the generation of knowledge.

In terms of hierarchy, the Sub-Commission understood itself from the start as an auxiliary body of the Commission and presented its resolutions and decisions for approval to its parent body. Yet at times it proposed activities without seeking formal endorsement, such as the organization of workshops or seminars, or directly addressed UN bodies other then the Commission (Lebakine, 2003: 661). It comes as little surprise that this led to tensions with the Commission and has given rise to fundamental questions regarding the legal relationship between inter-governmental bodies and their subsidiaries. One important issue at least was clarified by the UN Office of Legal Affairs in 1980, when the Sub-Commission's practice by seeking information directly from governments was confirmed as one within its mandate and competence (ibid.).

Regardless of its subordinate role, however, the Sub-Commission was meant to be an expert body free from political constraints, able to set new standards in the prevention of discrimination and the protection of minorities and to present proposals and drafts to the Commission for discussion and adoption. It has been successful in this endeavour, and many UN human rights documents bear its imprint (Eide, 1992: 242–5). Its research activities and analysis of new or contentious human rights issues has become an important contribution to an expanding understanding of human rights. This function, which could perhaps best be described as stimulating the further development of human rights law, is a significant contribution to the UN's human rights activities and reaches well beyond the UN into civil society and academia, making the Sub-Commission somewhat of a bridge between the academic world and the UN.

Critical observers, however, consider the increasingly 'political' approach of the Sub-Commission, in particular the discussion of human rights situations and the adoption of respective resolutions, as a duplication of the Commission's work (Eide, 1992: 241; Kedzia, 2003: 21). Indeed, as soon as Sub-Commission members, most notably those who feel bound by the political constraints of their nominating governments, engage in repetitive accusations of other governments rather than submitting independent expert advice to the best of their knowledge, the Sub-Commission deviates from its mandate. As a consequence, it has been repeatedly called to order and told to debate only those country situations which were not under review in the Commission, to abstain from adopting resolutions on country situations, and not to refer to countries in its thematic resolutions (Kedzia, 2003: 20).

As with the Commission, calls for 'depoliticizing' the Sub-Commission have to be approached with caution. Surely, if 'politicization' of the Sub-Commission means the election of serving ambassadors disguised as academic experts who bring their diplomatic luggage rather than their university laptops to the sessions, this certainly has to be halted, and should never have occurred in the first place. It also makes little sense for a subsidiary body to duplicate work done by its parent body. One should bear in mind, however, that such calls to put an end to 'politicization' may at times be little more than attempts to silence critical voices, prevent the naming of human rights violators and avoid examination of the causes for and consequences of their actions. Restraining the Sub-Commission within its mandate as an independent think-tank must not be equated with calling on it to turn a blind eye to the realities of human rights violations. Even more troublesome, the Sub-Commission has occasionally been asked to make sure that in its standard-setting and research work it acts first and foremost upon a request by the (then) Commission and shows restraint in initiating new activities. For a body which has proven to stimulate research and analysis in areas of human rights yet unexplored, often in cooperation with outside experts and NGOs, this seems an excessive curtailment of a core value, namely the provision of independent and at times critical expertise from a place which enjoys some distance from political processes.

## Prospects

As with the Commission on Human Rights, suggestions for reform of the Sub-Commission with a view to smoothing their relationship have been plentiful. They ranged from the abolition of the Sub-Commission altogether, to placing it on a par with the Commission, to altering its mandate and to changing its name (Eide, 1992: 257–8). The Commission has addressed some of the critical issues in its reform process, initiated in 2000, but now the future of the Sub-Commission is in the hands of the Human Rights Council. General Assembly resolution 60/251 does not explicitly mention the Sub-Commission, but provides that the Council shall 'maintain a system of expert advice' (para. 6), leaving it up to the latter to decide which expert advice it will seek from now on. The Council is also required to review all mandates, mechanisms, functions and responsibilities, and this clearly includes the Sub-Commission. In its decision 2006/102, the Council decided that a final session of the Sub-Commission in the present form should take place in 2006, and it has allowed the annual sessions of the Sub-Commission's working groups and the Social Forum to go ahead.

The Sub-Commission itself has – little wonder – urged that it should be maintained, stressing that there is need for a 'representative independent expert body that is able to think collectively, free from specialized mandate constraints and political considerations, in order to initiate and pursue new and innovative thinking in human rights standards and implementation' (Sub-Commission on the Promotion and Protection of Human Rights decision 2005/114, Annex: para. 6). Other options are, however, on the table, including an advisory panel, as proposed in the report *In Larger Freedom* mentioned above, or the appointment of *ad hoc* experts (International Commission of Jurists, 2005: 23). A standing body the size of the present Sub-Commission, the establishment of a roster of experts from which the Council may choose as appropriate, or a mix of a standing body assisted by *ad hoc* experts are other suggestions (Abraham, 2006: 59). Some may dispute the need for a special UN institution to propose human rights initiatives and elaborate standards altogether, as the Council itself is able to do so. Still, there is truth in the Sub-Commission's view that a 'human rights research' or 'think-tank' which evaluates human rights norms and practice, identifies gaps and analyses new developments would complement the Council as the main policy-making forum and the Office of the High Commissioner as secretariat, both of which are bound by rules which do not allow for such an explicitly 'academic' approach. Such an institution, however, adds value to the UN human rights system only when the election of independent experts rather than government appointees is guaranteed and when it does not get entangled in scrutinizing country situations or mistakenly feels the urge to respond to each and every human rights violation.

# Commission on the Status of Women

The first time an international organization showed interest in the status of women was in 1937, when the League of Nations appointed a committee of experts to inquire into the legal status of women on a global scale. The committee held three sessions before it collapsed, together with the League of Nations, after World War II (Reanda, 1992: 265). As mentioned above, the UN had originally envisaged mandating a sub-commission of the Commission on Human Rights to consider the status of women. In its first session in 1946, however, this sub-commission expressed the fear that women's concerns would as a result not receive the necessary attention and would become marginalized in the work of the Commission on Human Rights. Consequently, it asked to be given the status of a functional commission of ECOSOC, just like the Commission on Human Rights. ECOSOC acceded to this request, and one year later established the Commission on the Status of Women (CSW) on the basis of Article 68 of the UN Charter (Humphrey, 1984: 19). While this move mitigated the fear of some that women's issues would be sidelined in the work of the Commission on Human Rights, it raised at the same time concerns that women's rights might now find themselves in a ghetto, with the links between the status of women and human rights severed (ibid.; Reanda, 1992: 267). Indeed, while giving focus to many concerns related to the status of women, the existence of these two separate regimes has allowed an ambiguous relationship between women's rights and human rights to develop, and this may have contributed to a neglect of women's human rights concerns in the general human rights debate (Ainetter, 2002: 4).

Initially composed of fifteen members, CSW now consists of forty-five members, or rather member states, elected by ECOSOC for a period of four years. As with the Commission on Human Rights, the idea that the individuals nominated by their governments would be carefully screened by the UN Secretary-General and ECOSOC to ensure balanced expertise has never been realized in practice, and CSW has become what is effectively a governmental body. As with the Commission, this has meant that concerns of women activists have had to give way to official governmental policies on many occasions. Considerations of geographical balance allow for thirteen members from Africa, eleven from Asia, four from Eastern Europe, nine from GRULAC, and eight from WEOG. The Commission meets annually for a period of ten working days, in New York. Thus, CSW and the Committee under the Convention on the Elimination of All Forms of Discrimination against Women are the only UN human rights bodies to meet outside Geneva. Unlike the Commission of Human Rights, CSW only occasionally makes use of such subsidiary bodies as working groups or special rapporteurs, with the latter having been appointed on only two occasions (Reanda, 1992: 270).

In resolution 11(II) of 1946, ECOSOC entrusted CSW with the mandate to prepare recommendations and reports to ECOSOC on the promotion of women's rights in the political, economic, civil, social and educational fields, and to make recommendations to ECOSOC on urgent problems requiring immediate attention in the field of women's rights. This was a far cry from what the 'nuclear' Sub-Commission on the Status of Women thought its functions should be:

> an investigative function, through a study of the condition of women both in law and in fact, to be carried out world-wide on the basis of information supplied not only by governments but also specialized agencies of the United Nations, women's organizations, academic institutions, trade unions, and others; a mobilization function, through the convening of a women's conference and a number of activities aimed at creating a 'world-wide public opinion'; a technical assistance function, including training of women leaders, the promotion of scholarships for women, international exchanges of women, and assistance aimed at facilitating women's participation in public affairs; and a clearing house function, meaning that all communications and information received by the United Nations concerning all matters of interest to women should be referred to the new organ, and that it should be consulted on all matters pertaining to women before any decision was reached [by ECOSOC]. (Reanda, 1992: 272–3)

Gradually, however, CSW moved beyond the original and limited mandate which ECOSOC had entrusted it with. This development took place in three significant phases, leading the Commission from a focus on equality and standard-setting activities to a concentration on development and finally to the mainstreaming of women's human rights (Reanda, 1992: 275–95; Ainetter, 2002: 11–21). In a first phase, from its establishment until the 1970s, the analysis of different areas of discrimination through a system of data-gathering led to the drafting of standards with particular relevance for women, including the Convention on the Elimination of Discrimination against Women of 1979. In the second phase, the Commission shifted its focus towards development. The move started in the 1960s, and peaked in International Women's Year, 1975, and the subsequent Women's Decade. This period also saw the creation of two other institutions, the International Research and Training Institute for the Advancement of Women (INSTRAW) in 1976 and the United Nations Development Fund for Women (UNIFEM) in 1984. In 1987 ECOSOC added the functions of 'promoting the objectives of equality, development and peace, monitoring the implementation of measures for the advancement of women, and reviewing and appraising progress made at the national, subregional, regional, sectoral and global levels' (ECOSOC resolution 1987/22). The third phase in the Commission's development started with the Fourth World Conference on Women in 1995, following which it was mandated by ECOSOC resolution 1996/6 to integrate a follow-up process to the conference into its activities, to regularly review critical areas of concern in the conference's Platform for Action, and to take up a catalytic role in mainstreaming a gender perspective across United Nations activities.

Like the Commission on Human Rights, and despite its limited mandate, CSW has from its inception both received communications on violations of women's human rights and struggled with how it should respond. In its first session in 1947 it suggested to ECOSOC that a confidential list of such communications should be compiled and brought to its attention. ECOSOC gave the same answer it had given to the Commission on Human Rights, namely that CSW had no power to take any action with regard to complaints (ECOSOC resolutions 75(V) and 76(V) of 1947). The Commission on Human Rights overcame this attitude and, as we have seen, later introduced the 1503 procedure, but nothing similar happened within CSW. It was only allowed to consider the list of communications in private meetings. Later, in 1950, a distinction was made between communications dealing with principles and others: the former could be dealt with publicly, the latter only in private meetings. From then onwards, CSW reported its findings and recommendations to ECOSOC, but was never allowed to take up either individual cases or urgent situations or to react in any meaningful way (Wörgetter, 1999: 187; Gaudart, 2002: 65–6). In essence, there has never been a substantial role for the Commission in addressing violations of women's human rights, and the verdict remains valid that 'the outcome has been primarily to expand the types of information reaching it, and not its powers to act on it' (Reanda, 1992: 302).

CSW's strengths, however, lie elsewhere (Gaudart, 2002: 58–60). In close relationship with NGOs, it has gathered and evaluated data on the status of women worldwide and transformed its findings into both law and policy. It has contributed significantly to the standard-setting on women's human rights, remains the main policy-making body in the UN on all questions relating to women, promotes women's human rights within and beyond the UN, prepares studies, devises programmes, holds seminars and provides technical assistance to governments, and continues to function as a clearing-house or catalyst for women's issues in the UN. In doing so, it was less concerned with (and less expected to be concerned with) accompanying the implementation of norms, scrutinizing non-compliance or remedying human rights violations, than with influencing social processes by shaping discourse, interpreting information and suggesting standards. By foregrounding these functions, CSW may demonstrate, in line with what Barnett and Finnemore have asserted (as discussed in chapter 2), how institutions which are powerless in terms of enforcement mechanisms nevertheless are able to contribute to constructing the social world.

## Economic and Social Council

We have repeatedly come across ECOSOC in discussing the activities of other UN human rights bodies. ECOSOC is the principal UN body to coordinate the economic, social and related work of the fifteen UN specialized agencies, eight functional commissions and five regional economic commissions and to consider the reports of UN programmes and funds. It is also ECOSOC's task to monitor and evaluate the implementation of overall strategies emanating from the General Assembly and to assist the General Assembly (Quinn, 1992: 58–9). The Council is composed of fifty-four member states, elected by the General Assembly for three years (Article 61, UN Charter). It holds a four-week session each July, alternating between Geneva and New York, within which a 'High-Level Segment' is devoted to a specific topic every year. Article 62 of the UN Charter mandates ECOSOC to engage in a range of human rights activities. In particular it may make or initiate studies, reports and recommendations on international economic, social, cultural, educational, health and related matters; make recommendations 'for the purpose of promoting respect for, and observance of, human rights and fundamental freedoms for all'; and prepare draft conventions for the General Assembly and organize conferences. It can also set up commissions in economic and social fields and for the promotion of human rights, and such other commissions as may be required for the performance of its functions. In addition, under Article 71 of the UN Charter, ECOSOC is entrusted with making suitable arrangements for consultation with non-governmental organizations which are concerned with matters within the Council's competence.

This impressive range of powers belies the Council's actual importance. Despite the determination shown by the drafters of the UN Charter to make it the centre of gravity for social and economic affairs in the UN (O'Donovan, 1992: 107–8), ECOSOC has never lived up to such expectations. In its early years – until the 1960s – it did play a role in the field of human rights, but it was that of a wolf in sheep's clothing. Rather than supporting its subordinate bodies entrusted with the promotion and protection of human rights, it launched onslaught after onslaught against them (ibid.: 113–14). In 1947 it affirmed that the Commission on Human Rights had no power to act in response to human rights violations. In 1951 it sought to abolish the (then) Sub-Commission on the Prevention of Discrimination and Protection of Minorities, a move that was only prevented when the General Assembly intervened. In 1952 it wiped out the Sub-Commission on Freedom of Information; and in 1963 it cancelled the session of the Commission on Human Rights scheduled for 1964 on account of alleged shortages of conference facilities. Last but not least, it should be remembered that it was ECOSOC which overturned the decision of the founders of the Commission on Human Rights to elect independent experts to the Commission and replaced them by governmental representatives. Here we see an institution which, despite being entrusted with human rights matters, uses its institutional weight and the powers conferred on it to cut back the UN's consideration of human rights. What appear to be entirely procedural and institutional decisions (responding to the lack of conference facilities or concern for institutional proliferation within the UN) are in fact decisions on the role and place of human rights in the UN.

What can be said on the positive side is that ECOSOC sought only occasionally to overturn the decisions of the Commission on Human Rights, and mandated the latter to deal with human rights violations under the 1235 and 1503 procedures. It has made little use of its power to undertake studies and reports and has left this to subsidiary bodies and specialized agencies (O'Donovan, 1992: 114). It has at times assisted in drafting human rights standards, such as the Genocide Convention, but has largely endorsed the texts emanating from the Commission on Human Rights. While this seems entirely justified given the level of expertise in its subsidiary bodies, ECOSOC has also failed in its coordinating tasks and in linking human rights with the wider social and economic field (ibid.: 122). Over the years, plans to reform it, by allowing for universal membership and by turning it into the central forum for discussion on social and economic matters and for devising global strategies and carrying out comprehensive policy reviews, have largely failed (ibid.: 123). More recently, the 2005 World Summit asked the Council to meet biannually as a high-level 'Development Cooperation Forum' (General Assembly resolution 60/1, 2005: para. 155), shifting its focus towards analysing and responding to development trends.

In the field of human rights, ECOSOC has long been overtaken by its subsidiary bodies, the Commission on Human Rights and CSW. With the creation of the Human Rights Council, ECOSOC's role in human rights matter has been further diminished; in fact it is no longer relevant for human rights matters in the UN. The only strength it still displays in the field of human rights is in its setting up of new subsidiary bodies. In 2000, ECOSOC followed a proposal by the Commission on Human Rights and established the Permanent Forum on Indigenous Issues (ECOSOC resolution 2000/22). With this decision, a voice has finally been given to indigenous peoples in the UN system, and a decade-long struggle to ensure representation of the unrepresented within the UN's human rights system has reached a new level (Daes, 2001. We will refer to the Forum again in chapter 6 when we discuss the participation of civil society organizations in developing human rights.

# General Assembly

## A 'grand debate' on human rights?

Article 10 of the UN Charter gives the General Assembly the overall competence to consider all matters covered by the Charter, which includes 'international cooperation in solving international problems of an economic, social, cultural, or humanitarian character, and in promoting and encouraging respect for human rights and for fundamental freedoms for all without distinction as to race, sex, language, or religion' (Article 3, UN Charter). More specifically, it is entitled to 'initiate studies and make recommendations for the purpose of [. . .] assisting in the realization of human rights and fundamental freedoms for all without distinction as to race, sex, language, or religion' (Article 13 (1)(b), UN Charter). In addition, and by virtue of Article 62 of the UN Charter, which mandates ECOSOC to put draft conventions to the General Assembly, it is entitled to adopt international conventions on human rights. As early as the San Francisco Conference in 1945 a vivid debate ensued on how the General Assembly should approach its mandate, much in line with the discussion on the Commission on Human Rights (Cassese, 1992: 25–7).

Subsequent practice gave shape to the General Assembly's attitude towards human rights. Today, four fields of human rights activities may be discerned: leadership and oversight of the UN human rights system; budgetary responsibility for UN human rights institutions; participation in standard-setting; and scrutinizing individual countries. A fifth function – the holding of an annual 'grand debate' on human rights, weaving law and politics into a coherent web for the promotion and protection of human rights, and based on ample information provided by subsidiary bodies, has remained wishful thinking. No such debate has even been held. If it were to be held it could assign the proper place to single human rights issues for the benefit of a holistic, coherent approach, draw up a road map for future development, and ensure sustainable development and growth of human rights in the UN. In theory, the General Assembly, with its universal participation, would be the ideal place for holding such a debate at given intervals, from which long-term policy-making might ensue. Yet human rights are but one out of more than 160 agenda items of the annual General Assembly meetings, and otherwise make an occasional, rather arbitrary appearance in agenda items such as 'children's rights', 'advancement of women', 'human rights in the Israeli occupied territory', or 'democracy and human rights in Haiti'.

## Leadership, budget, standards, scrutiny

The General Assembly leadership function is threefold – leadership in bureaucratic matters, leadership in policy-making, and acting as a 'moral' leader of the world community – but the verdict of observers on its leadership qualities in human rights matters is muted and occasionally harsh (Quinn, 1992: 56). Its position on top of the bureaucratic hierarchy allows the General Assembly to exercise oversight over subsidiary bodies, consider their reports and establish new bodies (Article 15(2) and 22, UN Charter). While the reports of the Commission on Human Rights used to be forwarded via ECOSOC, the General Assembly has now direct links with the Human Rights Council. The General Assembly also considers and approves the budget of the UN (Article 17(1), UN Charter) and endorses voluntary funds. This relates to all human rights activities which entail financial implications, and is the reason why the Office of the High Commissioner of Human Rights takes a very close look at all resolution with 'PBIs' (Programme Budget Implications), as the General Assembly has the final say on those. The litany of complaints on limited funding for the UN's human rights activities has thus properly to be addressed to the General Assembly, or rather its Fifth (Administrative and Budgetary) Committee, which was confronted with these grievances again and again (Quinn, 1992: 93). This, of course, reflects the tension between human rights as a concern of the whole of the UN (as laid down in the UN Charter) and assigning the task of 'dealing with' human rights to specific bodies, which not only work in isolation from the main political and financial decision-making bodies, but reside on the lower end of the intrainstitutional pecking order. Human rights are neither entrusted to a body akin in status to the Security Council, as UN Secretary-General Kofi Annan and others had suggested, nor are they truly acknowledged (other than in conference speeches) as a cross-cutting issue which affects all parts of the organization.

The General Assembly also develops public information and awareness-raising strategies, including on human rights. Its oversight of the UN Department of Public Information and the proclamation of International Years and Decades allow for the global spotlight to be put on human rights if the General Assembly so decides. Indeed, human rights have figured prominently among International Years and Decades, e.g., the Decade for Human Rights Education (1995–2004), the Decades to Combat Racism and Racial Discrimination, spanning thirty years (1973–2003), and the two International Decades of the World's Indigenous People (1995–2004 and 2005–14). The General Assembly has also been the convener of the two World Conferences on Human Rights, in Tehran (1968) and Vienna (1993).

Like the Commission on Human Rights, the General Assembly has both shied away from addressing individual cases of gross human rights abuses and chosen to dwell in the safer ground of standard-setting. Formally, all human rights conventions are adopted by the General Assembly as the highest UN authority. Usually, it simply gives its imprimatur to texts which emerge from the subsidiary bodies. While such rubber-stamping of the work of the Commission on Human Rights was the rule, the General Assembly has on occasion been active in drafting documents on its own, as was the case with the Declaration on the Right to Development or the Second Protocol to the International Covenant on Civil and Political Rights on the death penalty (Quinn, 1992: 65–6).

The General Assembly has taken a limited interest in scrutinizing human rights situations and monitoring the implementation of human rights obligations. It participates in the supervision of human rights treaties insofar as it receives the reports of the UN treaty bodies. In theory, this would put it in the unique position of being able to coordinate the work of the treaty bodies and to consider their reports in a holistic manner. This, however, is not the case, as the treaties do not reach beyond those states which have signed them, and there is understandable reluctance to place the General Assembly, as a charter-based body, in a position of influence over treaty-based procedures. As a consequence, the General Assembly does not coordinate the work of the treaty bodies, nor does it move beyond simply endorsing their findings. It has reluctantly moved closer to scrutinizing governments for exceptionally unacceptable behaviour, always mindful of the non-intervention principle as set out in Article 2(7) of the UN Charter. Once again, South Africa provided the incentive. In 1952, the General Assembly set up a three-member Commission on the Racial Situation in the Union of South Africa, which studied the situation and presented it with recommendations which were subsequently adopted. It went on to establish the Special Committee on Apartheid (General Assembly resolution 1761 (XVII) 1962), the Special Committee on Israeli Practices in Territories Occupied after the 1967 War (General Assembly resolution 2443 (XXIII) 1968), the Special Committee on the Situation with Regard to the Implementation of the Declaration on the Granting of Independence to Colonial Countries and Peoples (the 'Committee of 24', General Assembly resolution 1654 (XVI) 1961), and the Committee on the Exercise of the Inalienable Rights of the Palestinian People (General Assembly resolution 3376 (XXX) 1975) (Cassese, 1992: 35). Still, observers conclude that the success of the General Assembly in investigating gross human rights abuses lay only in 'not undoing the attempts made in this area by [its] subordinate bodies' (ibid.: 40). Neither standard-setting nor monitoring the implementation of standards is thus a function fulfilled by the General Assembly.

## Third Committee

Much of the General Assembly's work is done outside the plenary, in one of the six main committees. The 'institutional peculiarity' (Quinn, 1992: 95) of the UN system in separating human rights from legal matters has, however, led to a very limited role for the General Assembly's Sixth (Legal) Committee in considering human rights norms. The work is done mainly in the Third Committee (the Social, Humanitarian and Cultural Committee). Membership of this committee is universal, and NGOs do not participate in its work. The General Assembly allocates topics to the Third Committee as diverse as implementation of the outcome of the World Summit on Social Development, the follow-up to the International Year of Older Persons, crime prevention and criminal justice, drug control, the advancement of women, children's rights, indigenous peoples, refugees, racism and self-determination. Under the item 'human rights questions', which is identical to the item on the General Assembly's agenda, the Committee routinely discusses such matters as the implementation of human rights instruments, the follow-up to the Vienna Declaration and Programme of Action (VDPA), 'human rights questions, including alternative approaches for improving the effective enjoyment of human rights and fundamental freedoms', human rights situations and reports of special rapporteurs and representatives, and reports of the UN High Commissioner for Human Rights. The same reports which were available to the Commission on Human Rights were also submitted to the Third Committee, together with other documents by the UN Secretary-General. These reports are usually introduced by heads of UN departments, senior UN staff or rapporteurs and independent experts, followed by discussions in an unscripted format (Note by the Secretariat, UN doc. A/C.3/59/L.1, 2004). As this listing of the Committee's agenda items shows, not only are human rights issues clustered in an arbitrary way, but the issues allocated to the Third Committee as such reveal the same arbitrariness.

In principle, the Third Committee would be well placed to consider the links between human rights and other issues on its agenda, such as, for example, refugees. This could have made for a distinctive contribution of the Third Committee and ensured a more holistic approach to human rights, but it never happened. The Committee gave away this chance by largely repeating the work done in the Commission on Human Rights and ignoring intersectional links. With few significant governmental initiatives in the Committee, scarce availability of human rights expertise in New York (as compared to Geneva), the absence of any NGO involvement, and little media attention, the Third Committee has been reduced to a mere additional bureaucratic layer, occasionally tinkering with the resolutions of subsidiary bodies. Design, location and insulation together are to be blamed for this and demonstrate how form impedes function.

## Achievements

Apart from rubber-stamping and approving the work of subsidiary bodies, the General Assembly's merits are scarce as far as human rights are concerned. This is undoubtedly a lost opportunity. It could have considered human rights issues in a wider political and economic context, established human rights firmly as a cross-cutting issue for the whole UN system, or made the link between sections hitherto unrelated, such as refugee flows and human rights violations, armed conflict and human rights, etc. Its high profile could also have led to increased attention for and pressure on countries which are engaged in gross human rights violations. None of this has happened. The General Assembly and its Third Committee consider human rights in a fragmented, selective and unbalanced way. Despite its authority and the fact that – according to calculations by observers – one-third of the Assembly's resolutions deal with human rights (Weiss, Forsythe and Coate, 1997: 161), these resolutions seem to have brought about even less change than has the Commission on Human Rights. In fact, it has been observed that 'the more impotent the Assembly felt in the face of difficult problems, the more often it resorted to paper solutions' (Cassese, 1992: 51).

In matters of human rights, the rise of the Commission on Human Rights to a 'mini-General Assembly for human rights' has been paralleled by the decline of the General Assembly and its Third Committee, at least in human rights matters. It is only in budgetary decisions where the General Assembly, or rather the respective committee, is of utmost relevance. Tracing the way in which decisions on finance, but also on legal matters, are being taken by bodies well insulated from the world of human rights, and how they impact on the successes and failures of UN human rights bodies, might be an interesting area of future research, in order to demonstrate the consequences of the institutional peculiarities to which Quinn has alluded above. With the creation of the Human Rights Council as a subsidiary body of the General Assembly, a closer link has now been established between the two institutions and, eventually, the General Assembly may regain importance in matters of human rights. Being informed on human rights issues by the Human Rights Council directly rather than via ECOSOC, it may, one dares to hope, feel more responsible for human rights matters.

# United Nations High Commissioner for Human Rights

## A mandate between servant and shield

The idea of setting up what today is the High Commissioner for Human Rights dates back almost to the creation of the UN and is sometimes attributed to the French jurist, and later president of the European Court of Human rights, René Cassin, who in 1947 proposed to establish an 'Attorney-General for Human Rights' (Clapham, 1994: 556–9; Boyle, 2003: 24). Others consider John Humphrey, the first director of the (then) UN Division for Human Rights, as the father of this idea (Hobbins, 2001: 72). It took nearly half a century and the momentum of the Vienna World Conference on Human Rights in 1993 to put a proposal on the establishment of the post of UN High Commissioner for Human Rights to the General Assembly. After lengthy debate (Clapham, 1994: 559–63), the General Assembly adopted resolution 48/141, which established the post and defined the High Commissioner's responsibilities.

The said resolution assigns an exceptionally broad range of responsibilities to the High Commissioner in a mandate which has been referred to as a 'combination of vagueness and comprehensiveness' (Alston, 1997: 326). It is worth reproducing the full text of the relevant part of the resolution so as to instil the same sense of awe in the reader which must befall every mandate holder upon taking up his or her job:

> a) to promote and protect the effective enjoyment by all of all civil, cultural, economic, political and social rights; b) to carry out the tasks assigned to him/her by the competent bodies of the United Nations system in the field of human rights and to make recommendations to them with a view to improving the promotion and protection of all human rights; c) to promote and protect the realization of the right to development and to enhance support from relevant bodies of the United Nations system for this purpose; d) to provide, through the Centre for Human Rights of the Secretariat and other appropriate institutions, advisory services and technical and financial assistance, at the request

of the State concerned and, where appropriate, the regional human rights organizations, with a view to supporting actions and programmes in the field of human rights; e) to coordinate relevant United Nations education and public information programmes in the field of human rights; f) to play an active role in removing the current obstacles and in meeting the challenges to the full realization of all human rights and in preventing the continuation of human rights violations throughout the world, as reflected in the Vienna Declaration and Programme of Action; g) to engage in a dialogue with all Governments in the implementation of his/her mandate with a view to securing respect for all human rights; h) to enhance international cooperation for the promotion and protection of all human rights; i) to coordinate the human rights promotion and protection activities throughout the United Nations system; j) to rationalize, adapt, strengthen and streamline the United Nations machinery in the field of human rights with a view to improving its efficiency and effectiveness; k) to carry out overall supervision of the Centre for Human Rights. (General Assembly resolution 48/141 of 1993: para. 4)

Six clusters of responsibilities may be filtered out from this resolution: 1) a mandate to protect human rights, which means being accessible and responding to victims of human rights violations, but also involves managing large-scale human rights crises worldwide; 2) the promotion of human rights and support for human rights initiatives, which includes educational activities, awareness-raising campaigns and publications; 3) operational activities such as advisory services and technical assistance for governments; 4) leadership within the UN human rights system, including mainstreaming human rights into the work of UN agencies, programmes and funds, and driving on the reform of the UN human rights system, as well as 'moral leadership' for the global human rights movement; 5) the duty to service (as part of the UN secretariat) all UN human rights activities and to ensure the coordination of and consistency in the work of UN human rights institutions; and 6) being available for good offices and diplomatic initiatives in matters of human rights. Living up to all these demands at the same time seems something of a mission impossible: how to reconcile the quiet diplomat with the swashbuckling activist, the subservient secretary of state with the self-confident voice of human rights, the hands-on manager of a complex web of UN human rights bodies with the world's depository of human dignity? Most of all, it is the Janus-faced nature of the office – part servant at the disposal of governments, part shield against those very governments – which puts the High Commissioner in a very special and delicate position.

The High Commissioner is appointed by the UN Secretary-General and approved by the General Assembly. The first to fill the post was the Ecuadorian diplomat José Ayala-Lasso (1994–7), who was followed by the former president of Ireland, Mary Robinson (1997–2002). Sergio Vieira de Mello from Brazil, the third High Commissioner, was killed in his office in Baghdad in 2003. Currently, Louise Arbor (Canada) holds the post. The appointment takes place with due regard for geographical rotation, and for a period of four years, which is renewable once. It gives the High Commissioner the rank of a UN Under-Secretary-General with principal responsibility for United Nations human rights activities. The office holder is firmly entrenched in the UN institutional human rights framework: he or she discharges these responsibilities under the direction and authority of the Secretary-General and within the framework of the overall competence, authority and decisions of the General Assembly, ECOSOC and the Human Rights Council (formerly the Commission on Human Rights). The Office of the High Commissioner (OHCHR), also established by General Assembly resolution 48/141, is based in the Palais Wilson in Geneva with a liaison office at the UN headquarters in New York. In 1997, the staff of the human rights secretariat of the UN (the then 'Centre for Human Rights') was merged with the office. As of January 2005, 576 staff worked in the office, with more than 260 of them in the field.

The leadership function which the High Commissioner is meant to exercise is effectively threefold: it is managerial leadership of OHCHR, human rights leadership within the UN bureaucracy, but also some kind of vague 'moral' leadership of the global human rights movement. As head of OHCHR, the High Commissioner has to make sure that the office can offer high-quality expertise, advice and administrative services to the main UN human rights bodies. OHCHR provides support for the meetings of UN human rights bodies, ensures the communication flow between them, follows up decisions taken, and assists individual experts in investigating and reporting on human rights issues. As manager of the UN human rights system, the High Commissioner strives to ensure coordination and cooperation not only between UN human rights institutions but also between mainstream human rights in the UN system. Finally, the High Commissioner is also something of a figurehead of the global human rights movement. Whenever he or she issues public statements, visits countries to meet human rights activists, takes the side of victims of human rights violations, and supports human rights movements, initiatives and NGOs, national parliaments, courts and human rights institutions, the High Commissioner is likely to be seen as the movement's spearhead.

The High Commissioner's mandate, like that of the Human Rights Council, embodies the many functions which global human rights institutions can perform. More than this, it also reflects the expectations which the international community has towards such institutions. As is the case with high hopes, they often go unfulfilled. The High Commissioner is proof of two limitations which restrain global human rights institutions: overstretching them normatively and starving them out financially. The High Commissioner is affected by both. The extensive mandate of the post combines the legal with the moral and entails that the mandate holder is entangled in contradictory claims. And the High Commissioner's broad range of responsibilities contrasts with ludicrous financial support. The initial costs of implementing General Assembly resolution 48/141 were calculated at US$1,888,000 for the first two years, which observers calculated as being just sufficient for the salaries of the High Commissioner, two professional and three secretarial staff, and a travel allowance of US$50,000 (Clapham, 1994: 565) – not much for guaranteeing global respect for human rights. The 2006/7 regular budget as approved by the General Assembly is US$85.6 million (UN High Commissioner for Human Rights, 2006: 69). This means that currently only around 1.8 per cent of the regular UN budget is spent on human rights (UN, 2005: para. 126). The 2005 World Summit Outcome Document called for doubling this amount over five years (General Assembly resolution 60/1, 2005: para. 124). In previous years, the regular budget covered only around one-third of the office's activities, and voluntary contributions had to make up for the rest, which gave rise to concern over possible influence linked to such contributions. For 2006/7, the Office needs US$160 million from voluntary contributions to fulfil its mission (UN High Commissioner for Human Rights, 2006).

## From headquarters to the field

The move from headquarters to the field, initiated by the Rwanda genocide, is the most influential development to have occurred since the establishment of the post of the High Commissioner. As a matter of fact, the Rwandan tragedy made the High Commissioner learn crisis management and response to emergencies the hard way. One day after the first High Commissioner, José Ayala-Lasso, took up his position, on 5 April 1994, the presidents of Rwanda and Burundi died in an air crash, triggering the genocide. After having travelled to the region, he not only urged the Commission on Human Rights to meet in a special session and appoint a Special Rapporteur, but sent a mission of human rights officers to Rwanda, thus creating the first human rights field operation ever organized by the High Commissioner (Martin, 2001: 405–9; Ramcharan, 2002c: 75–6).

Today, field missions are crucial in translating international commitments into realities on the ground, integrating human rights into other UN activities such as development, peacekeeping and peacebuilding in post-conflict areas and generally contributing to the creation of a domestic culture of human rights. A variety of means could be developed and tested over the years: OHCHR offices, technical cooperation projects within United Nations Country Teams, OHCHR regional offices within UN Economic and Social Commissions, human rights advisers within United Nations Country Teams, and human rights components of UN peace missions (http://www.ohchr.org/english/countries/field/index.htm; Ramcharan, 2002c: 107–44). They give support to national human rights capacities and institutions; follow up recommendations of human rights bodies; monitor human rights situations; and provide technical assistance in areas such as legislative reform, human rights education, and the administration of justice (Gallagher, 1999b: 264). This technical cooperation programme of the office has grown exponentially over the past two or three decades (Mokhiber, 2001: 416–23). It comprises activities such as advice on ratifying treaties, constitutional reform, training for armed forces, electoral assistance, training of law-enforcement officials or the preparation of national human rights action plans (Mertus, 2005: 17–18). Field presences may also be an early-warning tool to prevent a human rights crisis from emerging (Schmidt, 1999: 171–5; Mukherjee, 2001: 395–6) and generally allow for a more proactive approach for international institutions (Howland, 2004). Altogether, the move from headquarters to the field demonstrates how international human rights institutions are becoming operational actors in their own right (Sucharipa and Theuermann, 1997: 246–54).

Some of the promotional activities of the High Commissioner entail technical cooperation, such as educational and training activities. However, OHCHR's outreach activities go beyond assisting governments at their request and include awareness-raising campaigns, research and publications. The office cooperates with NGOs, academic institutions and the private sector. Working with the UN Department of Public Information, OHCHR ensures that records of the meetings of human rights bodies are available to the media. The OHCHR website has become the main human rights portal of the UN, and it publishes the 'Fact Sheets' series and training material.

Given that field missions were a relatively new area for the OHCHR – despite some predecessors in peace operations (Martin, 2001: 403–5) – the office sought to professionalize these missions, adapt them to specific circumstances, and explore adequate exit strategies. In its action plan 2005 (UN High Commissioner for Human Rights, 2005b) it attempts to take all this further. Increased deployment of staff to countries and regions, developing standing capacities for rapid deployment, investigations, field support, human rights capacity-building, advice and assistance are priorities to ensure greater presence on the ground. Greater interaction with all parts of the UN human rights system is envisaged. Yet, without significantly increased funding from the regular UN budget these goals will remain aspirations.

# Treaty bodies

Seven major human rights treaties stand out among UN human rights documents: the two International Covenants, on Economic, Social and Cultural Rights (ICESCR) and on Civil and Political Rights (ICCPR), of 1966, the Convention on the Elimination of All Forms of Racial Discrimination (CERD, 1965), the Convention on the Elimination of All Forms of Discrimination against Women (CEDAW, 1979), the Convention against Torture and Other Cruel, Inhuman or Degrading Treatment (CAT, 1984), the Convention on the Rights of the Child (CRC, 1989) and the Convention on the Protection of the Rights of All Migrant Workers and Members of Their Families (CMW, 1990). Together with their respective optional protocols (Optional Protocol to ICCPR, 1966, which establishes an individual complaints procedure; Second Optional Protocol to ICCPR, aiming at the abolition of the death penalty, 1989; Optional Protocol to CEDAW, 1999, which establishes an individual complaints procedure; Optional protocols to CRC on the involvement of children in armed conflict, 2000, and on the sale of children, child prostitution and child pornography, 2000; and Optional Protocol to CAT, 2002, which establishes an inspection mechanism), they constitute what is commonly referred to as 'core UN human rights treaties'.

Under each of these seven treaties, a committee of independent experts monitors the implementation of treaty provisions by state parties. The Committee on the Elimination of Racial Discrimination was the first to be established, and since 1969 it has monitored the implementation of CERD (Wolfrum, 1999). The Human Rights Committee took up its work in 1976 and monitors the implementation of the ICCPR and its optional protocols. The Committee on Economic, Social and Cultural Rights has since 1987 carried out a mandate which before was entrusted to ECOSOC, and the Committee on the Elimination of Discrimination against Women (since 1979), the Committee against Torture (since 1987), the Committee on the Rights of the Child (since 1990) and the Committee on Migrant Workers (since 2004) monitor the respective conventions.

The number of experts serving on treaty bodies varies (eighteen for the committees under ICESCR, ICCPR, and CERD, twenty-three under CEDAW, and ten under CRC, CAT and CMW). They are elected for renewable four-year terms and meet periodically throughout the year at UN headquarters in Geneva (with the exception of CEDAW and the Human Rights Committee, in its March session, in New York). All of them are serviced by the OHCHR (with the exception of CEDAW, which receives support from the UN Division on the Advancement of Women). Experts fulfil their duties part-time. The treaties require them to be of high moral standing, knowledgeable and independent (in the sense that they are not supposed to represent their governments). Yet they are nominated and elected by the member states to the respective treaty, and such states are free in deciding whom they put forward for nomination. The treaty bodies have adopted (non-binding) guidelines for elections (Ghandhi, 2000: 405–6), but despite this ambassadors, heads of government departments and even foreign ministers have occasionally been elected 'independent' experts, making a mockery of the requirement of independence. After trailing through their CVs, Bayefsky found that nearly 50 per cent of the experts were employed by their government in some capacity (Bayefsky, 2001: 103). Difficult as it may be to draw conclusions as to their independence when acting on the treaty bodies, and with many individual experts enjoying a deservedly high reputation for their independence and expertise, the figure shows that many governments are not overly concerned with the requirement of independence.

In essence, the treaty bodies have four types of procedure at their disposal to monitor the implementation of treaty provisions: consideration of state reports, decisions on both inter-state and individual complaints, and on-site inquires. Treaty bodies also issue so-called General Comments, i.e., interpretations of specific treaty provisions.

## State reports

All core UN human rights treaties apply the state reporting system as the most basic tool to monitor compliance (Oberleitner, 1998;

Dimitrijevic, 2001). Under this system, states have to submit initial reports one year after joining the treaty (two years in the case of the CRC) and subsequent periodic reports, usually every four or five years. Special reports, allowing treaty bodies to react to current developments, are requested rarely. Only CERD routinely calls for such reports, but they remain troublesome as they divert from the principle of scrutinizing all states on equal terms, which includes equal time-frames (Bayefsky, 2001: 23–4). Thus, since 1965, each state party to human rights treaties is required to report on the legal, administrative and judicial measures it has taken to implement treaty provision and to point out factors and difficulties it has encountered in this process. The treaty body discusses these reports with governmental representatives, thus establishing a dialogue on treaty implementation. There is no uniform procedure, but all treaty bodies have adopted guidelines on the consideration of state reports, and some have drafted questionnaires and drawn up lists of issues to be discussed.

The process is often dismissed as shifting paper from a national to an international bureaucracy or as a dull bureaucratic exercise with no immediate effects. There is a truth in such allegations, and the shortcomings of state reporting are obvious. States are often sluggish in their obligations, and overdue or inadequate reports are the rule rather than the exception. Bayefsky's 2001 study of the treaty system found that, out of more than 1,600 reports considered to that date, over 1,200 were overdue, and over 70 per cent of states lagged behind with their reports, with more than a quarter not having submitted even an initial report (Bayefsky, 2001: 9). The treaty bodies face backlogs in considering reports, too, some more than two years (ibid.: 18). As a consequence, the treaty bodies have in practice abandoned the periodic reporting cycle and, because of the great number of overdue reports, accept whatever report is submitted, regardless of deadlines (ibid.: 17). Some of these shortcomings are remedied in the treaty bodies' practice, such as complementing or substituting missing or dubious governmental information by 'shadow reports' submitted by NGOs. Still, nowhere else in the field of human rights have bureaucratic requirements been so all-consuming as in the state reporting procedure; and nowhere else is success in bureaucratic terms closer to actually endangering rather than promoting observance of human rights. State reports are required not only under UN human rights treaties, but under ILO conventions and regional human rights treaties as well. States which scrupulously meet their reporting obligations have as many as four reports considered in one year (ibid.: 19). The multitude of these obligations poses a considerable and rising burden on state parties, in particular on developing countries, which may find themselves unable to set up an elaborate domestic bureaucracy to satisfy the appetite of international human rights bodies.

The merits of state reporting, in turn, are less obvious. First, as an obligatory procedure it is the cornerstone of compliance for monitoring international commitments. It paints a larger picture of both the status quo and the development of human rights in a given country. It traces and exposes structural rather than individual human rights violations. Because it is a 'soft' tool in comparison with an individual complaint and because, unlike complaint procedures or the procedures in the Commission on Human Rights, it is applied equally to all state parties, it does not give rise to accusations of double standards. It does not coerce governments, but gives them an opportunity regularly to take stock of their efforts, progress and failures in protecting and promoting human rights domestically. It also allows for the identification of shortcomings and the assessment of future needs. It is a tool for the development of policies and makes it possible gradually to harmonize national law and policy with the requirements of human rights treaties. The reporting system entails the establishment of ties between an international monitoring body and governments and thus allows states to hook into the multilateral system of human rights protection, often forcing such states out of a narrower domestic, subregional or regional corner and exposing them to a soft form of international scrutiny. It allows for the feeding back of knowledge and best practices into domestic political and legal processes, and there may be a socializing force in some of these dialogues. Clearly, the long-term perspective and low-key approach of the reporting system are less likely to generate immediate change. State reporting can be expected to have the greatest impact where human rights supervision is not critically needed, namely where the human rights situation is generally good (Donnelly, 2006: 88).

The consideration of state reports ends with the publication of the treaty bodies' findings (usually referred to as 'concluding observations' or 'concluding comments'). They are an assessment of human rights conditions as much as an evaluation of needs and priorities. Their quality varies and may be hampered by insufficient access to information or lack of research capacity or expertise on the part of individual experts. Altogether, however, there seems to be a move away from sweeping assessments to a substantiated and focused identification of obstacles to the implementation of treaty provisions (Bayefsky, 2001: 64–5). States are expected to inform the treaty bodies about the implementation of observations and comments in the next reporting cycle.

There are no means available to treaty bodies to enforce their recommendations other than to take up cases of non-implementation in the next reporting cycle. The development of concrete, practical and assessable follow-up measures, including technical assistance, is long overdue and crucial for enhancing the effectiveness of the reporting system. Linking the work of treaty bodies with other UN human rights bodies, field presences and UN specialized agencies, programmes and funds is a challenge that has not even begun to be realized. Likewise it is important to engage more domestic actors – civil society groups, parliamentarians, the media – in publicizing the findings of treaty bodies. Linking the two crucial elements of the reporting procedure – governmental self-assessment and feedback from an international expert body – with the formulation of national human rights action plans, rights-based development programming, national debates on human rights, UN technical assistance and a UN presence on the ground has yet to be achieved.

## Inter-state complaints

Four of the seven core human rights treaties allow states to complain to the treaty body about alleged treaty violations by another state party. The procedure is mandatory under CERD (Article 11), while Article 41 of ICCPR, Article 21 of CAT and Article 76 of CMW require a separate declaration of acceptance by state parties. To date, no state has ever made use of this procedure.

## Individual complaints

Allowing individuals to bring claims against states to international bodies is perhaps the most potent invention in all of human rights law. Four out of the seven human rights treaties (CERD, ICCPR, CEDAW and CAT) allow for individual complaints or, more accurately, 'communications'. (Under CMW, a communications procedure will become effective once ten states have made the necessary declaration under Article 77.) Under these four treaties, the procedure is facultative; in other words, states may decide to be bound by the respective human rights norms without being subjected to an individual complaints procedure. They have to 'opt in' if they think persons under their jurisdiction should benefit from the procedure. State parties to ICCPR and CEDAW must accept optional protocols, while CAT and CERD allow for state parties to make declarations to this end (Article 22, CAT;

Article 14, CERD). To date, 106 states have accepted the complaints procedures provided for in the Optional Protocol to ICCPR, seventy-eight those to CEDAW; sixty have made the respective declaration under CAT and forty-five under CERD.

What is sometimes wrongly seen as a judicial procedure with victims pursuing their case as plaintiffs and states as defendants is in fact based merely on 'petitions' (Lewis-Anthony and Scheinin, 2004). It would be mistaken to consider individual complaints procedures as standing in for a non-existent global human rights court. The procedure allows victims of human rights violations to inform a group of independent experts on alleged violations of treaty provisions. Those experts may, in turn, formulate their opinion on whether the treaty has indeed been violated and suggest, in non-binding form, remedies to the government concerned. Complaints under human rights treaties must also not be confused with complaints of gross and serious human rights violations under the 1503 procedure before the Human Rights Council (formerly the Commission on Human Rights) or with complaints addressed to 'the UN' in general, of which OHCHR, for example, receives more than 100,000 every year, most of which used to be channelled to working groups and special procedures of the Commission on Human Rights (Bayefsky, 2001: 108). The treaty bodies, in contrast, receive complaints only in their hundreds a year – minute figures considering the potential range of more than 1.5 billion victims in more than 100 countries (ibid.).

Compared to court procedures, the complaints procedure is simple (UN High Commissioner for Human Rights, n.d.). No legal representation is required, and there are few formalities. The treaty body decides on the admissibility of the communication and, in cases where irreparable harm would be suffered by the victim, may request the state party to take 'interim measures'. Communications to treaty bodies are subsidiary means of protection, and consequently the claimant must have exhausted all domestic remedies before submitting a communication. The treaty body then concludes whether or not a violation of treaty provisions has occurred. Treaty bodies sit in closed session and usually decide on the basis of written information, oral hearings being the exception. They do not, as a rule, attempt to verify factual information provided. Their decision is brought to the attention of the complainant and the state party and then made publicly available. No appeal is possible. The treaty bodies' conclusions consist of two elements: the decision on the violation of specific treaty provisions and recommendations on how to remedy the violation. Should the treaty body rule that a treaty provision has been violated, it calls upon the state party to supply information within a certain period of time on the steps it has taken, if any, to give effect to the treaty body's findings. While the treaty bodies have discretion as to what they suggest, they cannot award damages in the way the European Court of Human Rights can.

Decisions on individual cases are of relevance for the person(s) concerned, yet their importance goes beyond the respective case. By deciding on complaints, the treaty bodies give concrete meaning to specific human rights norms in concrete circumstances and thereby build up a kind of 'jurisprudence', which can guide governments, NGOs and inter-governmental organizations in interpreting and understanding the content and relevance of international human rights norms. The Human Rights Committee's 'views' (Article 5 Optional Protocol to the ICCPR) on violations of the ICCPR are perhaps the most widely known and most influential of such decisions. The Committee has built up considerable jurisprudence and its decisions are cited in courts and in scholarly writings (McGoldrick, 1994; Buergenthal, 2001; Young, 2002; Mavrommatis, 2001).

These views, like those of other treaty bodies, are not legally binding for state parties; nor can their implementation be enforced by the treaty body. To clarify this grey legal zone, at the Vienna World Conference on Human Rights in 1993, the treaty bodies proposed the insertion into the Optional Protocol to ICCPR of a provision reading: 'states parties undertake to comply with the Committee's views under the Optional Protocol'. Their proposal went unheard, so that the precise legal nature of such views remains uncertain (Ghandhi, 2000: 445–52; de Zayas, 2001: 117). In any case, follow-up procedures are essential to the credibility of the work of treaty bodies, but even within treaty bodies, such as the Human Rights Committee, there is disagreement on whether they would be competent to press for such a follow-up. In 1990, a decision was taken by the Human Rights Committee to install a Special Rapporteur for Follow-up (de Zayas, 2001: 118–19; Bayefsky, 2001: 32–4), which made clear what seems only logical, namely that treaty bodies should care for the implementation of their findings. Only innovative, sustained and targeted activities to follow up the non-implementation of treaty bodies' recommendations will translate their paperwork into visible changes on the ground (Schmidt, 2001). Raising the political costs of non-compliance with the findings of treaty bodies, however, is a task beyond their scope and would require efforts by higher political bodies.

## Inquiries

Treaty bodies meet in UN headquarters in Geneva and New York, and only rarely do the experts venture out to conduct on-site visits. CAT (Article 20) and CEDAW (Articles 8–10, Optional Protocol) allow their treaty bodies to initiate inquiries once they have received reliable information containing well-founded indications of serious or systematic violations of the respective treaty by a state party. Such inquiries may include visits to the territory of the state concerned, provided the state agrees. The inquiry procedures are confidential and the findings are transmitted to the state party together with recommendations. Such inquiries have been undertaken only occasionally (Soerensen, 2001: 172). With the adoption of the Optional Protocol to CAT in 2002, a more promising system of in-country inspection has been set up, which may replicate the successful activities of the European Committee against Torture. The protocol creates a Subcommittee on Prevention, which may visit places where people are deprived of their liberty. It combines on-site inquiries with a preventive mandate. Unlike the inquiry procedures of CAT and CEDAW, state parties to the protocol are legally obliged to allow such visits. The protocol is also innovative in that it requires states not only to accept an international monitoring body but also to set up (or maintain) national inspection mechanisms which are intended to work in conjunction with the Subcommittee. The procedure ends with the publication of a report on the Subcommittee's findings, which is made public (together with comments by the state) when the state so requests. Should the state not cooperate with the Subcommittee in its inquiries or fail to implement its recommendations, the report can be made public even if the state objects. Once the procedural arrangements for the Subcommittee are concluded, this new tool weaving together prevention, inquiry, reliance on domestic institutional structures and public pressure can demonstrate its strength.

## General Comments

Treaty bodies are entitled to clarify the content of treaty provisions in the form of 'General Comments' ('General Recommendations' in the case of CERD and CEDAW). These interpretational acts may relate to substantive provisions (such as the right to life) or cross-cutting issues (such as violence against women), give procedural advice to state parties, or clarify the treaty bodies' methods of work. Their legal

character is somewhat ambiguous and lies between authoritative interpretations of treaty provisions and advisory opinions. Despite their
unassuming name, and notwithstanding the critique that they are
sometimes sweeping assertions rather than substantiated interpretative
statements, they have proven to be significant and influential tools with
the ability to strengthen human rights norms (Alston, 2001: 763).

## Achievements

The establishment of seven treaty bodies rather than one central monitoring institution for all treaty obligations is a mixed blessing. It allows
for tailored assessments of specific human rights provisions, but leads
to a degree of incoherence, puts a higher burden on states, and stresses
the service capacity of the UN secretariat. Enhancing the effectiveness
of the treaty system is a reform priority for the UN, as indicated by
the UN Secretary-General in his 2002 report (UN, 2002: paras. 52–4).
Many proposals for reform are on the table (Bayefsky, 2001; Alston,
2000), a number of which have been alluded to in this chapter: curtail-
ing excessive state reporting; speeding up the procedure; ensuring
follow-up to decisions in individual cases; making on-site visits possible; increasing cooperation and coordination among treaty bodies;
communicating the findings of treaty bodies to other human rights
bodies; and ensuring sufficient resources are the major concerns.
Ensuring that treaty bodies and the special procedures of the Human
Rights Council work hand in hand is particularly important to avoid
overlapping and contradictory recommendations to governments
(Rodley, 2003). Similarly, overlap between treaty bodies themselves
presents a challenge to the consistency and coherence of international
human rights law (Tistounet, 2000).

Technical suggestions on the micro-level, such as relocating the
CEDAW committee to Geneva; harmonizing terminology, document
symbols and reporting cycles; more 'cross-referencing' in reports; and
using 'core documents' rather than duplicate information, are pitted
against changes on the macro-level. These include asking for one
'super-report' instead of individual state reports or merging all seven
treaty bodies into one. The latter suggestion was put forward by the
High Commissioner for Human Rights in a concept paper in 2006 (UN
doc. HRC/MC/2006/2). As with the whole of the UN human rights
system, there is a scarcity of financial resources for OHCHR to support
the treaty bodies (Evatt, 2000: 461). Yet, ironically, money alone is no
remedy. Were the OHCHR to receive the necessary funding to support
the treaty bodies with maximum efficiency, it would collapse under the

number of reports and complaints it could suddenly be required to consider; and the same would happen if effective incentives were to lead to states submitting all their reports in time (Schmidt, 2000: 497).

The crisis that many commentators see in the treaty body system (Bayefsky, 2001: 8), and which has led to the flurry of reform proposals just mentioned, is, however, partly also a sign of success (Crawford, 2000: 3). It shows how accepted the system has become not only by victims of human rights violations, but also by NGOs, which participate in different formal and informal ways in the work of treaty bodies and are crucial for the functioning of the system (O'Flaherty, 1993: 1–16). Even where the system fails to deliver 'justice' in the complaints procedures, it keeps producing the one and only corpus of global human rights jurisprudence available on which governments and academia can build their understanding of international human rights norms. And even where it trundles along in reviewing inadequate state reports, it keeps states engaged in a continuous dialogue on the progressive implementation of international human rights norms and insists on bringing home the message to them that human rights violations are breaches of international treaty law rather than excusable collateral damage of domestic policies.

Treaty bodies have been able to assert themselves as autonomous actors which stand up to their masters, the states, more than other UN human rights bodies, in particular when it comes to speaking out on individual human rights violations. Bodies such as the Human Rights Committee set up under ICCPR are indeed the closest the UN has yet come to any such thing as an independent human rights tribunal. In its strictly legal approach based on international treaty law, it avoids the political quagmire which characterizes charter-based UN institutions and is better able to fulfil a core function of international institutions (as described by Simmons and Martin, 2002: 198, and discussed in chapter 2), namely constraining the behaviour of states. The reason lies in the system's design: treaty bodies are set up under treaties, to which states are free to accede (or not), with the individual complaints procedure requiring a separate declaration of acceptance to come into force. In effect, this allows groups of states to move faster towards achieving and implementing common norms. It must not be overlooked, however, that there is a price to be paid for such a design. Realistic as it is in its reflection of an international system which lacks a constitutional order, this approach replaces the universal acceptance of human rights norms with a model of layered acceptance of such norms.

# 5 MAINSTREAMING HUMAN RIGHTS

## From mandate to mainstreaming

International organizations manage a great range of global social, economic, humanitarian, technical and political issues. Over the past decades they have proliferated in the fields of development, trade, investment, humanitarian relief, health, food security, intellectual property, telecommunications and crime prevention, to name but a few. Most of these institutions are members of the large 'UN family' of organizations, agencies, programmes and funds. Unlike the institutions discussed in the previous chapter, their mandates do not, or not explicitly or solely, relate to human rights. The extent to which human rights permeate these institutions differs, as does the level of practical experience they have in human rights, as well as the consequence of exposure to human rights for the institutional framework and activities and the resulting changes in self-perception.

The ILO, the discussion of which starts this chapter, may (as we have already said) be called the first ever international human rights institution, albeit limited to a particular sector of human rights. Other institutions presented in the following pages, such as UNESCO, are mandated to protect or promote certain human rights alongside other duties. UNDP and UNICEF have embraced human rights and have reoriented their activities along international human rights law. UN-HABITAT (the United Nations Human Settlements Programme), WHO and FAO continue to perceive themselves as institutions for the pursuance of social concerns such as housing, health and food. Yet, as international human rights law provides for the right to housing, health and food, these institutions have begun to explore the impact of international human rights law on their work. Still others, in particular international financial institutions, such as the World Bank and the IMF, cling to their self-perception as 'non-political' institutions, which, they argue, exclude human rights from their mandate. But the fiction that their activities have no repercussions on human rights has long been shattered and given way to the quest of understanding better the place of human rights in international financial institutions. Beyond those institutions, the belief that 'technical' institutions simply 'don't do human rights' is as widespread as it is questionable.

Mainstreaming human rights has become the catch-phrase for integrating human rights into all these institutions. The process was launched in 1997, when the UN Secretary-General presented his reform programme for the UN, *Renewing the United Nations: A Programme for Reform* (UN, 1997; Pennegard, 2001: 57–8; Nowak, 2003: 75). According to Kofi Annan, the time had come to accept that human rights were no longer extraneous to UN activities such as development, peacekeeping or child welfare. The stage was set that same year with the restructuring of the UN secretariat into four executive committees reflecting the main activities of the organization: peace and security, economic and social affairs, humanitarian affairs, and development cooperation. Rather than creating a fifth 'human rights' committee, human rights were to be integrated ('mainstreamed') into all of the UN's work (UN, 1997: para. 28). The process built on the establishment in 1992 of the Inter-Agency Standing Committee (General Assembly resolution 46/182, 1992), which is the primary mechanism for inter-agency coordination of humanitarian assistance. In his 2002 report *Strengthening of the United Nations: An Agenda for Further Change*, the UN Secretary-General confirmed that 'the promotion and protection of human rights is a bedrock requirement for the realization of the Charter's vision of a just and peaceful world' (UN, 2002: para. 45). Subsequently, thirty-six actions for reform were identified. 'Action 2' and the resulting 'Action 2 Plan of Action and Work Plan', adopted by twenty-one heads of UN departments and agencies, aimed, *inter alia*, to integrate human rights throughout the UN system in its humanitarian, development and peacekeeping work and to apply a human rights approach to programming. The OHCHR was entrusted with overall responsibility for driving forward the policy of mainstreaming human rights, in particular into peace operations and development activities.

Mainstreaming human rights represents the deliberate infusion of human rights into the work of organizations, including their organs and bureaucracy. The process still lacks conceptual clarity, there are disagreements as to its scope and utility, and its achievements and failures so far are often difficult to measure. Mainstreaming human rights is sometimes expressed as a 'rights-based approach' (e.g., as a 'rights-based approach' to development). In the understanding of the OHCHR this means that 'the process of human development [. . .] is normatively based on international human rights standards and operationally directed to promoting and protecting human rights' (http://www.unhchr.ch/development/approaches.html).

Misunderstandings and disagreements prevail as to both the process of mainstreaming and its desired outcome. Often, differing perceptions of human rights are at the core of such disagreements. Human rights may either be acknowledged as a comprehensive international legal framework which lays down concrete entitlements, rights, duties and responsibilities, or be perceived as a set of values and policy goals an institution may choose to follow (or not). In the former case, a normative framework is introduced into policies and programmes; in the latter, human rights are added on to already existing policies and programmes as an optional element. When mainstreaming human rights is meant to be more than a 'do good, feel good' approach and to go beyond rhetorical exercises in conference speeches, its far-reaching legal and practical implications must be tackled in earnest.

The difficulties of translating international human rights norms, standards and principles into the policies and programmes of global institutions which lack a specific mandate on human rights are plentiful. Mainstreaming human rights is a challenge because it means departing from the 1945 model of splitting up the management of 'global commons' to separate specialized agencies on development, environment, human rights, etc. It is more than a process of institutional reform and may also require an 'integration approach' (Petersmann, 2001: 1) that has yet to be developed. It may impact on an institution's self-perception, leading it to question its very mandate. It may also necessitate changes in the structure and internal organization or entail budgetary consequences. UN Secretary-General Kofi Annan outlined four different challenges in 1997: mainstreaming must involve the adoption of a rights-based approach to an institution's activities; it must lead to the development of specific programmes or projects on human rights; it requires the reorientation of existing programmes towards human rights; and it must ensure that the UN human rights programme is included in the broader UN policy development (Gallagher, 1999a: 154–5).

The practical requirements of mainstreaming human rights are equally demanding – training staff, changing the infrastructure and bureaucratic practices, acquiring human rights expertise in implementing, monitoring and evaluating programmes, and so on. There are many factors which mean the process follows a long and winding road: the great range of actors in the UN system; uncertainties on how to integrate international legal norms into policy- and programme-type activities; little understanding of the implications of international human rights law; and doubts about the precise aim of mainstreaming. Yet, as discussed in this chapter, sufficient practice has accumulated over the past decade to provide some street lighting along the way.

# International Labour Organization

As one of the oldest existing multilateral organizations, the ILO is a survivor, and a successful one for that matter. As we have seen above, it was set up by the Peace Conference in Paris in 1919 and is a living legacy of the Treaty of Versailles. In the years following its establishment it quickly set itself apart from the League of Nations and did not share the League's fate of disappearing from the global institutional landscape. The ILO lived through World War II and the Cold War, continually expanding its membership and adapting its mandate to the needs of a globalized world. The organization can now look back at more than eight decades of experience in managing global issues, first and foremost in the area of labour rights and working conditions, but lately also the globalization of markets and labour. It can also look down – sometimes a bit too literally, perhaps – from its headquarters above Lac Léman in Geneva to the Palais des Nations, the seat of its younger sister, the UN, because to some extent the ILO paved the way for the creation of the UN human rights regime. The ILO's founding documents laid the ground for the Universal Declaration of Human Rights. René Cassin, the principal author of the Universal Declaration, saw the ILO's constitution of 1919 as the first instance of an international contractual arrangement to secure individual freedoms (Valticos, 1998: 135). Driven by humanitarian, political and social considerations, the ILO constitution reaffirms that universal and lasting peace cannot be achieved without social justice. In 1944, the ILO's aims and purposes were redefined in the Declaration of Philadelphia, which holds that labour is not a commodity, that freedom of expression and association are essential to economic progress, that poverty constitutes a danger to prosperity, and that 'all human beings, irrespective of race, creed or sex, have the right to pursue both their material well-being and their spiritual development in conditions of freedom and dignity, of economic security and equal opportunity' (Article II).

Today, the ILO serves a twofold purpose: it helps promote economic growth by recommending good labour market policies and practices, and it protects the individual from coercion or abuse by both states and employers (Charnovitz, 2000: 183). The latter is achieved by prescribing minimum standards for workers as legal obligations. From its very first days, the ILO engaged in developing and adopting such international labour standards: 187 Conventions and 198 Recommendations form an impressive body of international standards known as the International Labour Code. With now 179 member states, the organization has achieved a quasi-universal status. In 1946, it became the first specialized agency of the UN. While the ILO was awarded the Nobel Peace Prize in 1969, with the remarkable explanation that it is 'one of the rare institutional creations of which the human race can be proud' (http://www.ilo.org/public/english/bureau/inf/download/brochure/pdf/page6.pdf), and has been praised as 'social science of the world', it has been sidelined by others as 'not terribly interesting' and has been dismissed as outdated for its 'corporative orientation and command-and-control culture' (quotations taken from Charnovitz, 2000: 148–50 and 183).

In its institutional design, the ILO is unique. Its tripartite structure allows it to accommodate governments and employers' and workers' organizations with an equal voice, thus firmly including non-state actors in its decision-making processes. The result is a continuous dialogue between governments and social partners, e.g., in the International Labour Conference, the main gathering of ILO member states. Tripartism also prevails in the ILO Governing Body (with twenty-eight government members and fourteen workers' and fourteen employers' members), which calls on the support of the International Labour Office, the ILO's secretariat, with its more than 2,500 staff and more than forty field offices.

The question as to whether the ILO is a human rights organization has been discussed for some time (Jenks, 1960). Today, the ILO leaves no doubt about its self-perception: it sees itself as an organization 'which seeks the promotion of social justice and internationally recognized human and labour rights' (http://www.ilo.org/public/english/about/index.htm). The organization, however, was created before the term 'human rights' was widely used. It is built around the idea of social justice and based on the expectation that social justice is best secured by combining economic growth and workers' rights (Charno-vitz, 2000: 183). Indeed, 'international labour standards, as a body, constitute a special category of human rights' (Valticos, 1998: 136–7). It seems fair to call the ILO not only a human rights institution with universal reach, but also the first global human rights institution.

The ILO is a busy production facility for labour standards, continu-ally covering most areas of social concern with a growing number of conventions (Samson and Schindler, 1999: 191). Basic labour rights remain the focus, such as the right to organize, the rights of trade unions, freedom of association, collective bargaining, abolition of forced labour, equality of opportunity and treatment, child labour, conditions of work, labour administration, social security, and safety and health at work. The organization has a long track-record in dealing with occupational safety, work-related diseases, hazardous occupa-tions, violence at the workplace, maternity protection, labour inspec-tion, and the protection of migrant workers. Among the most prominent legal texts are Convention No. 29 on forced labour, No. 87 on freedom of association and the right to organize, No. 98 on collec-tive bargaining, No. 100 on equal remuneration, No. 105 on the aboli-tion of forced labour, No. 111 on discrimination in employment and occupation, and No. 138 on the minimum age of employment.

Today, the organization takes a broader interest in areas such as social security, children's rights, gender equality, and indigenous rights. On the last issue, it is the ILO, and not the UN, which has the only two legally binding documents on indigenous rights, the Indigenous and Tribal Peoples Conventions No. 107 (1957) and No. 169 (1989). They aim to protect traditionally disadvantaged groups of workers, to reduce poverty among indigenous peoples and to improve their employ-ment opportunities and conditions. The ILO is a vigorous contributor to the international debate on child labour and bolsters its respective legal obligations (such as Convention No. 182 of 1999, on the worst forms of child labour) with expertise and assistance in the International Programme on the Elimination of Child Labour (IPEC), the world's largest technical cooperation programme on child labour. In order to tackle gender inequality it has developed an integrated approach based on capacity-building, policy analysis, awareness-raising and targeted practical interventions to address problems faced by women within and beyond the workplace. It has responded to the need to reach out to multinational enterprises and ensure their accountability for labour rights and workers' rights. With the Tripartite Declaration of Princi-ples Concerning Multinational Enterprises and Social Policy of 1977, the ILO set out principles on employment, conditions of work and industrial relations. More recently, it has taken an interest in the consequences of globalization for workers' rights (Cox, 1999: 456). Since the establishment of a working party on the social dimensions of the liberalization or international trade in 1994 (later renamed the Working Party on the Social Dimensions of Globalization), the organization has engaged in the discussion on the inclusion of 'social clauses' in trade agreements (Swepston, 2003: 107–8; Charnovitz, 2000: 157–63).

This impressive list of activities combines alertness, innovation, sound theoretical frameworks and workable tools in a way which other global institutions find difficult to replicate. With the adoption of the ILO Declaration on Fundamental Principles and Rights at Work at the fiftieth anniversary of the Universal Declaration of Human Rights in 1998, the ILO member states reaffirmed their commitment to respect, promote and realize four core ILO standards: freedom of association and the recognition of the right to collective bargaining; elimination of all forms of forced or compulsory labour; abolition of child labour; and elimination of discrimination in respect of employment and occupation. The commitment to these standards does not depend on signature or ratification of the respective ILO Conventions. With this Declaration, the ILO was able to prioritize its work in the areas mentioned (Swepston, 2003: 94). In a follow-up procedure to this Declaration, established by the International Labour Conference, member states are reviewed annually and an annual Global Report is prepared, in which the core standards are examined on a rotating principle. The value of the Declaration is thus threefold: it reaffirms the commitment of both governments and social partners or the universality of fundamental principles and rights, it adds to the promotional activities of the organization, and it leads to a reorientation of the ILO's resources towards new priorities (Kellerson, 1998: 227).

Innovative standard-setting is accompanied by a supervisory system for the application of its standards, established as early as 1926 (Swepston, 2003: 95–8; Leary, 1992: 595–612; Samson and Schindler, 1999: 196–213). The system allows for diverse mechanisms to ensure compliance with ILO standards. These include examination of governmental reports by independent experts; investigation by an independent commission of inquiry; complaints lodged by governments and social partners; fact-finding; conciliation; condemnation of gross violations of core labour rights; 'Global Reports' on core labour standards; action by the ILO Governing Body and the International Labour Conference; direct dialogues with governments; technical assistance; and recourse to the ICJ. No other institution can show an equally broad and multi-faceted approach to the supervision of the implementation of international commitments.

As in the UN, state reporting is the cornerstone of supervision. Each ILO member state has to present periodic reports on the implementation of the Conventions it has ratified. The reports are examined by the Committee of Experts on the Application of Conventions and Recommendations, composed of twelve independent experts in the legal and social fields. The Committee submits an annual report to the International Labour Conference, which has set up a tripartite committee to prepare recommendations on the basis of the experts' views. Complaints procedures supplement the reporting mechanism. Different avenues are on offer: employers' and workers' organizations can initiate so-called representations against an ILO member state for alleged non-compliance with a Convention it has ratified. The Governing Body then appoints a different tripartite committee, the conclusions and recommendations of which are brought to the attention of the Governing Body. An ILO member state can also lodge a complaint against another member state which has not implemented a convention satisfactorily. In this case, the Governing Body may set up a Commission of Inquiry. The same can be initiated by the Governing Body itself or by a delegate to the International Labour Conference. If governments refuse to accept the recommendations made by the Commission of Inquiry, the case may be submitted to the ICJ.

A further procedure related to freedom of association is unique to the ILO. It was set up in 1950 and allows governments or employers' or workers' organizations to submit a complaint against a member state even if that state has not ratified the relevant convention. This is possible because freedom of association is not only regulated by Conventions, but is also laid down in the ILO Constitution, to which every ILO member state subscribes. This procedure allows either for a Fact-Finding and Conciliation Commission (which is based upon the consent of the concerned state and functions in a way similar to the Commission of Inquiry) or for the appointment of a Committee on the Freedom of Association (a tripartite Committee set up by the Governing Body). Since its first establishment, the Committee on Freedom of Association has dealt with more than 2,000 cases. While all these mechanisms are geared towards rectifying shortcomings in the implementation of specific treaty provisions, the ILO has lately also shown greater willingness to confront gross and persistent violations of its core standards. In a step unprecedented in its seriousness, the ILO condemned Myanmar in 1999 for violations of Forced Labour Convention (No. 29) and for failing to respond to recommendations by the ILO supervisory bodies (Bollé, 1998; Charnovitz, 2000: 154).

The launch of technical cooperation programmes after World War II complements the ILO's standard-setting and supervisory activities (Swepston, 2003: 100). Today, the ILO provides technical assistance in a range of areas, including vocational training and rehabilitation, employment policy, labour administration, labour law and industrial relations, working conditions, management development, social security, labour statistics, and occupational health and safety.

In the mainstream discourse on human rights as well as in the academic literature, little attention is devoted to the ILO's standards and procedures. Leary attributes this to the mistaken perception among human rights scholars and activists that the organization is concerned only with labour standards and not with human rights, and to the limited possibilities it allows for participation of NGOs (Leary, 1992: 580). Given its impressive record, one cannot but deplore such lack of interest. Observers willing to engage with the ILO from a human rights perspective acknowledge that it has 'the most highly developed inter-governmental system for the protection of human rights' (ibid.), and 'the most effective and well-developed mechanisms for human rights protection in the international system' (Swepston, 2003: 91). The supervisory mechanisms have been considered a model for other institutions (Valticos, 1994: 112). Indeed, the detailed legal obligations, together with the elaborate and well-tested supervisory system and the targeted programme of technical assistance, set standards for other institutions. True, the tripartite structure – as the key to the ILO's success – cannot be replicated easily. One lesson to be learned from the ILO, however, is that any supervision of legal obligations must be systematic, regular and consistent in order to yield results in the long run. Unlike the case with the UN, this allows the ILO to harvest the fruits of its work more often. And the ILO conveys another message: despite being perceived as an organization concerned with social rights, it has in fact adopted an integrated approach to human rights (Dao, 1993: 141). In applying the same procedures and putting the same emphasis on the civil, cultural, economic, political or social rights of workers, it is able to avoid the dichotomy between civil-political and socio-economic rights which is such an intrinsic part of other human rights systems (Leary, 1992: 590–4).

On the downside, the ILO lacks an individual complaints procedure and allows only limited access to NGOs. These are areas in which UN human rights institutions fare better. Victims of violations of workers' rights are thus present only insofar as they are represented by their workers' organizations. While this gives national trade unions a powerful tool to ensure workers' rights on the international level, it excludes the individual person from the ILO's procedures (Donnelly, 2003: 146). Although it is willing to listen informally to NGOs, take advantage of their knowledge and expertise, and work with them in technical assistance programmes or in the framework of a Commission of Inquiry (Swepston, 2001: 499–500), better access to the ILO for NGOs beyond the social partners has been identified as one of the challenges ahead (Charnovitz, 2000: 177). Like some other human rights institutions, the organization has also become a victim of its own success: pinning down its ideas of social justice and human rights has resulted in more than 7,000 ratifications of ILO conventions so far, and both member states and the ILO itself find it difficult to handle the resulting huge number of periodic reports on the implementation of legal obligations (Swepston, 2003: 106).

The ILO is indeed a 'pioneer' of human rights. (Freeman, 2005: 136). Looking back at more than eighty years of standard-setting and implementation, observers generally judge the impact of the ILO's work on the human rights situation in member states as substantial and covering a wider range of labour rights and workers' rights, with an increasing focus on tackling negative consequences of a globalized economy (ILO, 1976; Swepston, 2003: 101–4; Valticos, 1998: 144–5).

## United Nations Development Programme

Created in 1965 and present in 166 countries, UNDP is the world's largest development organization and has long emancipated itself from being a mere UN 'fund'. The Executive Board, composed of thirty-six member states, oversees UNDP's activities, which are guided by the UN Millennium Development Goals (MDGs) and focus on democratic governance, poverty reduction, crisis prevention and recovery, energy and environment, and combating HIV/AIDS. The UN Capital Development Fund, UNIFEM and the United Nations Volunteers (UNV) work under the umbrella of UNDP. The UNDP Administrator is also head of the UN Development Group (UNDG), in which other UN programmes and funds cooperate, and manages the UN Resident Coordinators. The UNDP's flagship publication, the annual *Human Development Report*, is a cornerstone of the international debate on development.

UNDP was the first institution to respond to the Secretary-General's call to mainstream human rights. In 1998, it adopted a policy paper on integrating human rights into its work: *Integrating Human Rights with Sustainable Development* (UNDP, 1998) soon became a landmark document on why and how human rights should guide the policy and practice of institutions other than the core UN human rights bodies. In this document, UNDP acknowledged that human rights are already part of its work and identified the challenges that it saw lying ahead:

> UNDP already plays an important role in the protection and promotion of human rights, both in its country activities and through its participation in national, international and multilateral meetings and conferences. Its programme is an application of the right to development and addresses primarily the economic, social and cultural rights of citizens. In some countries the programme has expanded into civil and political rights. There is a need, however, to more systematically address and focus the programme's human rights content and dimensions. (UNDP, 1998)

Ever since this initiative, UNDP has continued to play a leading role in applying a rights-based approach to development. The organization considered that several of its strategies have particular relevance for human rights: sustainable human development programming with a focus on eliminating poverty; targeting disadvantaged or excluded groups (women, children, minorities, migrant workers, people with HIV/AIDS); linking social justice, discrimination and development; promoting partnerships with NGOs and civil society organizations and encouraging people's participation; addressing governance issues such as corruption, the rule of law, participation, democratization and accountability; strengthening institutions of governance and developing human rights capacity within such institutions; and supporting legislative and judicial systems (UNDP, 1998).

Also in 1998, UNDP was the first organization to sign a memorandum of understanding with OHCHR. Other key documents and strategy papers have since accompanied and spelled out the human rights-based approach of UNDP, such as the Administrator's note of September 2000 on implementing UNDP policy on human rights in the new millennium, the training manual on human rights and sustainable human development, and the Global Programme on Human Rights Strengthening (HURIST). The last is a joint programme of UNDP and OHCHR designed to test guidelines and methodologies and to identify learning opportunities and best practices for the development of national human rights policies (Ramcharan, 2002c: 51–3). The programme helps in developing national human rights action plans and in strengthening human rights capacities, reviewing UNDP country programmes, and disseminating learning experiences with regard to a human rights-based approach. Within the HURIST framework, a number of policy papers and strategies have been adopted, e.g., the Common Understanding of a Human Rights based Approach to Development Cooperation, which was subsequently endorsed by the UN, the Draft Guidelines of Human Rights Reviews of UNDP country programmes, the Practice Note on Poverty Reduction and Human Rights, and the Asia/Pacific Access to Justice Programme. In 2005, UNDP adopted the strategy paper *Human Rights in UNDP: A Practice Note* (UNDP, 2005) with the aim of confirming its policies along a human rights-based approach and elaborating – on the basis of its experience since 1998 – how such a policy should be implemented in the three strategic areas of its work: supporting the strengthening of national human rights institutions, promoting the application of a human rights-based approach to development programming, and enhancing cooperation with the UN human rights machinery. The paper is meant to make further concrete practical steps in human rights mainstreaming possible. No other institution shows a comparably serious engagement with the challenges of mainstreaming human rights.

Human rights have become a key component not only in strategy, but also in the daily work of UNDP. It seems that today the organization finds it unimaginable that its activities – strengthening of electoral systems; supporting national parliaments; ensuring access to justice; supporting local governance and public administration; working towards accountability and transparency; combating corruption; enabling civil society participation in decision-making processes; reducing poverty; and fighting HIV/AIDS – could be based on anything other than human rights. The reason it gives for this is compelling. It considers human rights 'an important and objective normative tool to address the inherent power issues underlying many of the contemporary development problems' (UNDP, 2005: 8). In practice, it is also an indispensable partner of other human rights institutions, on account of its partnership with governments based on dialogue, its strategic partnership with the donor community and civil society, its presence on the ground in 166 countries, its network of 'communities of practice', and its role as facilitator and manager of the UN Resident Coordinator System (ibid.: 12). Yet it has put up fences around its activities: investigating, documenting and reporting human rights violations are considered outside the range of its responsibilities (ibid.: 11). The UNDP is an example of what mainstreaming human rights can mean in practice and how it enhances an institution's reach. It has proven that mainstreaming human rights needs neither to remain a lofty goal nor lead to the limitless spread of pseudo-activities beyond an institution's competence.

# United Nations Children's Fund

Like UNDP, UNICEF has also taken seriously the UN Secretary-General's call to mainstream human rights. Around the same time as UNDP, in 1999, UNICEF adopted its strategy to integrate human rights into its work in the form of a policy paper entitled *A Human Rights Conceptual Framework for UNICEF* (Santos Pais, 1999). It describes UNICEF's shift from being an institution active in development and responsive to emergencies towards a human rights-based organization and an implementing agent of CRC. Like UNDP, UNICEF does not consider this a dramatic change in its self-perception, but rather as flowing from an increased awareness that much of its work has in fact always been linked to human rights. The fundamental change, though, was one from 'needs' to 'rights': 'UNICEF's focus is no longer limited to meeting the needs of children, but on the recognition and realization of their rights' (ibid.: 5–6). UNICEF's mission statement – 'to advocate for the protection of children's rights and to strive to establish children's rights as enduring ethical principles and international standards of behaviour towards children' (http://www.unicef.org/about/who/index_mission.html) – now puts it firmly in a human rights framework. CRC and other UN conventions, in particular CEDAW, and further human rights standards and principles now guide the work of UNICEF (ibid.: 4).

The link between CRC and UNICEF is particularly close. It is not as if UNICEF had chosen overnight to adopt the convention to constitute its guiding principles. Rather, CRC, in Article 45, provides for a specific role for UNICEF as a partner in implementation: 'the United Nations Children's Fund [. . .] shall be entitled to be represented at the consideration of the implementation of such provisions of the present Convention as fall within the scope of their mandate, [. . .] to provide expert advice on the implementation of the Convention [. . .], to submit reports on the implementation of the Convention in areas falling within the scope of their activities.' UNICEF is also alerted by the Committee on the Rights of the Child when governments request advice or assistance. It uses CRC as a reference against which progress can be assessed and results compared, as guidance for its cooperation programmes and for advocacy and the development of partnerships, and to monitor progress in the situation of children (Santos Pais, 1999: 5). In its operational activities, it considers the use of CRC as helpful because it gives it a tool to assess the meaningfulness of activities undertaken, provides a precise agenda instead of a set of general principles, prevents its commitment from becoming fragmented, allows it to set benchmarks and identify suitable measures to achieve them in a given time-frame, and provides an opportunity to promote a self-critical monitoring process (ibid.: 15). UNICEF sees the conclusions of the Committee on the Rights of the Child as a 'golden opportunity' (ibid.: 19) for it to enhance its dialogue with governments on sensitive areas.

Like UNDP, UNICEF finds it advantageous for its activities, reputation, outreach and effectiveness to base its work on human rights. International human rights law has become a tool, a benchmark, a set of references against which UNICEF measures its own work, and which it finds convenient to use in confronting governments with their obligations towards children. Both institutions see the mainstreaming of human rights as a process in which the latter are understood not as an option for the UN system, but as the basic purpose of the UN and its institutions. They consider human rights as highly relevant for their operational activities and understand mainstreaming as a process which better informs UN institutions about the 'why' and the 'how' of their activities, i.e., on the reason for the adoption of specific strategies and policies as well as on the way to implement these strategies and policies. They have also to give something in return: the way in which human rights are being operationalized in their activities helps the appreciation, respect for and realization of the universality, indivisibility and interdependence of human rights not as a theoretical construct but as a practical consequence (Santos Pais, 1999: 1).

# United Nations Educational, Scientific and Cultural Organization

UNESCO was established in 1945 as a specialized agency of the UN to promote cooperation among member states in the field of education, science and culture and with the overall goal of contributing to peace. The General Conference, UNESCO's decision-making body, is comprised of the organization's 191 member states and meets every two years. It appoints the Director-General upon the recommendation of the Executive Board, its fifty-eight-member body entrusted with executive functions. The Director-General oversees more than 2,100 staff in the Paris headquarters and in more than fifty field offices. UNESCO makes use of a unique system of National Commissions in its member states and allows for broad NGO participation.

The organization is specifically mandated by its founding document, the UNESCO constitution, to promote respect for human rights in line with the UN Charter: 'the purpose of the Organization is to contribute to peace and security by promoting collaboration among the nations through education, science and culture in order to further universal respect for justice, for the rule of law and for the human rights and fundamental freedoms which are affirmed for the peoples of the world, without distinction of race, sex, language or religion, by the Charter of the United Nations' (Article I(1)). From the outset, UNESCO has contributed to standard-setting in the field of human rights. It assisted in drafting the Universal Declaration of Human Rights and some subsequent UN human rights treaties.

Several human rights provisions contained in UN human rights conventions, in particular the right to education and to participate in cultural life, the right of freedom of expression and opinion, the right to seek, receive and impart information, and the right to enjoy the benefits of scientific progress, access to information, cultural diversity and gender equality are of importance for UNESCO's respective work (Symonides, 2001b: 307–27). UNESCO considers the right to education a fundamental human right, and in its 'Education for All' initiative (under which the World Education Forum was held in Dakar in 2000) it seeks to ensure six main goals by 2015, all of which could also be expressed in human rights terms: expanding early childhood care and education; providing compulsory free primary education; increasing learning opportunities for youth and adults; improving adult literacy rates by 50 per cent; eliminating gender disparities in schooling; and improving all aspects of education quality. Likewise, cultural human rights are concretized in a threefold way: through specific norm-making (e.g., the 1952 Universal Copyright Convention), through protecting cultural achievements (e.g., in the 1972 Convention concerning the Protection of the World Cultural and Natural Heritage), and by generally acknowledging the importance of cultural diversity (e.g., in the 2001 Declaration on Cultural Diversity).

This last is part of UNESCO's attempts to promote a dialogue among cultures and civilizations and to build a 'Global Alliance for Cultural Diversity' (http://www.unesco.org/culture). The promotion of cultural and linguistic diversity and UNESCO's focus on overcoming the 'digital divide' between developed and underdeveloped countries in information and communication technologies tie in with this activity. In the field of communication and information, the organization sees itself as a watchdog for press freedom. It promotes freedom of expression and freedom of the press as basic human rights, in particular in countries in transition and in conflict zones. In the area of science and biotechnology, UNESCO adopted the Universal Declaration on the Human Genome and Human Rights in 1997 and the International Declaration on Human Genetic Data in 2003.

While it seems fair to say that, in the light of these standard-setting and other activities, UNESCO is usually underrated as a contributor to international human rights law, the organization's attempts to monitor the implementation of these standards are feeble in comparison. Its constitution provides for a general reporting obligation on member states' 'laws, regulations and statistics relating to its educational, scientific and cultural institutions and activities' (Article VIII), and the General Conference also considers reports submitted by member states on UNESCO conventions and recommendations (Article IV (6), UNESCO constitution). Some UNESCO conventions and recommendations contain specific reporting provisions (Symonides, 2001a: 511), the first being devised for the 1960 Convention against Discrimination in Education (Partsch and Hüfner, 2003: 112). Such reports are considered by the Committee on Conventions and Recommendations, which submits its conclusions, via the Executive Committee, to the General Conference. UNESCO also provides for a little-known complaints procedure, established in 1978 by its Executive Board (104 EX/Decision 3.3, 1978). The procedure is used infrequently compared to complaints procedures under UN human rights treaties; UNESCO's website indicates that there were 508 cases between 1978 and 2003, of which 315 have been resolved (http://portal.unesco.org/shs/en/ev.php-URL_ID=8044&URL_DO=DO_TOPIC&URL_SECTION=201.html).

The reasons for such a small number can be attributed to a lack of knowledge in the NGO community and among potential complainants, as well as to the confidential nature and general weakness of the procedure itself: 'at a minimum, the procedure makes the concerned government aware that the allegations are known outside the country. At best, the procedure may generate sufficient diplomatic or humanitarian pressure to obtain some form of redress' (Marks, 2004: 108–9 and 120). The communications procedure allows for victims or anyone with reliable knowledge about a violation to submit 'cases' or 'general questions' to UNESCO, which are then examined by the Committee on Conventions and Recommendations in regular or emergency sessions. The communication must relate to one of the rights within

UNESCO's sphere of competence, i.e., the right to education; to enjoy the benefits of scientific progress; to take part in cultural life; to information, freedom of opinion and expression; to freedom of thought, conscience and religion; to protection of the moral and material interests resulting from any scientific, literary or artistic production; and to freedom of assembly and association when connected with education, science, culture and information. The distinction between 'cases' and 'general questions' is the result of inter-institutional compromises and, in essence, means that 'questions' are, unlike cases, massive human rights violations, which are to be considered in public by the Executive Board and ultimately by the UNESCO General Conference (Partsch and Hüfner, 2003: 125–7). The aim of the procedure is to reach a friendly settlement with the state in question. Despite UNESCO's appraisal that confidentiality is an advantage of the procedure, its shortcomings make it a weak mechanism which operates in 'secrecy, isolation and obscurity' (Coomans, 1999: 228).

In 2003, the General Conference adopted the UNESCO Strategy on Human Rights (32/C/Resolution 27, 2003). Like the respective strategies of other organizations, it is based on the UN Secretary-General's reform proposals of 1997 and takes into account the VDPA and the MDGs. The strategy is closely linked to the UNESCO Integrated Strategy to Combat Racism, Discrimination, Xenophobia and Related Intolerance, also adopted by the General Conference in 2003 as a response to the Durban Declaration and Programme of Action of 2001 and to UNESCO's programme on gender equality and development. Through its Strategy on Human Rights, the organization seeks to ensure that human rights standards and the conclusions of UN treaty bodies are better integrated into its work, that staff are trained in human rights, that the design and evaluation of the outcome of projects is in line with human rights standards, and that its human rights profile is recognized. Four areas of particular relevance have been identified: policy-oriented research; human rights education and training; strengthening cooperation with various actors and networks; and integrating human rights into all UNESCO programmes. As concrete contributions, UNESCO plans, *inter alia*, to monitor human rights education as part of the right to education in all member states; to mainstream human rights education into national education systems; to integrate human rights education in the Education for All initiative; and to assist states in preparing national plans on human rights education.

Unlike UNDP and UNICEF, UNESCO has not yet provided any evidence to show that its operational activities benefit from these plans and goals. It has also not developed effective tools to contribute to the implementation of international commitments and has not yet found ways and means fully to realize the potential of mainstreaming human rights. Having said this, however, one must acknowledge that UNESCO has a specific human rights mandate which pre-dates the idea of mainstreaming human rights – a mandate which perhaps must be read in line with UNESCO's overall self-perception as an institution promoting, and not enforcing, a range of rights in the fields of culture, education and science. The organization's successes in drafting standards and the way in which it has, over time, dispersed human rights values and ideas into different communities may represent progress which can hardly be captured by criteria applicable to bodies such as the Human Rights Council and treaty bodies, or UNDP and UNICEF. If this holds true, then UNESCO is, in terms of its commitment to human rights, more a channel of communication, exchange and dispersion. If measured by other types of output, such as operation, enforcement or securing norm compliance, it lags behind other human rights institutions.

# United Nations High Commissioner for Refugees

The protection of refugees is secured mainly by the 1951 Convention Relating to the Status of Refugees and its 1967 Protocol rather than by human rights instruments. Despite this division of labour, the links between the two fields are close and manifold. After all, the Universal Declaration of Human Rights and many human rights treaties recognize the right to seek asylum. In turn, the Refugee Convention protects a number of human rights of refugees, such as non-discrimination (Article 3), religious rights (Article 4), access to employment opportunities (Articles 17 to 19), freedom of movement (Articles 26 and 31) and the right to housing (Article 21). UNHCR is specifically mandated to lead and coordinate international action for the protection of refugees and the resolution of refugee problems. Since its establishment in 1950, the organization has attempted to ensure that everybody can exercise their right to seek asylum, find refuge in another state, resettle or return home voluntarily. Originally entrusted with a three-year mandate to help resettle European refugees, the organization has since turned into the major global institution for refugee protection. Moreover, the range of activities has widened, and UNHCR is now also engaged in protecting stateless persons or persons whose nationality is disputed, persons who have found refuge on humanitarian grounds without legally qualifying as refugees, and internally displaced persons (IDPs) as well. The last group, numbering 20 to 25 million worldwide, does not benefit from the Refugee Convention, nor is human rights law able to ensure full protection. This in itself would suffice to demonstrate the necessity of both UNHCR and human rights bodies joining forces to fill this void.

With a staff of 6,540, UNHCR provides legal protection as well as material relief in emergencies to over 19 million people in 116 countries (http://www.unhcr.org/cgi-bin/texis/vtx/basics). The Executive Committee of sixty-six member states, which meets at headquarters in Geneva, decides on UNHCR's policies and programmes. The organization is funded almost entirely by voluntary and 'in-kind' contributions by governments and other donors, and receives less than 2 per cent from the United Nations regular budget for its administrative costs. It has developed from a small, geographically and temporarily restricted specialized agency into an organization whose tasks encompass legal protection, physical safety and material assistance. It has in some situations effectively acquired a leading role in coordinating relief efforts, thus stretching its mandate to assist refugees. UNHCR is a 'hands-on' organization: its 'Quick Impact Projects', for example – rebuilding schools and clinics and repairing road infrastructure, etc. – link emergency assistance with longer-term development cooperation. It has on occasion also deployed early-warning systems to monitor the outbreak of conflicts.

UNHCR sees itself as a 'humanitarian and social organization' (UNHCR Statute, General Assembly resolution 428 (V), annex 5, 1950). While human rights are not assigned a significant role in the statute, and its work is based on the said Refugee Convention and other refugee agreements, human rights are today as much part of UNHCR's mandate as refugee law. International protection, it says, in practice means ensuring respect for a refugee's basic human rights (http://www.unhcr.org/basics/basics/3b0249c71.html). Despite the close links between refugee protection and human rights, UNHCR's initial position towards the UN human rights system was diffident. The respective statement in its 1997 policy paper *UNHCR and Human Rights* may stand for the caution exerted by nearly all institutions whose mandates do not explicitly contain the protection and promotion of human rights (with the exception of UNDP and UNICEF):

> Extreme caution traditionally marked UNHCR's approach to any suggestion that it should cooperate and collaborate with established

mechanisms for the promotion and protection of general human rights principles. While being prepared to acknowledge its human rights origins, as well as the complementarity of refugee protection and human rights promotion, UNHCR nevertheless kept a deliberate distance from the proliferating and increasingly forceful UN mechanisms for monitoring and ensuring compliance with international human rights norms. Motivating this approach was the fear that greater activism would lead to politicization of UNHCR activities which would compromise our capacity to work with our government counterparts. (UNHCR, 1997)

It was only in 1990 that UNHCR for the first time addressed the UN Commission on Human Rights. The organization explains this change of attitude by pointing to its increased participation in multidisciplinary, inter-agency responses to complex emergencies, its heightened focus on prevention, the increasing awareness of refugee protection problems by treaty bodies, and the complementarities between human rights protection and refugee law (UNHCR, 1997). In a way, this is a utilitarian approach to mainstreaming human rights based on the acknowledgement that human rights violations produce refugees. This pragmatic approach was gradually refined. Today, UNCHR uses human rights on three levels (ibid.): it promotes, and is guided by, human rights standards; it uses and generates human rights information; and it cooperates with, and seeks the cooperation of, human rights mechanisms, institutions and field operations. The guidance it takes from human rights law is rigorous: the organization recognizes that its own goals and objectives must comply with human rights standards. Practically, this means that its staff must not compromise human rights standards and that it must try to enhance the observance of these standards by its governmental and NGO partners. The second area of activities – gathering and processing information – is a delicate one for UNHCR, which is not itself a monitoring agency but is guided by the principle of protection, which often entails confidentiality. Yet, the organization has an interest in human rights issues insofar as these impact on its mandate and activities. Balancing protection and information-gathering can, understandably, be an uneasy task. In turn, the third area – cooperation with other human rights institutions – is perceived as mutually beneficial for both UNHCR and other institutions.

Shifting from caution to embracing human rights allows UNHCR to focus more on the causes of refugee problems than on their manifestation, given that human rights violations are often the prime source for refugee flows (Gorlick, 2000). Today, the organization has incorporated a number of human rights principles and strategies into its policies and programmes, e.g., in the areas of legal rehabilitation, institution-building and law reform; enforcement of the rule of law; and protecting refugee women and children. In the *Agenda for Protection* (UNHCR, 2003), a strategic framework which came out of a twenty-month global consultation and deals with some of the most controversial topics in the debate on asylum and refugee protection, UNHCR sought to adopt guidelines for governments and humanitarian organizations to strengthen worldwide refugee protection. The *Agenda* also addresses those of its concerns which have a strong link to human rights or are effectively dealt with by UN human rights bodies, such as child soldiers, sexual and gender-based violence, and the protection of children's and women's human rights.

# United Nations Human Settlements Programme

The United Nations Human Settlements Programme (HABITAT) is the UN agency responsible for human settlements and is mandated to promote socially and environmentally sustainable towns and cities with the goal of providing adequate shelter for all. Established in 1978, subsequent to the Habitat I meeting in Vancouver, it seeks to put the effects on human well-being of urbanization and massive urban growth, especially in the developing world, on the agenda of the UN. The main guideline for its work is the Habitat Agenda, adopted by 171 countries at the Habitat II meeting in 1996. It contains over 100 commitments and 600 recommendations. With General Assembly resolution 56/206 of 2002, HABITAT was turned into a UN programme. This, together with Habitat's focus on the MDGs, has brought HABITAT closer to the UN's development agenda. More than that, Target 11 of Goal No. 7 of the MDGs (aimed at improving the lives of at least 100 million slum dwellers by the year 2020) is a task specifically mandated to HABITAT (http://www.unhabitat.org/content.asp?typeid=19&catid=10&cid=927).

HABITAT deals mainly with the downsides of urbanization – crime, pollution, poverty and disease in mega-cities where slum dwellers may soon be in the majority, often left without water, shelter or sanitation. In working towards urban poverty reduction, HABITAT sees itself guided by 'norms and principles [which] include, among others, sustainable urban development, adequate shelter for all, improvement in the lives of slum dwellers, access to safe water and sanitation, social inclusion, environmental protection and the various human rights' (http://www.unhabitat.org/content.asp?typeid=19&catid=10&cid=929). Its approach to human rights, as mirrored in this mission statement, is akin to that of other 'technical' and operational organizations, which seek to grasp the theoretical depths and practical implications of what they light-heartedly call 'various' human rights.

Yet, seen from a human rights point of view, the link is obvious, and it is even reflected in HABITAT's internal structure. The organization – headquartered in Nairobi with more than 200 staff working in regional offices – has three main divisions: the Shelter and Sustainable Human Settlements Development Division; the Monitoring and Research Division; and the Regional and Technical Cooperation Division. What sounds so off-track from human rights seems more familiar when one looks into the sub-units established under the Shelter and Sustainable Human Settlements Development Division: the Shelter Branch deals with the Global Campaign for Secure Tenure; the Water, Sanitation and Infrastructure Branch promotes access to basic services, water and sanitation; the Training and Capacity Building Branch aims at enhancing local authority and civil society management capacity; and the Urban Development Branch runs the Global Campaign on Urban Governance. Translated into the rights to adequate living, health, housing, water, and participation in the conduct of public affairs (as provided for in the 1966 UN Covenants), the Division suddenly is full of human rights.

HABITAT has recognized the human rights implications of its mandate and activities, and, as a visible result of inter-agency cooperation in human rights matters, the United Nations Housing Rights Programme (UNHRP) was launched in April 2002 as a joint initiative by HABITAT and OHCHR. The programme, which is based on Commission on Human Settlements resolution 16/7 and Commission on Human Rights resolutions 2001/28 and 2001/34, turns the right to housing into a concern to be jointly pursued by UN human rights bodies and HABITAT. The UN Special Rapporteur on adequate housing cooperates particularly closely with HABITAT. The programme aims to assist states to implement their commitments under the Habitat Agenda as a way of guaranteeing the right to adequate housing as provided for in international human rights instruments. A report on human rights legislation, which reviews international and national legal instruments from a human rights point of view, is the most prominent outcome yet (http://ww2.unhabitat.org/programmes/housingrights).

HABITAT stands as an example of a 'technical' organization which has accepted and increasingly appreciates the human rights implications of its mandate. The United Nations Housing Rights Programme, in particular, is one of the best models to date of how to combine the technical approach of a specialized UN programme with the mandate of the UN High Commissioner for Human Rights and the work of special procedures of the Human Rights Council.

# World Health Organization

In the UN system, health has figured under many agenda items in various bodies, but has hardly ever been referred to as a human right (Tomasevski, 1993: 185), despite the inclusion in the ICESCR (Article 12) of the right of everyone to enjoy the highest attainable standard of physical and mental health. WHO is the UN specialized agency entrusted with health issues. It was established in 1948 and today has 192 member states. Its constitution lays down the attainment by all peoples of the highest possible level of health as its primary objective, with health being defined as a state of complete physical, mental and social well-being and not merely as the absence of disease or infirmity. The organization's rhetoric on health as a human right has been strong from the beginning; after all, in the preamble of its constitution the enjoyment of the highest attainable standard of health is seen as one of the fundamental rights of every human being. Conceptualizing and realizing health as a human right, however, has proven more difficult. The reason lies partly in the complex nature of the right to health, which after all is a matrix of different human rights concerns. The overlaps between the right to health and the right to food, shelter, access to water, sanitation, education and information make the right to health perhaps the most multi-faceted topic in international human rights law.

As with other institutions, in WHO rhetoric gave way to a more concrete engagement with human rights only very recently. Appraisals by observers only a few years ago did not find any substantial place for human rights in the organization's work (Gallagher, 1999a: 166). Today, WHO may be on its way to becoming another example of how to overcome the 'sociopolitical role' (Tomasevski, 1993: 186) which purportedly holds an institution back from touching upon human rights. Health and human rights, as the WHO website prominently declares (http://www.who.int/hhr/en), have been designated a cross-cutting issue of the organization's work – or rather, in WHO-speak, 'Ethics, Trade, Human Rights and Law (ETH) fall within Sustainable Development and Healthy Environments (SDE)' (ibid.). The organization claims a leading role in providing technical, intellectual and political leadership in the field of human rights and health by integrating a rights-based approach to health and promoting the right to health globally. The areas in which WHO sees human rights as central are manifold, spanning from harmful traditional practices to torture, discrimination, participation, privacy and information, gender-based violence and child abuse, and are closely linked to the human right to food, water, shelter, housing and education. Gender and reproductive rights, the rights of persons with mental illness and HIV/AIDS and children's and adolescents' rights are considered priority areas (http://www.who.int/topics/human_rights/en).

The claim to be the lead institution on health as a human right may, however, be somewhat overzealous. It seems more appropriate to say that WHO has finally anchored itself more firmly in a matrix of institutions which protect and promote the right to health. In particular, WHO takes into account the findings of the UN Committee on Economic and Social Rights (e.g., the Committee's General Comment No. 14, UN doc. E/C.12/ 2000/4), which sets out the normative scope and content of the right to health, and cooperates with the UN Special Rapporteur on the Right to Health. There is no doubt, however, that WHO has in fact become active in human rights matters. It has given itself a human rights advisor, and the range of human rights-related activities seems to be gradually expanding, including a publication series and a database on health and human rights. WHO publishes promotional and research material on the right to health, such as the Health and Human Rights Working Paper Series. It compiles and disseminates 'best practices' of a human rights-based approach to health, strives to integrate human rights norms and principles in WHO technical programmes, and attempts to identify indicators to monitor the progressive realization of the right to health (http://www.who.int/hhr/en).

More recently, the organization has gone further than this, adopting a vision of how it wants to protect and promote the right to health. It has identified three ways to do so: to apply a human rights-based approach in its own activities work; to support governments in adopting and implementing a human rights-based approach to health development; and to advance the right to health in international law and development processes (WHO, 2005). No concrete activities seem to have come from this, nor has any more specific forward-looking strategy been communicated by the organization. Ideas and visions on how it should realign its policy and programmes seem to speak for a thorough process which WHO wants to unleash within which both member states and the organization itself have firmly to locate health policies and programmes within a human rights framework (Nygren-Krug, 2005). Transiting from rhetoric to reality should be the next step.

# Food and Agriculture Organization

FAO, established in 1945, is dedicated to fighting hunger in the world, or, more accurately (as laid down in its constitution), to raising levels of nutrition and standards of living, improving agricultural productivity, bettering the life of rural populations, and ensuring humanity's freedom from hunger. Its mandate is principally to provide technical advice, and it sees itself as a centre of knowledge which collects, analyses and disseminates data. The organization seems keen to emphasize its role as an assistant of governments which deploys its knowledge to devise agricultural policies, draft legislation, and adopt strategies to end hunger and malnutrition. FAO employs more than 3,450 staff in its headquarters in Rome and its regional, sub-regional and liaison offices in around eighty countries. Since a major reform programme was initiated in 1994, it is emphasizing food security, moving staff to the field, and strengthening links with the private sector and civil society organizations (http://www.fao.org/UNFAO/about/index_en.html).

Article 1 of the FAO constitution requires the organization, *inter alia*, to collect, analyse, interpret and disseminate information on nutrition, food and agriculture, fisheries, and marine and forestry products; to promote scientific, technological, social and economic research on nutrition, food and agriculture; to improve the administration relating to nutrition, food and agriculture and the conservation of natural resources; to improve the processing, marketing and distribution of food and agricultural products; and to adopt policies for the provision of adequate agricultural credit and international policies on agricultural commodity arrangements. One might think this leaves little space for considerations of food as a human right. Yet the FAO has a remarkable history in terms of human rights.

Under its then Director-General, B. R. Sen, the organization was instrumental in introducing the human right to food as Article 11 of the International Covenant on Economic, Social and Cultural Rights of 1966 (Moore, 2005: 140). Despite its close involvement in the drafting of the Covenant, the FAO then withdrew from human rights until the World Food Summit in 1996, when it again participated in discussion on the implementation and realization of the right to food. In the interim period, the right to food received little attention and had little weight as a motivating force for FAO's work (ibid.: 142). Even now, the organization gives the impression of being extremely cautious when using human rights language, despite the increased awareness of human rights which some observers have reported finding (Vidar, 2001: 521–2). For FAO, fighting hunger is more a matter of providing technical expertise and putting itself at the disposal of states as 'a neutral forum where rich and poor nations can come together to build common understanding' (http://www.fao.org/UNFAO/about/activities_en.html).

This self-perception, however, is not quite in line with the Rome Declaration on World Food Security and the Summit Plan of Action, the outcome of the 1996 World Food Summit (http://www.fao.org/wfs). Both documents would give the FAO strong grounds for applying a rights-based approach to fighting hunger. The Declaration reaffirms the 'right of everyone to have access to safe and nutritious food, consistent with the right to adequate food and the fundamental right of everyone to be free from hunger' (para. 1 of the Declaration). In the Summit Plan of Action, Objective 7.4 calls for the content of the right to adequate food and the right to be free from hunger to be clarified. The primary responsibility for following up the Plan of Action was assigned to the OHCHR and the UN treaty bodies rather than to the reluctant FAO, which had to be pushed for some more years. In 2000, when the Commission on Human Rights established the Special Rapporteur on the Right to Food, it mandated him to cooperate with FAO, and in 2002 the 'World Food Summit: Five Years Later' (http://www.fao.org/worldfoodsummit) took a slightly more decisive step. It set up an Intergovernmental Working Group which elaborated voluntary guidelines to support member states in achieving the progressive realization of the right to food in the context of food security. The guidelines were adopted by the FAO Council in 2004 and finally drew the organization closer to the UN's human rights activities – the place where it had started before its decision to idle on the fringe some forty years before. While FAO is still struggling fully to acknowledge the right to food as a basic human right and a guiding principle of its work (Moore, 2005: 153), the adoption of the voluntary guidelines is an important move towards a rights-based approach to food security and to combating hunger globally.

# World Bank and International Monetary Fund

Established in 1944, the 'Bretton Woods institutions' the World Bank and the IMF are entrusted with guaranteeing stability in the international economy through monetary and exchange-rate regulations (IMF) and reconstruction and development (World Bank). What is commonly referred to as the World Bank is in fact the World Bank Group, composed of the International Bank for Reconstruction and Development (IBRD), which focuses on middle-income countries; the International Development Association (IDA), which deals with the poorest countries; the International Finance Corporation (IFC); the Multilateral Investment Guarantee Agency (MIGA); and the International Centre for the Settlement of Investment Disputes (ICSID). IFC finances private-sector investments and provides technical support and advice to governments, MIGA provides guarantees to foreign investors against loss caused by commercial risks, and ICSID is a facility for settling investment disputes between foreign investors and their host countries. Headquartered in Washington, DC, the World Bank has offices in more than 100 countries, with about 7,000 staff in Washington and more than 3,000 around the world, and a membership of 184 countries. Members are shareholders of the Bank, with shares equalling votes, and the United States is the largest single shareholder (16 per cent). The Bank sees itself as 'banker' (allowing governments to borrow from IBRD and IDA), 'broker' (facilitating loans and grants from wealthier nations and administering trust funds and covering risks), 'donor' (overseeing grant facilities in the area of rural development, health, education, economic policy or environmental protection) and 'adviser' (in areas such as development economics, poverty, trade, globalization, health, education, financial services, law, etc.) (http://siteresources.worldbank.org/EXTABOUTUS/Resources/wbgroupbrochure-en.pdf).

The IMF was established to promote international monetary cooperation, exchange stability and orderly exchange arrangements, to foster economic growth and high levels of employment, and to provide temporary financial assistance to countries. It deploys three main mechanisms (surveillance, technical assistance and lending) to meet these objectives. Surveillance means a regular dialogue between the Fund and member countries and includes policy advice. Once a year, the Fund conducts an in-depth appraisal of each member state's economic situation. Technical assistance is offered in areas such as fiscal policy, monetary and exchange-rate policies, banking and financial system supervision and regulation, and statistics. The Fund offers financial support through its lending facility – the Poverty Reduction and Growth Facility (PRGF), the Exogenous Shocks Facility (ESF) – and through debt relief under the Heavily Indebted Poor Countries Initiative (HIPC) and the Multilateral Debt Relief Initiative (MDRI). It sees itself as an instrument to prevent crises in the economic system by encouraging countries to adopt certain economic policies, and it is also a fund for members which are in need of temporary financing to address balance of payments problems. Together with the World Bank, it has its headquarters in Washington, DC and a membership of 184 countries. The IMF's resources come from member states, primarily through payment of quotas reflecting each state's economic size (http://www.imf.org/external/np/exr/facts/glance.htm).

The IMF and World Bank are sister institutions which collaborate regularly and are involved in several joint initiatives. The terms for this cooperation were set out in a concordat in 1989. Such activities include the HIPC and the use of Poverty Reduction Strategy Papers (PRSP). PRPSs are prepared by country authorities in consultation with civil society and other development partners, which describe an economic, structural and social policy framework that is being implemented to promote growth and reduce poverty. In 2004, the Fund and the Bank together initiated the Global Monitoring Report, which assesses progress on policies and actions needed to achieve the MDGs.

What is the role of human rights in this impressive mesh of bodies, tasks, strategies, policies and programmes? Human rights are not part of the mandate of either the World Bank or the IMF; on the contrary, these have for long been seen as 'political' issues within the domestic realm of member states – issues which must not occupy any space in the Bank's or the IMF's economic decision-making processes. As for the World Bank, this view stems from the founding document: 'the Bank and its officers shall not interfere in the political affairs of any member; nor shall they be influenced in their decisions by the political character of members concerned. Only economic considerations shall be relevant to their decision' (Article IV, Section 10, IBRD Articles of Agreement). Similar language can be found in the Articles of Agreement of IDA (Article V, Section 6). The IMF bases its hostile position towards human rights on the obligation that it 'shall respect the domestic and social policies of members' (Article IV, Section 3, IMF Articles of Agreement).

At the same time, however, it is now widely recognized and accepted that many policies, programmes and decisions by the World Bank and the IMF have repercussions for human rights, most prominently perhaps the Structural Adjustment Programmes (SAPs) (e.g., Skogly, 1999: 233). The increasing critique of human rights groups and civil society organizations, together with the UN Secretary-General's request to mainstream human rights, have initiated a reconsideration of the human rights responsibilities of international financial institutions, a process which also finds support in the framework of 'human development' and is fuelled by the MDGs. Yet it should be recalled that, for the World Bank at least, these challenges are not new. As early as in the 1960s it was asked to take a position on human rights when lending to South Africa and Portugal in defiance of UN resolutions condemning their respective apartheid and colonial policies. It refused to take any such position (Brodnig, 2005: 4).

Today, the World Bank and IMF are more prepared to engage in discussions on the role of human rights in international financial institutions. The dilemma they face was expressed by the former World Bank president, James Wolfensohn, in his statement to the 71st meeting of the Bank's Development Committee: 'The Bank is currently reviewing its role with a view to making a more explicit link between human rights and our work, while at the same time remaining fully in compliance with our Articles of Agreement' (Wolfensohn, 2005). As we shall see, the Bank is, in this respect, more forthcoming than the IMF.

As a matter of fact, the distinction between 'economic' and 'political' considerations in the World Bank has never been fixed. Rather, the Bank has long been expanding its interpretation of what an 'economic' matter is. Today, it considers goals such as development, poverty reduction and gender equality, together with the tools to achieve such goals, e.g., legal reform, as part of its mandate. While it refrains from wording these activities in human rights language, it is in effect actively promoting a number of human rights, such as the right to development, the right to be free from poverty, the right to education and health, women's human rights, the rights of refugees and involuntary resettled persons, and environmental rights (Oestreich, 2004: 61–3). It has also drafted several Operational Directives relevant to human rights, such as those on involuntary resettlement (1990), poverty reduction (1991) and indigenous peoples (1994) (Skogly, 1999: 234). In addition, with the rights-based approach to development more accepted and the Bank being mandated to contribute to development, human rights necessarily become part of the World Bank's consideration and activities (Brodnig, 2005: 8–19). The

Bank seems prepared to accept this, as stated by Robert Danino, then senior vice-president and general counsel, in 2004: 'the Bank [. . .], in my opinion, [. . .] can and must take into account human rights violations in its process of making economic decisions. Moreover, because of the way international law has evolved with respect to concepts of sovereignty and interference, and the range of issues considered to be of global concern, in doing so the Bank will not fall foul of the political prohibitions of the Articles' (Danino, 2004: 11).

Critics rightly point out that much of this was forced upon the Bank from outside and that the underlying rationale for the Bank's increased concern for human rights remains utilitarian. Indeed, it helps the Bank to insulate it from NGO criticism and makes human rights a means to improving development effectiveness, guaranteeing stability, enhancing project quality and creating an environment conducive to investment (Oestreich, 2004: 65–6 and 71). Still, the Bank has clearly rejected the idea that it has nothing to do with human rights. Now it is struggling with the consequences of this development as, to date, the new openness towards human rights is still more a reflection than action, as a survey of the Bank's current human rights-related activities reveals. These are declared to be 'the launch of a human rights mapping process which aims to match existing World Bank activities against the provisions of the three [sic!] core human rights treaties that comprise the International Bill of Rights'; 'continuing empirical work by the World Bank Institute on the links between human rights and development outcomes which will help the Bank in establishing its global advocacy priorities'; and consideration of how the Bank 'might strengthen human rights indicators in [the] assessments of country performance' (http://web.worldbank.org/WBSITE/EXTERNAL/EXTSITETOOLS/0,,contentMDK:20749693~pagePK:98400~piPK:98424~theSitePK:95474,00.html). None of this sounds like a convincing strategy. As a matter of fact, while there is practical evidence that human rights matters for the Bank (e.g., in indigenous peoples' affairs, the development of HIV/AIDS strategies, social policy initiatives, children's rights or judicial reform), there is no comprehensive human rights policy based on international human rights law.

The closest the World Bank has come to this is the 1998 document 'Development and Human Rights: the Role of the World Bank', which sees human rights as important for good governance and access to services. Yet, with this narrow approach, the Bank still shies away from deploying a rights-based approach rooted in the acceptance of internationally recognized human rights standards (Skogly, 2005: 165).

This remains the crux of the Bank's involvement in human rights: if we leave to one side the rhetoric and declarations of the importance of human rights, we can see that it has never accepted any *legal* obligation in the field of human rights. While 'an ever increasing number of units within the Bank seem cautiously to be fluttering around the flame of human rights [. . .] in circles of ever diminishing radius' (Darrow, 2003: 22), the Bank continues to resist basing its actions and policies on international human rights law. Statements such as 'the Bank is concerned by human rights in Chad and elsewhere, but its mandate does not extend to political human rights' (the World Bank Inspection Panel on the Chad pipeline project in 2001; quoted from Horta, 2002: 227) remain symptomatic and render its approach contradictory. Even when human rights are allegedly respected and promoted by the Bank, closer analysis reveals that these are assumptions made without testing project or programme outcomes against human rights indicators (Skogly, 1999: 234).

The IMF declines any obligation in the field of human rights altogether more firmly than the World Bank. Sweeping and simplifying assertions by the IMF such as 'if one looks beyond the surface, all of the IMF's activities contribute directly or indirectly to reducing poverty and fostering human rights' (Pereira Leite, 2001) are of little help to understanding why and how international financial institutions should contribute to the protection, fulfilment and promotion of human rights. In 2001, the IMF's legal counsel rejected the view that the International Covenant on Economic, Social and Cultural Rights could be in any way applied by the Fund, and went on to explain that this

> does not mean that the Fund does not contribute to the objectives of the Covenant. The Fund's contribution to economic and social human rights is essential but indirect: by promoting a stable system of exchange rates and a system of current payments free of restrictions, and by including growth as an objective of the framework of the international monetary system, as well as providing financial support for balance of payment problems, the Fund contributes to providing the economic conditions that are a precondition for the achievement of the rights set out in the Covenant. (Gianviti, 2001: para. 57)

Skogly remarks that this mirrors the statements of the World Bank's counsel a decade earlier (Skogly, 2005: 162).

The question of whether or not there is an obligation on the part of international financial institutions to respect human rights remains controversial, and in particular the IMF seems not inclined to change its aversion towards human rights. As for the World Bank, the Bank's

Inspection Panel, established in 1993, may contribute to clarifying its position towards human rights. The three-member panel receives requests for inspection from an affected party in the territory of the borrower aimed at demonstrating that 'its rights or interests have been or are likely to be affected by an action or omission of the Bank as a result of a failure of the Bank to follow its operational policies and procedures' (Executive Directors resolution No. 93–10, 1993). Despite having been praised as a means to promote access to justice for individuals whose rights have been impaired (Boisson de Chazournes, 2001), it is not a body to which general complaints can be filed about the Bank's violating human rights, precisely because there is no World Bank human rights policy which it could fail to follow (apart from the mentioned Operational Directives). To date, twenty-seven formal requests have been received by the panel, often relating to large infrastructure projects such as the Arun III Hydroelectric Project in Nepal (the first request in 1994), the Cartagena Water Supply, Sewerage and Environmental Management Project in Colombia, or the Chad Petroleum Development and Pipeline Project, as well as natural resource management projects, e.g., the Rondonia Natural Resources Management Project in Brazil. In some of these cases, the panel had already had to consider human rights, yet they were most often couched in terms of environmental concerns (Skogly, 1999: 240). Empowering the World Bank Inspection Panel so that it can effectively redress the problems it has identified has been proposed as an important step towards increased accountability (Clark, 2002).

The debate on whether or not international financial institutions are bound to respect international human rights law has implications beyond those institutions, as it will lead to a more fundamental reappraisal of the human rights obligations of all international institutions. Three main lines of argument are advanced in this debate (Skogly, 2003, 46–68; Clapham, 2006: 137–59). First, because both the World Bank and the IMF are subjects of international law, they are bound by international legal obligations, including human rights obligations. While different from the obligations of states, they are obligations nevertheless. Second, the two institutions are specialized agencies of the UN and – despite not being directly bound by the UN Charter – are under the obligation to adhere to the aims and principles of the UN, which include human rights promotion. And, third, they are institutions composed of states which have adhered to a number of human rights treaties, so that it seems unreasonable that either should be allowed to engage in activities from which their member states are barred. Identifying the concrete obligations which these arguments would impose on international financial institutions must follow suit, but this is difficult in the absence of a systematic evaluation of their policies from a human rights perspective (Skogly, 2003: 78).

What is also required is a shift from the perception of human rights as 'add-ons' (Darrow, 2003: 299) towards their acceptance as entitlements. First steps towards accepting human rights as legal obligations have been taken by the World Bank, but they are biased in favour of a small range of civil and political rights and exclude treaty-based obligations (Skogly, 2005: 163). Observers have repeatedly noted that what is possible in environmental matters – namely that the Bank will not finance projects that contravene international agreements to which member states are party – must also be possible for human rights (Skogly, 2005: 165). Skogly has rightly stated that

> human rights are not a 'social good' that is achieved through a shift in budgetary allocations. If the institutions are sincere in their new 'interest' in human rights, they need to explicitly recognise that there are legal obligations (rather than moral) that pertain to these rights and their role in individuals' ability to enjoy these rights. (Ibid.)

# World Trade Organization

The regulation of trade and the protection of human rights were disconnected fields for much of their existence. This is no longer true. With trade regulation moving beyond trade in goods and covering intellectual property and services, the link between trade and human rights becomes ever more visible (Cottier, Pauwelyn and Bürgi, 2005: 2–3). Resolution 1998/12 of the UN Sub-Commission on the Promotion and Protection of Human Rights called for human rights to be recognized as the primary objective of trade, investment and financial policy. Such demands form part of a debate on whether the principle of open trade, on which the international trade regime is based, means elevating property interests above human rights or whether trade liberalization and human rights protection are compatible goals. Just as with the World Bank and the IMF, the place of human rights in WTO law has become a disputed topic (Cohn, 2001; Petersmann, 2003), yet the debate over human rights in the WTO 'has hardly progressed since it started, even though the terms "human rights" and "WTO" are more frequently juxtaposed, and the number of participants is rising' (Dommen, 2005: 53).

The multilateral trading system of which the WTO is the core was developed through a series of trade negotiations, or rounds, held under GATT, the General Agreement on Tariffs and Trade. The WTO is the outcome of the 'Uruguay Round' trade negotiations (1986–94) and was established in 1995. Headquartered in Geneva, with a membership comprising 150 countries and a secretariat staff of more than 600, the WTO administers the WTO trade agreements, provides a forum for trade negotiations, deals with trade disputes, monitors national trade policies, and provides technical assistance for developing countries. The WTO is as much a set of rules as it is a forum for negotiations and dispute settlement. The WTO agreements are the legal ground-rules for international trade, covering areas as diverse as trade in textiles, intellectual property rights, agriculture, banking, telecommunications, government purchases, food sanitation regulations, industrial standards and much more. GATT is the principal among the trade agreements and regulates trade in goods. It is supplemented by rules dealing with trade in services (General Agreement on Trade in Services – GATS) and intellectual property (Trade-related Aspects of Intellectual Property Rights – TRIPS). The WTO Agreement is the umbrella agreement to which the other agreements are attached, making up a set of about thirty agreements and other commitments running over some 30,000 pages. The fourth WTO Ministerial Conference in Doha, Qatar, launched the latest round in 2001, which focuses, *inter alia*, on a range of issues of concern for developing countries known as the Doha Development Agenda.

The potential of WTO agreements to impact on human rights is undisputed. Intellectual property rights, agricultural rules and the provision of essential services are three areas of concern. The TRIPS rules, for example, can have detrimental effects on the ability of developing countries to ensure access to medication (Ovett, 2007: 273–4): they grant patent owners twenty years of exclusive commercial rights and thus monopoly over the making and selling of products, keeping prices high. So visible were the impacts of TRIPS rules that in 2001 the Doha Declaration on TRIPS and Public Health emphasized the importance of public health on the international trade agenda (WTO Ministerial Meeting Declaration on the TRIPS Agreement and Public Health, WT/MIN(01)/DEC/2, 2001). GATS, to name another example, regulates sensitive areas such as the provision of water, electricity, infrastructure, financial services, education, etc. The 'Cochabamba water war' in Bolivia in 2000 serves as one striking example, where the privatization of water services, attributed to World Bank conditionalities and GATS requirements, led to a 200 per cent increase in water prices and subsequent massive protests (Olivera, 2004). It seems interesting to note, in this respect, General Comment No. 15 on the right to water, adopted by the UN Committee on Economic, Social and Cultural Rights two years later (UN doc. E/C.12/2002/11), which succinctly pointed out that water is a social good, not a commodity.

Labour standards are another controversial issue in the WTO. In the first WTO Ministerial Conference, in Singapore in 1996, the issue was deferred to the ILO as the proper institution, yet the question remains whether labour standards should also be debated within the WTO. Should the trade regime be used as a means of putting pressure on countries which violate core labour rights? The debate on whether or not it is wise to insert a general 'social clause' in WTO agreements which would prevent this continues, since the idea was advocated by many NGOs in the run-up to the Singapore meeting in 1996. The suggestion may also serve as an example of the undesired institutional consequences of a convergence between trade rules and human rights (and perhaps of the challenges inherent in mainstreaming human rights in general) as, somewhat ironically, a decade later NGOs questioned the wisdom of the suggestion on the grounds that such a clause would give the WTO 'undue jurisdiction to adjudicate human rights matters' (International Federation for Human Rights, 2005: 9).

The WTO is only beginning to take up the challenge of mainstreaming human rights and, compared to the institutions discussed above, is most remote from this process (Benedek, 2007: 230). Part of the reason is that it is not a specialized agency of the UN, and that there is comparable scarce NGO participation in WTO institutions which would push such mainstreaming (Benedek, 1999). Yet it seems somewhat remarkable that, despite a vigorous public debate, and although many of the issues of which the WTO is in charge are in fact also human rights concerns (labour standards, health services, access to pharmaceuticals, intellectual property, development, etc.), there is no official WTO text which refers explicitly to human rights, nor is there any body in charge of human rights within the institution.

In contrast, trade issues have, since 1998, repeatedly been brought before UN human rights bodies on the grounds of their allegedly negative impact on human rights (Grant, 2006: 134–8; Benedek, 2007: 232–8). The trade system, however, continues to remain hostile to the acceptance of human rights implications for trade rules. Some put this down to the international trade regime being inherently flawed, as its rules 'assume an equality of bargaining power between all countries that engage in trade' and 'ignore the fact that the greater percentage of global trade is controlled by powerful multinational enterprises.

Within such a context, the notion of free trade is a fallacy' (Oloka-Onyango and Udagama, 2001: para. 14). Others see only one thing worse than a world with the WTO: a world without the WTO, in which no regulatory framework for trade exists. 'The WTO', they note, 'is a better guarantor of human rights and public interest-consistent outcomes than the absence of international trade rules, or than bilateral trade agreements' (Dommen, 2005: 58). If one accepts the necessity of a global regulatory framework for trade, and this seems a wise choice, then the problem is not that free trade itself contradicts human rights, but that trade rules and policies based on WTO principles are disconnected from international human rights law.

Even within the generally reluctant attitude towards human rights in the WTO, however, areas of progress for human rights advocates have been discerned (Walker, 2005: 75–7). Acceptance that WTO law must not be interpreted in isolation from international law, including human rights law, seems to be growing (Marceau, 2002). Indeed, specific provisions in WTO agreements can be used to promote and protect human rights. The compulsory licensing in TRIPS, given as an example of the negative impact on human rights, allows countries in certain circumstances to reduce the costs of HIV/AIDS treatment in a way that is consistent with both the TRIPS agreement and human rights norms (Sub-Commission on the Promotion and Protection of Human Rights, UN doc. E/CN.4/Sub.2/2001/13, paras. 51–8). The general exception clauses in WTO agreements, to give another example, provide some flexibility for WTO members to meet their obligations under human rights law. Under such clauses, governments can take measures to protect 'public morals' and 'public order' or for the protection of life and health. Arguments have been put forward in support of an interpretation of these notions in terms of human rights (UN High Commissioner for Human Rights, 2005a).

The debate on whether or not the WTO should be bound by international human rights law rests on much of the same arguments that have been put forward for the World Bank and IMF (Clapham, 2006: 162–5). And, as with the World Bank, hope is put into the WTO dispute settlement mechanism for repositioning human rights within the WTO and balancing WTO members' obligations under trade agreements with international human rights law (Marceau, 2006). Disputes in the trade regime may arise when a WTO member takes a trade policy measure or other action which another WTO member believes to be in breach of trade agreements. In this case, the WTO Dispute Settlement Body (DSB), which is based on the Dispute Settlement Understanding, establishes an expert panel. The panel's findings, which can be appealed to the standing Appellate Body, are accepted (or rejected) by the DSB. The DSB also monitors the implementation of its decisions and may authorize retaliation when a country does not comply with its ruling. WTO panels or the Appellate Body, however, have jurisdiction only over claims under WTO agreements. Although NGOs have invoked human rights arguments in amicus curiae briefs, it is disputed whether or not human rights law can be invoked before these bodies (Pauwelyn, 2005: 212).

In the WTO, just as in international financial institutions, neither innovative conceptual approaches nor the application of human rights in dispute settlement procedures have yet yielded convincing success in terms of obliging these institutions to respect human rights. As for the WTO, the question whether human rights law can, or should, 'safeguard the legitimacy of the multilateral trade system' (Dommen, 2006) has yet to be answered. The isolationist attitude which the organization still displays, however, when it comes to human rights, the exclusive authority it has assumed in defining the scope and content of trade rules, and its aversion to greater participation of civil society actors will not only make the mainstreaming of human rights a long and difficult process, but is reminiscent of the pathologies of international bureaucracies as discussed in chapter 2.

# Challenges ahead in mainstreaming human rights

We have seen that, in the areas of promoting social, cultural and scientific progress, caring for the rights and welfare of vulnerable groups, furthering the standard of living, and ensuring the provision of essential goods (such as food, health and housing), mainstreaming human rights has yielded results. In contrast, the worlds of finance, investment and trade remain largely diffident or even hostile towards human rights. Beyond the attempts documented above, however, even less attention is paid to mainstreaming human rights in other institutions of the UN family. The polite negligence of human rights as displayed on the website of the World Intellectual Property Organization serves as an example: 'WIPO continues to follow closely relevant developments in human rights' (http://www.wipo.int/tk/en/hr). Other (successful) initiatives are singular events. FIFA (the international football association), for example, participated in the publication of the booklet *HIV/AIDS – Stand up for Human Rights* (UN High Commissioner for

Human Rights, 2005c). What was meant as a contribution to Human Rights Day 2005, in a joint effort with WHO, UNAIDS (the Joint United Nations Programme on HIV/AIDS) and OHCHR, at least found its way via FIFA's national football associations to readers in several African countries.

There may be other areas where obvious linkages with human rights may be strengthened in the future, such as in protecting personal security. In the UN system, the Commission on Crime Prevention and Criminal Justice, which was established as a functional commission of ECOSOC in 1992, is mandated with combating national and transnational crime, organized crime, economic crime and money laundering, with crime prevention, and with the improvement of criminal justice administration systems. Some of these issues, together with concerns such as trafficking in human beings and fighting corruption, which are being dealt with in the framework of the Crime Programme of the UN Office on Drugs and Crimes, have clear human rights implications. The norms and standards elaborated in this framework, such as the UN Standard Minimum Rules for the Treatment of Prisoners (1995), the Code of Conduct for Law Enforcement Officials (1979), the so-called Beijing Rules for the Administration of Juvenile Justice (1985), and the Basic Principles on the Use of Force and Firearms by Law Enforcement Officials (1990), embody human rights norms and, in turn, are used by other human rights bodies in giving interpretative views on human rights treaty provisions (Nowak, 2003: 121–2). Such specific standards, principles, rules, codes and guidelines are an important contribution to translating often vaguely formulated international human rights norms into detailed and practical guidance for police officers or law-enforcement personnel, which reflect the circumstances of their work and are applicable in concrete situations.

In contrast, the International Telecommunication Union (ITU) serves as an instructive example of how challenging the process of mainstreaming human rights continues to be. In the framework of the World Summit on the Information Society (WSIS, a UN-sponsored global conference on information and communication as global challenges, which took place in stages from 2001 to 2005), ITU occupied a leading role as the UN specialized agency in the field. ITU, which perceives itself as a 'non-political' and 'technical' UN institution, was taken by surprise when all of a sudden civil society groups began introducing human rights as a matter of concern. What began as a conference on managing technological change forced ITU to take a stand on human rights (Leuprecht, 2005: 42). It had anticipated that social issues or economic and environmental questions would arise, but was taken aback when the human rights implications of telecommunications were suddenly brought to the forefront. It had not expected to discuss freedom of opinion and information, data protection, the right to privacy, intellectual property rights, non-discrimination, the right to participation in scientific progress, child pornography, cultural rights, or the right to education. What seemed obvious to human rights groups – that a technological process entails a number of human rights considerations – was a new experience for a specialized technical agency, ten years after the process of mainstreaming human rights had begun (Oberleitner, 2007).

## United Nations Security Council

The Security Council, one of the six 'principal organs' of the UN mentioned in the Charter, is composed of five permanent members and ten non-permanent members elected by the General Assembly for two-year terms. Article 24 of the UN Charter entrusts the Security Council with the primary responsibility for the maintenance of international peace and security. This mandate does not make any reference to human rights, yet today the Security Council frequently speaks out on human rights violations. In a painstakingly slow process over more than half a century it has left behind much of its ignorance towards human rights and has begun to acknowledge the links between peace, security and human rights. Notwithstanding its continuing structural and procedural shortcomings, first and foremost the veto power of the permanent members, the Security Council is today prepared to act in favour of human rights in at least five important areas: it considers human rights violations as threats to international peace and security; integrates human rights components in peace operations; uses human rights language to support democratization; denounces violations of international humanitarian law and protects civilian victims of armed conflict; and holds perpetrators of human rights violations accountable by setting up international tribunals. Most of this was inconceivable a few decades ago. In a sixth area of utmost importance, however, the prevention of gross human rights violations such as genocide, the Council has failed abysmally. Yet, it remains centre stage in a vivid discourse on humanitarian intervention, on the responsibility of the international community to protect victims of genocide and gross human rights violations, and on supplementing national security with human security.

## Safeguarding international peace and security

The Security Council has to carry out the task ascribed to it in Article 24 of the UN Charter (maintaining international peace and security) 'in accordance with the Purposes and Principles of the United Nations' (Article 24(2), UN Charter). Among these purposes and principles, further outlined in Chapter I of the Charter, are equal rights and self-determination of peoples (Article 1(2)) and the 'promotion and encouragement of respect for human rights and for fundamental freedoms for all without distinction as to race, sex, language, or religion' (Article 1(3)). Other principles the Council has to consider are the sovereign equality and territorial integrity of all its members and the principle of non-interference in matters which are essentially within the domestic jurisdiction of member states (Article 2). As a consequence, in each of its decisions it is confronted with a matrix of often conflicting demands: maintaining global peace and stability, respecting the national sovereignty of member states, guaranteeing self-determination of peoples and encouraging respect for human rights. What is the role of human rights in this environment?

The evidence of the past fifty years is that the principles of non-intervention and national sovereignty have trumped human rights in the Council more than once. Concerns over the stability and security of member states have outrivalled calls for preventing humanitarian disasters, remedying human rights violations, combating impunity and holding perpetrators accountable. In effect, save on a few occasions, human rights concerns were virtually excluded from the Council's decisions until the 1990s, a situation which in the end proved both 'impossible and unwise' (Mertus, 2005: 115). Indeed, the reasons why the Council must consider human rights when safeguarding international peace and security have been expressed many times over: human rights violations are often the root causes of armed conflict; the cross-border consequences of human rights violations, such as refugee flows, lead to instability; and neglecting human rights violations in peace negotiations may be the source of future conflict. Whenever the Council strives for durable peace rather than merely silencing the weapons, ensuring respect for human rights is an essential element.

No doubt the Council knows all this, yet its practice tells a different story. Security Council action on human rights was sporadic over the better part of the past half century: before the 1990s it acted on human rights issues in an 'adventitious, sporadic and inconclusive' way (Bailey, 1992: 305–6). Actions on Hungary in 1956, the Congo in 1961 and the

Dominican Republic in 1965 are exceptions which never became a rule (Weschler, 2004: 56). Still, as Sidney Bailey has shown (Bailey, 1994), human rights concerns were present throughout the Council's existence like a background noise, hardly audible but irritating to most governments, while human rights activists and interested governments struggled to grasp the volume control so that the sound would swell, and slowly it did. The Council spoke out on decolonization and self-determination, e.g., in Angola, Mozambique, Guinea-Bissau, Zimbabwe and Namibia (ibid.: 2–9). It laid down, in a series of resolutions from 1988 onwards, a framework for self-determination in Western Sahara (Ramcharan, 2002b: 90–3). Southern Rhodesia and South Africa stand out as major cases; in the former the Security Council supported the right to self-determination of peoples, in the latter it condemned apartheid. In taking a stand against apartheid it couched human rights violations in terms of threats to peace and security in an ambiguous manner. Yet this paved the way for a line of reasoning that increasingly saw gross human rights violations as constituting a threat to the peace in the sense of the UN Charter (Bailey, 1994: 10–11). Altogether, however, the Council's approach remained inconsistent. Most importantly, even when it saw the need to speak out on human rights violations within a given state, it would wait for cross-border conflicts to become discernible (or construct such a conflict in its arguments) so as not to deviate from the very words of the Charter which required it to act solely on international conflicts.

With the Cold War over and world media and transnational pressure groups making it harder for it to turn a blind eye to an ever greater number of internal conflicts involving gross human rights violations, the Council took more courageous steps. Resolution 688 (1991), which allowed for the creation of 'safe havens' in Iraq to protect the Kurdish population from the repression of Saddam Hussein's regime, is often seen as a watershed (Mertus, 2005: 124). Authorizing the provision of humanitarian assistance and, if necessary, military action to prevent human rights violations within a nation-state – even in the absence of the state's consent – showed a new line of argument in the Council, which gave raise to hopes that it might become a more effective tool to stop gross violations of human rights. Soon afterwards, with resolution 794 (1992), it authorized the use of force to restore peace, stability and law and order in Somalia. The Council considered that 'the magnitude of human tragedy caused by the conflict in Somalia [. . .] constitute[s] a threat to international peace and security.' The resolution allowed member states to 'use all necessary means to establish as soon as possible a secure environment for humanitarian relief operations in Somalia' (para. 10). The Council's authorization to intervene in Somalia, based primarily on human rights violations (albeit in the context of relief operations) without mentioning cross-border effects, was out of line with many previous decisions and made for a strong argument that human rights violations alone could trigger a response by the Council (Mertus, 2005: 125). Subsequent events – the killing of US soldiers, the pull-out of peacekeepers and the failure to bring peace and stability to Somalia – kept the Council from repeating such decisions. Observers at that time, however, concluded that – based on such practice – the Council was entitled to authorize coercive military measures under Chapter VII of the UN Charter to respond to human rights violations within the territory of a state (authors quoted ibid.: 124).

Part of the reason why the Council was increasingly prepared to accept human rights violations as threats to peace and security in the 1990s is often attributed to the Secretary-General's influence (Mertus, 2005: 117–20; Weschler, 2004: 63–4). Boutros Boutros-Ghali's *Agenda for Peace* (UN, 1992) was based on the understanding that human rights violations may be the cause of conflicts and called for human rights to be taken into account in peace operations. When Kofi Annan became Secretary-General in 1997, human rights moved from their 'institutional exile' (Weschler, 2004: 64) to the centre of the stage. In what later came to be known as the Annan doctrine, the Secretary-General in effect made clear that considerations of national sovereignty must not hinder the prevention of crimes against humanity, and that the Security Council would have to respond more effectively to gross human rights violations.

## Genocide, the responsibility to protect and human security

The promise that the Security Council, freed from the constraints of the Cold War, would effectively deploy all means necessary to protect individuals from gross human rights violations did not hold for long. Unhindered ethnic cleansing and atrocities in Bosnia-Herzegovina from 1992 onwards and the 1994 genocide in Rwanda presented to the world an impotent and ignorant Security Council, entangled in procedural discussions and strangled by the unwillingness of its members to make it act. While these abysmal failures put an end to rising hopes that the Council might in a consistent way consider human rights violations as threats to peace and security and act accordingly, they have led to much soul-searching and opened the way for a debate on the duty and right to intervene. The report of the independent inquiry into the actions of the UN during the 1994 genocide in Rwanda (UN doc.

S/1999/1257) highlighted a number of shortcomings and emphasized that the Council must be better prepared to prevent genocide and gross human rights violations, and the report of the UN Secretary-General on the fall of Srebrenica (UN doc. A/54/549 of 1999) equally dissected the UN's failures.

In 1999 there began a thorough and in-depth reassessment of the link between state sovereignty, human rights and UN intervention, which to date is not concluded. UN Secretary-General Kofi Annan argued for territorial sovereignty to be complemented by individual sovereignty (Annan, 1999). An expert panel produced what later became to be known as the Brahimi Report on the minimum requirements for successful UN peace operations (UN, 2000). In 2001, the International Commission on Intervention and State Sovereignty (ICISS), a group of academics and practitioners funded by the Canadian government, came out with its report *The Responsibility to Protect*, which aimed at reconceptualizing state sovereignty as a state responsibility and argued that a failure to protect their own citizens and guarantee human rights would open states to humanitarian intervention: 'Where a population is suffering serious harm, as a result of internal war, insurgency, repression or state failure, and the state in question is unwilling or unable to halt or avert it, the principle of non-intervention yields to the international responsibility to protect' (ICISS, 2001: xi).

Parallel to this debate, UNDP introduced, in the *UNDP Development Report 1994*, the notion of human security as a new way of thinking about security, provoking a debate which did not leave the Security Council unaffected. 'Whose security are you protecting?' is the core question the Council has been faced with since. Canada responded to this challenge to redefine security and the Security Council's responsibilities during its membership in the Council from 1998 to 2000. As a consequence, the Council took innovative decisions on the protection of civilians in armed conflict and on the trafficking of small arms and blood diamonds in Angola (Oberleitner, 2005: 192–3).

The balance between the Council's obligation not to intervene in internal affairs and to act to protect human rights is shifting in academic discourse as well as in state practice, and it is tilting towards the Council's responsibility to act on gross human rights violations. Accommodating this shift to the Council's outdated post-war decision-making structure is the challenge ahead in Security Council reform. The Council is at the centre of a reassessment of security, which sees the latter as an important element of a stable global inter-state order as well as an individual human right. The challenges of the early twenty-first century are balancing national with individual sovereignty, introducing the responsibility of the international community and the Security Council to protect victims of human rights violations, and linking security and human rights through the concept of human security. Diverse as those challenges are, they show in an ever more convincing way that the protection of human rights forms part of the Council's duty to uphold international peace and security, and that it must do so in a more systematic, coherent and predictable way.

## Peace operations

Peacekeeping forces were deployed for the first time sixty years ago in order to separate warring factions and supervise the observation of ceasefires on request of the parties involved. Since then, they have gradually evolved into complex peace operations which weave together peacemaking, peace-building and peace enforcement with long-term conflict prevention; they include tasks such as electoral assistance, reintegration of former combatants, reform of the domestic security sector, and reconciliation. In some cases, such as in Cambodia, Bosnia-Herzegovina and Kosovo, the UN took over the entire administration of post-conflict territories. Today, more than 90,000 personnel serve in eighteen peace operations worldwide under the guidance of the UN Department of Peacekeeping Operations (DPKO) (http://www.un.org/Depts/dpko/factsheet.pdf).

The role of human rights in these missions has changed considerably over the past half century. ONUSAL, the UN Observer Mission in El Salvador (established in 1990), was the first comprehensive approach to make human rights part of a peace operation's mandate (Weschler, 2004: 56). Other early examples include UNOMIL, the UN Observer Mission to Liberia (1993–7), which was mandated to investigate and report human rights violations; UNOMOZ, the UN Operation in Mozambique (1992–4), which entrusted the UN civilian police with monitoring human rights in prisons and police stations and investigating complaints; UNOMIG (UN Observer Mission in Georgia), established in 1993, where the task of reporting on human rights violations was entrusted to a human rights office; and UNOMSIL, the UN Observer Mission in Sierra Leone (1998–9), which allowed for the reporting of human rights violations as well as assisting the country in addressing its human rights needs. In his 1997 *Programme for Reform*, UN Secretary-General Kofi Annan stressed that human rights must be a 'key element in peacemaking and peace-building efforts and should be addressed in the context of humanitarian operations' (UN,

1997: para. 199). In 1999, the DPKO and OHCHR concluded a Memorandum of Understanding in order to better integrate human rights into peace operations (Ramcharan, 2002b: 107–11), and in 2000 the Brahimi Report repeatedly endorsed the Secretary-General's proposals (UN, 2000). Today virtually all peace operations contain human rights components (Ramcharan, 2002b: 115–16). Most recently, UNMIS, the UN Mission to Sudan, was based on the explicit mandate to protect the human rights of all people in Sudan (Security Council resolution 1590 of 2005).

## Democratic legitimacy

From the 1990s onwards, the Council has shown an interest in democratic legitimacy and has responded to situations in which democracy was under threat. It repeatedly used the language of human rights to support democratization processes and stress elements of democracy such as free and fair elections, participation in public life and adequate representation (Bailey, 1994: 16–58). In 1994 it adopted resolution 940, in which (acting under Chapter VII of the UN Charter) it authorized member states to 'use all necessary means to facilitate [...] the restoration of the legitimate authorities of the Government of Haiti' (para. 4). This was the first time the Security Council had used its power to safeguard international peace and security for the sake of restoring democracy (Malone, 1998: 1). It has also on occasion reiterated its support for democratically elected governments, e.g., in presidential statements or resolutions on Burundi (1996), Liberia (1996) and Guinea-Bissau (2000) (Ramcharan, 2002b: 23 and 98). Only when the elected government in Sierra Leone was overthrown, however, did the Council, in resolution 1131 of 1997, invoke Chapter VII again and impose economic and other sanctions under Chapter VII of the UN Charter, but it refrained from authorizing member states to use military means.

## International humanitarian law and civilians in armed conflict

Over the past decades, the Council has in some cases invoked Chapter VII of the UN Charter to find violations of international humanitarian law and to threaten sanctions. The plight of civilians caught up in armed conflicts has made it adopt a number of resolutions urging the parties to a conflict to protect civilians (Bailey, 1994: 59–89; Ramcharan, 2002b: 40–1).

More recently, the use of child soldiers and the role of women in armed conflict has led to innovative efforts to protect civilians. These attempts link international humanitarian law with human rights and human security. Driven by pressure groups and a number of interested governments and inter-governmental bodies, the Security Council has adopted a number of resolutions on child soldiers, the most prominent being resolution 1539 (2004). This condemns the recruitment and use of child soldiers and proposes a long-term strategy to end the practice, which violates human rights and humanitarian law and is a threat to peace and security. Consequently, the Council invoked provisions in international humanitarian law, the UN child rights convention, the optional protocol to this convention on the involvement of children in armed conflict, and a number of codes of conduct and guidelines of international organizations on civilian police and peacekeeping personnel. It combined these norms with the outcome of various studies, in particular Graça Machel's pertinent work *The Impact of Armed Conflict on Children* (Machel, 1996), and with the work of the UN Special Representative for Children in Armed Conflict, thus building a comprehensive edifice to protect children from being coerced to become soldiers.

The Security Council's willingness to head this process seems a remarkable new approach. Yet, in 2005, the Council proceeded to the operational stage, and with resolution 1612 established the first comprehensive monitoring and reporting system to enforce compliance among groups using children in situations of armed conflict. The system obliges such groups immediately to create and implement concrete and time-bound action plans for ending the use of child soldiers and for setting up a monitoring and reporting task force comprised of UNICEF, DPKO, UNHCR, OHCHR, OCHA, UNDP and non-governmental organizations active in this area. While it lies still at the discretion of the Council to take action once the task force presents its findings, another step in making human rights protection an undisputed task of the Council has been taken. Moreover, by reaching out to other UN bodies, the creation of a more coherent institutional web for the protection of human rights is less utopian than it seemed only a few years ago.

In a way the Council has repeated its efforts on protecting children's rights by adopting resolution 1325 (2000), on women, peace and security. Acknowledging the role of women in peace processes, conflict prevention and post-war reconstruction, the Council again takes a broad view on international peace and security and the linkages between women's human rights, humanitarian law, peace processes and regional and international stability. These two examples are welcome steps by which the Council transcends self-imposed limitations on its mandate and places human rights more firmly at the centre of its considerations. It has yet to prove that such a view can take hold in areas other than children's and women's rights and permeate all its decisions on international peace and security.

## Criminal justice for human rights violations

In establishing *ad hoc* criminal tribunals for the former Yugoslavia (1991) and Rwanda (1994) as well as a special court for Sierra Leone (2000), the Council took decisive steps towards combating impunity and holding perpetrators of gross human rights violations accountable. In doing so, it responded, albeit *ex post facto*, to genocide, violations of international humanitarian law, war crimes and crimes against humanity. The conditions and consequences of this development will be examined in chapter 6.

## Cooperation, transparency and the role of NGOs

More than anything it was the almost complete lack of cooperation between UN human rights bodies and the Security Council which undermined the image of a coherent web of UN institutions for the protection of human rights. It was only in 1992 that the Council for the first time ever invited a Special Rapporteur of the UN Commission on Human Rights to present his views. The appearance of Max van der Stoel, the Special Rapporteur on Iraq, led to a furious response by the ambassador of India to the effect that the Council 'cannot discuss human rights situations *per se* or make recommendations on matters outside its competence' (Weschler, 2004: 58). Also in 1992, and again for the first time, the Commission on Human Rights requested of the Secretary-General that the reports of the Special Rapporteur on ex-Yugoslavia, Tadeusz Mazowiecki, be made available to the Security Council. It took nearly half a century to establish such direct links between the Security Council and the Commission on Human Rights. It took even longer, until 1999, for the UN High Commissioner for Human Rights, Mary Robinson, to be permitted to speak before the Council for the first time (ibid.).

The ignorance which the Council has displayed for so long not only towards human rights bodies but, in particular, towards NGOs, was challenged with the introduction of the so-called Arria formula in 1992. The then president of the Council, Venezuelan ambassador

Diego Arria, wanted a Croatian priest (who had previously addressed him) to convey information on the Balkan conflict to the Council. As he could not find a formal way to do so, he invited interested fellow ambassadors to retreat to the delegates' lounge with his guest. Some attended, and 'Arria formula' briefings were born (Weschler, 2004: 62). It still took until the late 1990s for NGO briefings to become more regular and acceptable to the Council. With the creation in 1995 of the NGO Working Group on the Security Council, off-the-record briefings for Council delegates became routine (Mertus, 2005: 135–6), slowly ensuring more transparency in the decision-making processes of the Council and allowing them to be permeated by human rights concerns.

## Prospects

As we have seen, the Security Council, when acting to protect and promote human rights, accepts human rights as part of the overall legal framework which obliges it to guarantee peace and security, sees them as useful in managing conflict and post-conflict situations, considers them as elements of promoting democracy, invokes them for purposes of achieving accountability through criminal justice, or accepts an increasing convergence of human rights and humanitarian law. Yet, it seems correct to describe the Council's attitude towards human rights as 'convulsive' (Weschler, 2004: 66) and as provoking hopes and frustrations at the same time (Ramcharan, 2002b: 15). The Council is restrained not only by the veto power of its permanent members, but also by a number of fundamental principles it has to consider, as discerned by Ramcharan: a 'confidence-building principle' (the need for it to strive for pragmatic compromises with those in power on the expense of 'moral' considerations), a 'political principle' (the fact that it is the place for the most powerful nations of the world to engage with each other, which brings underlying struggles for power and influence to the forefront), and a 'power principle' (the fact that on occasions those powerful nations may wield their power in disregard for human rights and justice principles) (ibid.: 2–3).

Despite these limitations, the Council's practice on human rights over the past half century has pushed doors open. The Council now routinely considers gross human rights violations (including in internal conflicts) a threat to international peace and security, deploys peace missions with human rights mandates, strives to integrate human rights into peace negotiations, is concerned with protecting the individual in armed conflict, establishes criminal tribunals, and supports democratization. Today's greatest challenge for the Security Council lies in balancing its fight against terrorism as a threat to security while guaranteeing respect for human rights. When it adopted resolution 1373 (2001) in the wake of the terrorist acts of 9/11 and called upon states to cooperate in combating terrorism, it also set up a Counter-Terrorism Committee to monitor action on this matter. At that time, human rights were not a matter of great concern for the Committee, and it took numerous appeals from UN human rights institutions to establish some links between them and the Committee and strive for placing human rights concerns on a par with security considerations. With resolution 1456 (2003) the Council presented a more balanced view and held that states must ensure that counter-terrorism measures must comply with obligations under international human rights law. Once more, these wavering motions of the Security Council serve to prove that human rights have not yet found the place in its deliberations that they deserve.

# 6 WORLD COURTS AND HUMAN RIGHTS

## International Court of Justice

The ICJ, with its seat in The Hague, is the principal judicial organ of the UN and is entitled to settle disputes between states in accordance with international law and give advisory opinions on legal questions. Its role in human rights litigation is restricted in a number of ways. Most importantly, Article 34(1) of its statute allows only states to be parties in cases before the Court; individuals, judicial persons and non-governmental organizations are excluded. Even state parties have specifically to consent to their cases being brought before the Court. The ICJ has no special mandate to adjudicate claims involving human rights violations, and the judges, while international legal experts, are not required to have specific knowledge of human rights law. Consequently, the ICJ deals with the rights of individuals only to the extent that they are implicated by an inter-state dispute brought before it by states or in requested advisory opinions – a right which so far pertains only to the five other principal organs of the UN, most importantly the General Assembly and the Security Council, and the UN specialized agencies.

As of November 2006, the Court had handed down ninety-two judgments and twenty-five advisory opinions, with thirteen more cases (all contentious) pending. While it is by no means a human rights court, the ICJ has nevertheless taken decisions on human rights in both its adjudicatory and advisory capacity. The respective decisions have been important for the development of international law, but were often scarcely noticed by the global human rights movement.

The reasons lie in the way in which the Court approaches human rights.

The Court's predecessor, the Permanent Court of International Justice (1921–45), contributed solely to the development of minority rights. In the absence of human rights norms before 1945, this was what could be expected, and was entirely in line with the inter-war emphasis on minority and group rights rather than individual rights. The PCIJ helped to clarify the content and scope of minority rights (Higgins, 2002: 163–6). It spoke out on minorities in Upper Silesia (e.g., PCIJ *Minority Schools* case, 1928) and in Poland (PCIJ *German Settlers* case, 1923), on Polish nationals in Danzig (PCIJ *Polish Nationals in the Danzig Territory* case, 1932) and on minority schools (PCIJ *Minority Schools in Albania* case, 1935).

After 1945, the ICJ had a greater range of human rights norms on which to adjudicate. The increase in human rights treaties adopted thereafter, however, did not lead to a significant rise in cases before the Court (Higgins, 2002: 167). Three reasons may be discerned. First, few such treaties contain clauses overtly referring disputes to the ICJ. Second, regional treaties establish human rights courts, and some of the universal treaties provide for a complaints procedure which allows not only individuals but also states to come forward with claims, thus effectively rendering the ICJ superfluous, as inter-state disputes can be settled within those treaty regimes. And third, the fact that no inter-state complaint has ever been filed under a UN treaty (and very few under regional treaties) demonstrates that states are actually not overly eager to accuse other states of human rights violations before tribunals or other bodies.

In essence, therefore, a rather limited range of human rights concerns, such as apartheid, genocide, the death penalty, and the right to life, together with the application of international humanitarian law, have been brought to the ICJ, and only in a handful of these cases have states explicitly claimed violations of international human rights law by other states. While the Court's case law does demonstrate that the principles and laws of human rights have been referred a number of times, they have hardly ever taken centre stage, but have been intertwined with issues such as diplomatic protection, armed conflict, interpretation of treaty law, immunity, etc. On the other hand, human rights have sometimes been invoked by the Court itself in cases which at first sight seemed distant from international human rights law. In the *Barcelona Traction* case (1970), for example, what was at stake was the protection of Belgian shareholders in a company (Barcelona Traction) which was incorporated in Canada and provided electric power to Catalonia. The Court went beyond the boundaries of the case and developed the doctrine of *erga omnes* obligations (obligations in the protection of which all states have an interest). It went on to reason that such obligations are also to be found in human rights, such as slavery, racial discrimination and genocide. In essence, it used this case to state that 'the international community is founded on a set of common values the transgression of which it cannot accept' (Tomuschat, 2003: 196).

The 1948 Genocide Convention was perhaps the human rights treaty which most often received notice from the Court. In the ICJ *Reservations to the Convention on Genocide* case (1951) the General Assembly had asked the Court to give an advisory opinion on the scope of reservations made by states on signing or ratifying the Genocide Convention. The Court, while not touching upon genocide itself, held that the principles underlying the Convention are recognized by civilized nations as binding on states even without any conventional obligation. In 1993, the Court began consideration of a case brought before it by Bosnia-Herzegovina on the application of the Genocide Convention in the territory of the former Yugoslavia (Hurlock, 1997; Tomuschat, 2003: 193–5). It an ambivalent judgment handed down on 26 February 2006 (*Application of the Genocide Convention* case), the Court found Serbia responsible for not having prevented the genocide of Srebrenica and for having failed to punish the perpetrators, but did not find it guilty of having actually committed genocide. In the *Arrest Warrant* case (2002) the Court had to consider an application by the Democratic Republic of the Congo against Belgium. The dispute between the two states arose when in 2000 a Belgian investigating judge, in application of Belgian law, issued an arrest warrant against the then minister for foreign affairs of the Democratic Republic of the Congo on counts of genocide. The ICJ upheld the principle that under international law foreign ministers enjoy absolute immunity against any such charges brought forward by courts in other states.

In the *South West Africa* case (1971), the Court held, in an advisory opinion requested by the Security Council, that the presence of South Africa in what today is Namibia constituted a violation of international law. South Africa's presence in South West Africa was considered illegal, and the introduction of apartheid in South West Africa was seen as a fundamental denial of fundamental human rights and of the principles of the UN Charter. With this, the ICJ gave substance to the vague Charter provisions on human rights which have been seen as no more than a feeble appeal to states (Higgins, 1998: 694).

Protecting human dignity and specifically the right to life was repeatedly a matter the Court had to deal with. In the *Nicaragua* case, for example, Nicaragua asked for interim measures to be ordered in 1984 so as to protect the lives of Nicaraguan citizens, and the ICJ acceded to this request (Grimheden, 2001: 475). Regarding the *United States Diplomatic and Consular Staff in Tehran* case (1979) on the hostage-taking in the US embassy in Tehran, it was argued that the Court, while ordering interim measures to ensure diplomatic rights, aimed in effect to protect human dignity (ibid.). In the *Nuclear Weapons* case (1996) the ICJ had to consider more specifically Article 6 of the International Covenant on Civil and Political Rights (the right to life) in the context of armed conflict. While it found that under the specific circumstances the *lex specialis* of international humanitarian law prevailed, it also emphasized the importance of human rights law (ibid.: 478).

The Court also issued two advisory opinions on Special Rapporteurs of the UN Commission on Human Rights. In both cases it confirmed that Special Rapporteurs are entitled when carrying out their mandate to privileges and immunities under the UN Convention on Privileges and Immunities. The cases concerned Special Rapporteur Mazilu, who faced prosecution by his home country Romania, and Special Rapporteur Cumaraswamy, who faced legal proceedings before Malaysian courts (*Applicability of the Convention on the Privileges and Immunities of the United Nations (Mazilu)* case, 1989; *Difference Relating to Immunity from Legal Process of a Special Rapporteur of the Commission on Human Rights (Cumaraswamy)* case, 1999).

In a string of more recent cases involving the death penalty in the USA, including the *LaGrand* case (2001) and the *Avena* case (2003), the ICJ had to rule on the lack of consular notification of foreign nationals before US courts. It did not determine the question of the death penalty as such; rather it was the failure of US authorities to inform the respective consulates of the trials against their citizens. In these cases, the Court did not speak out on whether or not the death penalty is a human rights violation. However, in requesting an interim measure, namely to hold the executions of the said individuals until the Court could take a final decision, it effectively aimed to protect their lives. Article 41 of its statute ('The Court shall have the power to indicate, if it considers that circumstances so require, any provisional measures which ought to be taken to preserve the respective rights of either party') entitles the ICJ to do so, and it has used those powers in these and other cases. Although the USA did not follow the Court's order and carried out the executions (Rieter, 1998), such interim measures, weak as they are, are perhaps the Court's most immediate contribution to the protection of human rights (Iwamoto, 2002; Duxbury, 2000). Rosalyn Higgins, in a detailed account of the evolving jurisprudence of the ICJ on the right to life and physical integrity, concludes that the evolving scope and application of interim measures shows indeed 'a growing tendency to recognize the human realities behind disputes of states' (Higgins, 1997: 103).

In 2002, the Democratic Republic of the Congo brought an application before the ICJ which, based on human rights treaties, accused Rwanda of massive human rights violations on Congolese territory between 1998 and 2002. In 2006, however, the Court decided that it had no jurisdiction in this matter, as none of the bases for such jurisdiction which the Democratic Republic of the Congo had put forward could be upheld (*Armed Activities on the Territory of the Congo* case, 2006).

In its latest advisory opinion, the *Legal Consequences of the Construction of a Wall in the Occupied Palestinian Territory* case (2004), the Court was very outspoken on violations of human rights and invoked specific provisions of human rights treaties. It found that the wall erected by Israel violates, *inter alia*, the liberty of movement as guaranteed under the International Covenant on Civil and Political Rights and the right to work, health, education and an adequate standard of living as proclaimed in the International Covenant on Economic, Social and Cultural Rights and in the CRC (para. 134 of the Advisory Opinion). While setting this decision in the larger context of the situation, and mindful of the limitations and exceptions which human rights law allows to be applied by Israel, the Court, with a vote of 14 to 1, was very clear on this matter (para. 163 of the advisory opinion).

It is obvious from its sixty years of jurisprudence that the ICJ never pretended to be a human rights court. Only in adopting interim measures, and not in its judgments and advisory opinions, has it ever attempted directly to protect human rights (Higgins, 1998: 697). It has delivered such decisions as could be expected from a court which is called upon to adjudicate the totality of international law in inter-state cases. In the words of Christian Tomuschat, it has

first of all made a contribution to determining the strategic place of human rights in the international legal order by a number of advisory opinions. Never has it been requested to say whether an alleged human rights principle does exist or how it has to be understood. Thus, human rights has never occupied the centre stage in a legal proceeding with which it was seized. But in its advisory opinions one finds a number of the crucial propositions which fix the coordinates for any discussion on the relevance of human rights. (Tomuschat, 2003: 192)

While the ICJ has never shied away from invoking human rights law, it has also never given primacy to human rights in its considerations. It has successfully invoked human rights law to develop international law, but it has not been eager to use international law to promote human rights. Proposals have been put forward to allow access for NGOs or individuals to the Court to seek to remedy this situation, to make it more susceptible for human rights arguments and also to entrust it with the protection of human rights (Garland, 2001: 401; Grimheden, 2001: 483; both with reference to the respective authors). This, however, would be a misinterpretation of the Court's role. Turning it into an institution where individuals can seek redress would diminish its role as the main judicial forum in which states can peacefully settle their disputes. The ICJ's function in the international legal order is too valuable to make it stand in for a non-existent world court on human rights.

# International Criminal Court

International human rights law is a protective shield against the abuse of power by states and defends the individual against acts committed by governments and their agents. Hence it is the state, and not individual perpetrators of human rights violations, which answers to human rights institutions. Notwithstanding recent debates on the human rights obligations of non-state actors, it is states which take on the responsibility for violations and which are supposed to call their agents to order. By setting up international criminal tribunals, however, individual perpetrators of human rights violations rather than the social construct 'the state' are summoned to court and held to account. This presents a major shift towards ending impunity and punishing human rights violators.

The post-war Nuremberg and Tokyo tribunals provide the foundations of today's attempts to hold individuals accountable for crimes against peace, war crimes and crimes against humanity. Notwithstanding the critique that the tribunals represent victor's justice, the fact that they were convened, the way in which they conducted business, and the judgments they delivered mean that they remain the cornerstones on which criminal responsibility under international law rests. The development of international criminal law, however, was all but stalled for nearly half a century after Nuremberg and Tokyo and took up speed only in the 1990s. It needed the atrocities in the territory of the former Yugoslavia and the genocide in Rwanda to make the international community respond, and it was not the codification attempts of the International Law Commission but the Security Council's decision to create two *ad hoc* criminal tribunals which for the first time since Nuremberg and Tokyo put perpetrators in the dock.

The International Criminal Tribunal for the Former Yugoslavia (ICTY) in The Hague was given jurisdiction over grave breaches of the 1949 Geneva Conventions, violations of the laws or customs of war, genocide, and crimes against humanity. The International Criminal Tribunal for Rwanda (ICTR) in Arusha can hear cases on genocide, crimes against humanity, and violations of Article 3 common to the Geneva Conventions and of Additional Protocol II to the Geneva Conventions. Their statutes blend violations of the laws of war, human rights violations and crimes against humanity. As a matter of fact, the focus of both tribunals is more on what could be termed 'human rights crimes' (Schabas, 2003: 281) than on actual war crimes. The linkages between the two fields of law in which these two types of crime reside, human rights law and international humanitarian law, are still ambiguous (as is the concept of crimes against humanity itself), but the tribunals continue to make significant contributions to clarifying their respective scope and their interrelatedness (Abi-Saab, 1999: 651). Despite their jurisdiction being limited in time and space, both the ICTY and the ICTR contribute to the development of human rights law in a global perspective.

The adoption of the Rome Statute in 1998, which set up the ICC, did away with the *ad hoc* nature and limitations of previous attempts to hold perpetrators accountable. The Court has jurisdiction over 'the most serious crimes of concern to the international community as a whole' (Article 5, ICC Statute): genocide, crimes against humanity and war crimes. Crimes against humanity encompass murder; extermination; enslavement; deportation or forcible transfer of population; imprisonment or other severe deprivation of physical liberty in violation of fundamental rules of international law; torture; rape, sexual slavery, enforced prostitution, forced pregnancy, enforced sterilization, or any other form of sexual violence of comparable gravity; persecution of groups on political, racial, national, ethnic, religious, gender, or other grounds impermissible under international law; enforced disappearance; apartheid; and other inhumane acts of a similar character which cause great suffering or serious injury to body or mental or physical health (Article 7, ICC Statute). The statute contains a number of limitations: jurisdiction does not extend to events before 1 July 2002 or, for a state joining the Court thereafter, before the entry into force of the statute for that state; the Court can only exercise jurisdiction if the accused is a national of a state party (or the state has otherwise accepted the jurisdiction of the Court), if the crime was committed on the territory of a state party, or if the UN Security Council refers the situation to the prosecutor; and the Court complements national courts rather than replacing them and assumes jurisdiction only when a state is unwilling or unable to prosecute perpetrators.

The surprisingly swift establishment of the ICC in 1998 after two years of negotiations, the number of countries voting in favour (120, with twenty-one abstaining and seven, namely China, Libya, Iraq, Israel, Qatar, Yemen and the USA, voting against), and the ratification of the statute by 102 states as of November 2006 are hailed by many as representing the dawn of a new era for international law. Despite the limitations of the ICC, human rights organizations and activists worldwide, in particular, have welcomed its creation as a decisive step towards ending impunity for serious crimes, providing incentives and guidance for states that wish to prosecute perpetrators, and deterring potential human rights violators. Has a new era for international human rights law begun?

Indeed, unlike the governmental and expert bodies discussed above, courts give teeth to human rights law, and so will the ICC. In their jurisprudence, international courts flesh out the meaning and content of human rights law and set precedents on the basis of elaborate procedural rules. They complement and remedy the shortcomings of other types of human rights institutions. Governmental bodies are usually concerned with systematic and gross human rights violations, and the way in which they go about their work is peppered with bias, selectivity and double standards. When UN special procedures address individual human rights violations in their urgent appeals, they do so in a humanitarian rather than a legal way. And treaty bodies, despite often posing as quasi-judicial institutions, lack procedural clarity and core elements of fair trial and due process. Finally, none of those institutions deliver legally binding judgments. Courts such as the ICC act on firmer legal ground, apply established rules of evidence, and adhere to the requirements of fair trial.

Yet for international human rights law the ICC may not represent the enforcement revolution some have hoped for. The Court puts an end to the impunity on which dictators, *genocidaires* and war criminals could previously rely. This is an achievement one cannot praise enough – one that will, in the long run, boost the acceptance of human rights as enforceable entitlements rather than aspirations. Still, the jurisdiction of the ICC spans only a narrow range of crimes. International criminal courts such as the ICC may bring individual perpetrators to justice, but they do not address global inequalities, such as extreme poverty. The Court also has little to contribute to local justice or to the empowerment of local movements. Like the ICTY, it may run into the danger of being seen as a remote and elitist institution. The potential deterrence factor of international criminal justice for human rights violators has yet to be proven, and altogether it is not obvious whether the legalistic approach of individual criminal responsibility is the proper response to political evils. Critics have also pointed out that the expense of conducting court proceedings to hold a handful of perpetrators accountable exceeds the resources devoted to remedy structural human rights violations such as poverty or illiteracy. The ICC envisages budgetary needs of €93 million (US$117 million) for 2007, but has only just started its first trial. The massive imbalances between the budgets of the ICTY and the ICTR and the OHCHR are, for the time being, more striking. For 2006/7, the UN General Assembly approved the regular budget of the ICTR at US$270 million and of the ICTY at US$276 million (http://69.94.11.53/default.htm, http://www.un.org/icty/cases-e/factsheets/generalinfoindex-e.htm). The combined expense for holding perpetrators accountable in all but two places in the world (US$536 million) makes the 2006/7 regular budget of US$85.6 million, as approved by the General Assembly for the OHCHR's manifold global responsibilities, look minute in contrast (http://www.ohchr.org/english/about/fundraising.htm).

Since the ICC statute entered into force in 2002, three states (Uganda, the Democratic Republic of the Congo and the Central African Republic) have brought situations on their territories to the Court. A fourth situation on the territory of a non-state party, Darfur/Sudan, has been referred by the Security Council. The first person to be formally charged by the prosecutor is Thomas Lubanga Dyilo, a former militia leader in the Ituri district of the Democratic Republic of the Congo. He is accused of enlisting and conscripting children under the age of fifteen to participate in an armed conflict, and the charges brought against him are at the intersection of international humanitarian law and international human rights law. This is noticeable proof that the convergence of human rights, humanitarian law and international criminal law, as attempted in the Court's statute (Mendez, 2000: 73), changes our assumption that only bodies such as the UN Human Rights Council or UN treaty bodies are 'human rights institutions'. It shows that the promotion and protection of human rights is now effectively the task of a great range of multilateral institutions in formerly separated areas.

## Towards a world court of human rights?

Given that the ICJ is not accessible to individuals, the ICC has jurisdiction over only a range of human rights violations, and UN treaty bodies are not an effective judicial remedy, does this not call for the establishment of a world court of human rights? Or is this too utopian a suggestion? The idea of establishing such a court was floated at the Vienna World Conference on Human Rights in 1993 (Strohal, 1999: 166), but whatever enthusiasm there may once have been has declined since, not least because of the excitement the establishment of the ICC generated. There are arguments and experiences, though, upon which such a vision may be based. As mentioned, 102 states accept the ICC's competence to adjudicate on crimes committed on their territory or by their citizens. Furthermore, altogether eighty-six European, American and African states have submitted themselves to the jurisdiction of their respective regional human rights court. While the mandates of such regional human rights courts accommodate specific conditions and expectations of state parties, those states have nevertheless in principle accepted international human rights adjudication. Communications procedures under UN human rights treaties have been accepted by a respectable group of states, too (106 under ICCPR, seventy-eight under CEDAW, sixty under CAT and forty-five under CERD). Add the states for which ILO and UNESCO complaints procedures are applicable, and what emerges is a considerable number of states which are, one way or another, routinely scrutinized in individual complaints procedures. Notwithstanding the differences between many of those procedures and a proper court proceeding, this indicates the willingness of those governments to allow individuals under their jurisdiction to seek remedy in international institutions. A large number of states should thus have no principled objections that an international judicial institution should speak out on human rights violations and ask for them to be remedied.

Of course, the difficulties in setting up such a court should not be underestimated. Which human rights would fall within its remit? What procedure would be applied? How would its competences be fenced off from regional human rights courts and the ICC? What would the standing of non-governmental organizations be? How would it relate to the Human Rights Council and the Security Council? Would it have jurisdiction over all human rights, civil/political as well as social? Who would ensure that its decisions are implemented? Difficult as these questions are, it is not an impossible task to find answers. Decades of experience with the Inter-American and European regional human rights court can enlighten the drafters of such a statute for a world court of human rights. There are as yet only sporadic and cautious speculations among human rights scholars on the setting up of such a court – some rather confident (Nowak, 2006), some more pessimistic (Trechsel, 2003) – and no governmental initiatives in this respect are in sight. As the example of the ICC has shown, however, it is not impossible to overcome the legal, political and financial constraints in setting up a global court. The way in which regional human rights courts have changed, over time, the human rights landscape in their regions also seems to bode well for a world court on human rights. One must neither downplay the challenges these courts continue to face nor overlook the fact that regional experiences cannot simply be replicated at the universal level. Yet they demonstrate that international human rights jurisdiction is not a utopian concept, just as a world court on human rights would not be a utopian institution, but rather would be consistent with development processes in international human rights law. The creation of such a court could be achieved in realistic steps, leaving it to states whether or not they accept its jurisdiction and giving them leeway with regard to the scope of rights that could be invoked (Nowak, 2006: 65).

It is true that 'judicial romanticism' (Forsythe, 2006: 90), which overestimates the role of courts in the protection of human rights, is inappropriate. After all, human rights remain an essentially political issue, and their promotion and protection, even where it means pursuing justice for human rights violations committed, does not always require criminal justice. Apologies, mediation, and truth and reconciliation commissions may often be more appropriate avenues. Successful as human rights courts may be in adjudicating individual cases and compensating victims, they find it next to impossible to remedy, let alone prevent, gross serious human rights violations. Pitting the judicial protection of human rights against other means to ensure respect for human rights, however, misses the point. Courts are but one element in the global architecture of human rights institutions. In contributing to constraining the behaviour of states, delegitimizing deviant behaviour, and constructing the social world, they display indispensable elements which make global human rights institutions effective and autonomous actors. And while their decisions should first and foremost benefit the victims and coerce wrongdoers into changing their behaviour, they contribute decisively to shaping a culture of human rights, both domestically and internationally.

# 7 NON-GOVERNMENTAL ORGANIZATIONS

## Independence between law and politics

Over the past half century, the spread of inter-governmental human rights institutions has been accompanied by the emergence of an ever greater number of non-governmental organizations devoted to the promotion and protection of human rights. The organization of individuals who pursue goals on the international level is not a new phenomenon and has been traced back to the mid-1800s (Charnovitz, 1997). The rapid growth of civil society movements, though, in particular in the field of human rights, is essentially a striking global phenomenon of the past decades (Rice and Ritchie, 1995: 245). From small, local, grassroots-level groups to worldwide membership organizations, from single-issue pressure groups to large networks, NGOs have become central to the world of human rights. A number of factors have accelerated this development, most recently the revolution in telecommunications and electronic media, which allows civil society groups around the globe to gather and share information and exert an influence which is sometimes way beyond their size or financial power.

The 2004 *Yearbook of International Organizations* gives a total number of 7,306 international non-governmental organizations, a number which rises up to more than 13,600 when 'internationally oriented national organizations' and others are included, but it is less clear on the number of human rights NGOs. Indeed, there is no overall accepted definition for a 'human rights NGO'. Even the very term 'non-governmental organization' is contested. Alston has rightly noted that defining them 'in terms of what they are not combines impeccable purism in terms of traditional international legal analysis with an unparalleled capacity to marginalize a significant part of the international human rights regime' (Alston, 2005: 3). There is no clear-cut distinction between 'human rights NGOs' and NGOs working in other areas. Some would say that the former include only organizations with the very *raison d'être* of promoting and protecting human rights (Wiseberg, 2003: 349), but in light of the contribution often made to human rights by NGOs with a broader mandate, it seems perhaps reasonable to be more lenient on such definitions.

The precarious status of NGOs under international law, their independence and their opposition towards governments are often considered characteristic. They have been defined as 'private organisations (associations, federations, unions, institutes, groups) not established by a government or by intergovernmental agreement, which are capable of playing a role in international affairs by virtue of their activities' (Rechenberg, 1997: 612), and they are governed by national legislation rather than international law – with the exception of the International Committee of the Red Cross, which possesses international legal personality (ibid.: 617). The debate on their status under international law is ongoing (most recently Lindblom, 2006) and proceeds on two levels. First, what are the specific conditions and consequences of the special legal status they already enjoy under international law, e.g., as 'consultative' bodies for inter-governmental organizations? And, second, can or should NGOs obtain international legal personalities on a par with states and international organizations? Despite attempts to grant legal personality to NGOs as early as 1910, no progress has been made on this front (Charnovitz, 2006: 355–6).

Unlike inter-governmental institutions, which are set up and funded by governments, NGOs are independent actors. It is not surprising that the vague criterion of 'independence' has allowed for a range of questionable organizations to consider themselves NGOs. Alan Fowler, in his study on NGOs in development, came up with a remarkable list of such organizations, which includes GONGOs (government-operated or government-owned NGOs), BRINGOs (briefcase NGOs), CONGOs (commercial NGOs), FANGOs (fake NGOs), CRINGOs (criminal NGOs), MANGOs (Mafia NGOs), PANGOs (party NGOs) and others (Fowler, 1997: 32). Sometimes NGOs are referred to as 'non-profit organizations' (NPOs), meaning that any profits they make are invested back into the mission of the organization and are not distributed for the benefit of shareholders. In the absence of legal criteria or procedures to differentiate between various types of NGO, the

World Association of Non-Governmental Organizations (WANGO) has developed a voluntary code of ethics and conduct for NGOs (http://www.wango.org/codeofethics.aspx), which explores the above-mentioned criteria in greater detail.

States and NGOs are usually pitted against each other, with the latter pushing the former to respect human rights. Hostility towards NGOs and repression of NGO activists is indeed a matter of routine for many governments. Yet the relationship is often more complex than this: at times, human rights NGOs work in formal or informal partnership with governments (e.g., in supporting additional information to human rights bodies, consulting, carrying out government-financed projects, etc.); at times NGOs are, in cooperation with governments, important contributors to human rights capacity-building on the ground and serve as a bridge between policy and experience (Hegarty, 1999: 276–80). Some countries acknowledge and seek the input of domestic and international NGOs in their human rights policy and even aim for continued movement between NGO staff and governmental personnel. While this offers new opportunities for action, such cooption can also be used to silence human rights activists (Wiseberg, 2003: 364).

Human rights NGOs are not only considered independent, but are sometimes also said to be, or describe themselves as, 'non-political'. While this may attract people discouraged from party politics or domestic politics in general to join and support NGOs, this label is misleading (Mutua, 2001: 157–9). NGOs are apolitical (in the sense that they do not represent any particular political position) and they are non-partisan (in the sense that they do not depend, financially or otherwise, on the support of political parties); but they are fundamentally political, as 'the very act of appealing to governments for changes in their human rights policies is very much a political one' (O'Byrne, 2003: 97).

## Consultation, cooperation, compensation, competition

Inter-governmental human rights institutions and human rights NGOs are ploughing the same furrow. What difference is there in the way in which they seek to enhance respect for human rights? Obviously, one would assume when inter-governmental organizations are nothing more than instruments of governments, NGOs will find themselves in opposition to such institutions, just as they confront governments. Yet, in reality the relationship between inter-governmental human rights institutions and human rights NGOs is remarkably close and sometimes even symbiotic. There is, however, a scarcity of literature exploring the commonalities between the two, which is somewhat surprising given that, after all, they are both frameworks within which human rights become ever more institutionalized (exceptions are Thakur, 2001, and the authors quoted therein).

The importance of NGOs for the functioning of international human rights institutions has been highlighted in the previous chapters, and the specific contributions they make have been acknowledged in a number of studies (Chinkin, 1998; Brett, 2001; Alger, 2003; Gaer, 2003; Wiseberg, 2003). NGOs have assumed their present role gradually, and the may in which NGOs now participate in UN affairs was inconceivable in the early days of the organization (Das, 2001: 15). In examining their position towards international institutions, one may today discern at least four different roles for NGOs (Charnovitz, 2006: 357–63): they act as consultants for international human rights institutions, they are partners in cooperation, they compensate for what inter-governmental bodies fail to deliver, and they compete with such bodies.

Their consultative role is most clearly prescribed in the UN Charter, which allows for consultative status with ECOSOC (Article 71: 'the Economic and Social Council may make suitable arrangements for consultation with non-governmental organizations which are concerned with matters within its competence'). A strict regulatory mechanism is in place to vet the performance of NGOs and control their access to various UN bodies, including human rights bodies – a mechanism which leaves room for many questions and doubts as to both its legitimacy and its effectiveness (Breen, 2005). More than 2,700 organizations have achieved consultative status with ECOSOC to date, and therefore had to declare (according to ECOSOC resolution 1296 (XLIV) of 1968, updated by ECOSOC resolution 1996/31) that they have been officially registered with government authorities for at least two years, have established headquarters, a democratically adopted constitution, authority to speak for their members, a representative structure, appropriate mechanisms of accountability, and democratic and transparent decision-making processes, and that their resources come mainly from members' contributions. Once ECOSOC is satisfied that these criteria are fulfilled, NGOs are granted either general consultative status (for international NGOs whose activities cover most of the issues on ECOSOC's agenda and those of its subsidiary bodies) or special consultative status (for NGOs with a special competence in a few of ECOSOC's activities). NGOs fitting in neither category can be included in the 'roster', a list of NGOs with a narrow or technical focus or that have formal status with other UN bodies or specialized agencies, but which are nevertheless expected to contribute to ECOSOC's work. The decision on granting consultative status is taken by the Committee on Non-Governmental Organizations, a standing committee of ECOSOC. Once this process has been successfully concluded, NGOs may designate persons to represent them at the UN.

Consultative status allows NGOs to make oral statements or present papers to human rights bodies, participate in sessions, have their documents circulated as official UN documents and regularly receive UN documents. In the UN Commission on Human Rights, for example, NGOs have used these possibilities to carve out considerable public space in an otherwise inter-governmental institution. Several NGOs have also gained the confidence of delegations and have acted as trusted and experienced advisers and exerted considerable influence in the drafting of texts. Consultative status brings a certain degree of prestige and legitimacy which many NGOs find helpful. Outside the scope of ECOSOC, the participation of NGOs is organized in different ways. The ILO is a special case as it includes, in its tripartite system, delegates of employers' and workers' organizations in both its highest bodies, the International Labour Conference and in the Governing Body. While opening the doors wide to these organizations, the system has in effect excluded other human rights NGOs from participating in the ILO. UN specialized agencies also grant observer status to NGOs. UNESCO for example allows participation for nearly 600 NGOs (Bennett and Oliver, 2002: 291). Yet, 'the latitude accorded to NGOs within the human rights and environmental arenas has not translated into similar acceptance elsewhere' (Chinkin, 2000: 146).

Often, NGOs transcend their roles as mere 'consultants' and are partners in cooperation. Much of what inter-governmental human rights bodies plan or recommend can only be realized because NGOs take over, provide support and supply the necessary means. Many of the operational and educational functions discussed below, as well as the process of accompanying the implementation of international commitments, are tasks carried out jointly by governmental and non-governmental bodies. Sometimes, NGOs have to stand in for functions which other global human rights institutions do not offer. In the absence of global human rights tribunals, for example, NGOs have repeatedly conducted and participated in so-called peoples tribunals which publicly denounce human rights violations. The Italian Lelio

Basso International Foundation for the Rights and Liberation of Peoples, for example, has organized thirty such events since 1979 (http://www.grisnet.it/filb/filbeng.html), and in 2000 the Women's International War Crimes Tribunal considered acts committed by Japanese military and political officials in the 1930s and 1940s (Chinkin, 2001). Such mock trials are perhaps the most striking examples of NGOs pointing out the lacunae in international efforts to tackle human rights violations.

Finally, when NGOs pit their independence against the political bargaining common in inter-governmental institutions and their flexibility against the human rights bureaucracy, there is an element of competition in the relationship between them and international human rights institutions. Whose reporting is more accurate, whose studies are more comprehensive, whose recommendations more to the point? Such competition is not only about being faster and more efficient (and thus about securing donors' funding). It also embodies the (problematic) claim to hold morally higher ground than inter-governmental institutions and to be more representative and better legitimated to drive global governance based on global values, a claim that will be examined further below. The fact that states allow such competitors access to inter-governmental institutions, which are after all their creation, instrument and arena, is somewhat puzzling, and different explanations have been put forward (Charnovitz, 2006: 362–3, and the authors quoted): NGOs provide essential expertise, enhance public support for inter-governmental organizations, assist in translating norms developed in these organizations into realities on the ground, and guarantee mutual legitimacy. Thus, partnership and competition can go hand in hand.

# Functions

Whether under the umbrella of consultation, cooperation, compensation or competition, NGOs perform a variety of specific tasks. Diverging categorizations of such functions have been put forward. Weiss and Gordenker emphasize operational, educational and advocacy functions (Weiss and Gordenker, 1996), while Charnovitz finds NGOs to be active in all 'decision functions': intelligence (gathering and processing of information and data), promotion (advocating policy alternatives), description (designing policies), invocation (describing deviant behaviour and asserting control), application (giving effect to prescriptions in concrete disputes), termination (pressing for an end to unacceptable governmental activities) and appraising (evaluating the degree to which policies are achieving the desired end) (Charnovitz, 1997: 271–4). Welch describes standard-setting, information, lobbying and assistance as core functions of NGOs (Welch, 2001a: 3–6). In the following, their activities will be considered insofar as they are linked to inter-governmental human rights institutions, first and foremost UN institutions: NGOs manage information so as to have the power of definition and mobilization and contribute to agenda-setting, norm-making and policy development. They accompany the implementation of norms and policies adopted by international institutions and engage in operational activities with or on behalf of international human rights institutions, and they use international human rights institutions for their advocacy work.

## Information, definition, mobilization

Managing information is the essence of NGO activities (Wiseberg, 2003: 355–8). Fact-finding missions, research or interviews produce information, which is evaluated, analysed and put in context before it is disseminated or published. Reliance on NGO information, while still seen as disrespectful in some governmental circles, has long become routine (Welch, 2001b: 275). Often, NGOs know what inter-governmental institutions do not know. Together with media reports, their information often provides the basis for the activities of other human rights institutions, whether such information is accepted under procedural rules or communicated over a cup of tea in the cafeteria. But managing information is not usually an aim in itself. It leads to definition and mobilization. Information allows a problem to be defined in terms of human rights. Assessing information and data against the background of international human rights law turns sta-tistics and stories into human rights issues. In this ability to define events (killings and starvation in Darfur) as human rights violations (genocide in Darfur) lies great power for NGOs. And information is geared towards mobilization: lobbying the experts in treaty bodies to raise certain issues in their discussion with governmental representa-tives, challenging governments to correct their reports, asking members to write letters and sign petitions, or bringing people out on the streets. Eyewitness accounts, academic papers or statistical informa-tion in the hands of NGOs are tools for achieving change. As a con-sequence, the accuracy, reliability and timeliness of information are essential concerns which NGOs must meet in order to remain credible. Indeed, in the absence of other regulatory mechanisms to guarantee the independence of NGOs they are the only means for judging their work. By combining information, definition and mobilization, NGOs are able to put human rights issues on the agenda of inter-governmental institutions. In the absence of universally accepted rules on this process, however, the approach of NGOs resembles that of inter-governmental institutions (Kennedy: 2002, 121–2): they turn this problem but not that one into a human rights issue, call for intervention here, but not there. While overall their approach covers more topics and more places on the globe, it may well reveal much of the same arbitrariness we have encountered in inter-governmental human rights institutions.

## Agenda-setting, norm-making and policy development

What has been described above as information, definition and mobilization is followed by the search for solutions together with (or against) inter-governmental institutions. The way in which NGOs go about this business has been described as engaging in 'strategic framing processes to set the agenda in three stages: the definition of problems, the development of solutions or policies, and the politicisation' (Joachim, 2003: 268). Creating norms and policies is the preferred method, and NGOs have become essential contributors to creating norms and proposing policies. They are consultants and partners in conceptualizing, developing, debating and adopting human rights norms, standards and principles and are now present in all stages of making and applying international human rights law – in its development, interpretation, judicial application and enforcement (Charnovitz, 2006: 352–5). They initiate normative developments, cooperate formally and informally in the law-making process in international forums, draft interpretative documents and submit amicus curiae briefs to courts. Even when they do not immediately participate in law-making, they raise the stakes for such processes by campaigns and by mobilizing their members and the public. Amnesty International's successful campaign for the abolition of torture in the 1970s, which greatly contributed to the adoption of the UN Convention against Torture in 1984, may serve as an example (Wiseberg, 2003: 351–2).

NGOs seek to input two essential elements in law-making and interpretative processes in inter-governmental institutions. One is expertise, which stems both from their control over theoretical knowledge and from practical experience, and is not (or not in sufficient quality or quantity, or not timely) otherwise available to governments. The other element is legitimacy, based on the claim that they represent those 'concerned', the victims, or general moral problems which would otherwise go unheard in inter-governmental law-making processes. While the former element (expertise) can be proven or rejected in the course of creating the respective norms, the latter (legitimacy) remains a problematic claim, which we will consider further below.

## Accompanying implementation

Inter-governmental human rights institutions are particularly weak in ensuring the domestic implementation of norms and policies they have devised and the decisions and recommendations they have made. NGOs assist in this process and are cooperative partners in implementing international commitments. They point to violations of norms and deviant behaviour of states or call for individual perpetrators to be held accountable before human rights bodies. Rooted in domestic environments as most of them are, and linked to local media, they are better suited than remote bureaucratic institutions to influence domestic affairs. They transmit between the local and the global not only by bringing domestic deficiencies to the knowledge of international institutions, but also by feeding the results achieved in these institutions into the domestic sphere.

## Advocacy, education and operation

Many NGOs engage in practical assistance for victims of human rights violations. They invoke procedures provided in international human rights institutions, represent individuals before international bodies, provide legal aid, etc. (Hannum, 2004: 28–9). A variety of formal and informal ways of participating in proceedings before treaty bodies, tribunals and other forums have been developed, including the submission of amicus curiae briefs. Other NGOs have become centres of education, training, learning and sharing experiences and run education and training programmes and courses, write user manuals, provide advice on how to set up human rights databases and human rights centres, etc. By doing so, they are actively promoting human rights and integrating international norms into social processes. More specifically, such NGOs hook up organizations and individuals with global institutions and their processes. The Geneva-based International Service for Human Rights, to give an example, was established in 1984 specifically to assist and empower human rights defenders in accessing international institutions, understanding their internal organization and functions, and using their procedures (http://www.

ishr.ch). Finally, some NGOs carry out operational activities together with or on behalf of international institutions, such as emergency relief or trial observations.

# Legitimacy

Their claim to represent ('the victims', 'our constituency', 'universal values', 'the conscience of the world', 'mankind', etc.) is what gives NGOs appeal, strength and authority; yet it rests on fragile assumptions. Why should NGOs be allowed to participate in the creation of community norms? Why are they entitled to represent victims? Why should they be allowed to define a human rights problem? Boli and Thomas have pointed out that the authority of NGOs is informal and cultural, not organizational, allowing them to act 'as if they were authorised in the strongest possible terms' (Boli and Thomas, 1997: 181). Little wonder the legitimacy of NGOs is frequently questioned, and not only by oppressive governments. On whose behalf do they operate? In the wake of the 'Battle of Seattle', the 2000 protests against the World Bank meeting, *The Economist* asked

> who elected Oxfam? [. . .] Bodies such as these are, to varying degrees, extorting admissions of fault from law-abiding companies and changes in policy from democratically elected governments. They claim to be acting in the interests of the people – but then so do the objects of their criticism, governments and the despised international institutions. In the West, governments and their agencies are, in the end, accountable to voters. Who holds the activists accountable? (*The Economist*, 23 September 2000, quoted in Slim, 2002: para. 1).

Human rights NGOs would respond that what they represent in the first place are arguments which preserve the international human rights framework. Still, the more NGOs impact on processes of global governance, the more pressing it is to find answers to crucial questions about their legitimacy (Baehr, 1998; Slim, 2002; Charnovitz, 2006: 363–8). Is it moral or legal legitimacy that NGOs seek? To what extent do they have to make their organizational processes transparent? Does their organization have to be based on democratic principles or on representativeness, and what does either mean in an NGO context? Coming to terms with such questions is particularly important in light of attempts to prevent NGOs from bringing information into the public domain on the grounds that they are not legitimized to do so or that doing so would lead to their being held accountable. Such arguments seek to exploit legal shortcomings to silence critical voices.

In his salient critique of the human rights movement, David Kennedy assembled a great number of such concerns which led him to ask whether or not the movement is 'more part of the problem in today's world than part of the solution' (Kennedy, 2002: 101). Others see human rights NGOs as too deeply rooted in Western, liberal conceptions of human rights and dependent on the moral, financial and social support of Western liberal elites to claim global representativeness (Mutua, 2001).

While claims of representation remain a frail foundation on which to build arguments for their participation in human rights matters, the accuracy, reliability and impartiality which independent NGOs bring to such discussions are important contributions and complement the work of inter-governmental institutions. Yet, even in these fields, recent research seems to be shattering some illusions. An empirical study of Amnesty International's reporting of human rights violations concluded that the accuracy of its reporting is not in question, but that the choice of information is influenced not only by the severity of human rights violations, but by factors such as a country's prominence in the Northern media, the organization's chance of maximizing its advocacy and the desire to raise its own profile, the respective country's link to US military aid, and other factors. Some of these were found to be part of Amnesty's decision-making processes, while staff members in charge were not consciously aware of others (Ron, Ramos and Rodgers, 2005). Allegations of false priorities and of adopting a selective approach, very much akin to those levelled against inter-governmental human rights institutions, are sure to follow such findings.

# Challenges

Despite the spread of NGOs and their impressive impact on international human rights institutions, a number of challenges lie ahead. Assigning NGOs an international legal status which would allow them increased rights of participation and enhance their legitimacy, while at the same time preserving their independence, is one of them. This cannot be a simple replication of the successful ILO tripartite system. Institutional changes such as creating an NGO assembly for the UN, parallel to the General Assembly, also remain a vision. Suggestions to this end, e.g., in the report *Our Global Neighbourhood* (Commission on Global Governance, 1995), which recommended setting up a parliamentary body for civil society representatives, never materialized. It is not only governmental resistance that is to blame for this; indeed, the assumed identity between NGOs and civil society is questionable (Bennett and Oliver, 2002: 294–5). Great care must be taken in the process of reforming NGO participation, as the eagerness with which some governments seek to eliminate critical voices from their meetings makes it likely that any international treaty would result in cutting back effective NGO participation instead of enhancing it (Charnovitz, 2006: 357). Rather than adopting a one-size-fits-all methodology for assigning NGOs enhanced legal status, the gradual expansion of their participation in various forums seems a more realistic goal. Improved access for NGOs to international financial institutions, the WTO and UN specialized agencies, programmes and funds, remains an essential demand.

Enhancing NGO access to international institutions, however, does not automatically guarantee improved access for underrepresented or unrepresented groups. The establishment of new, innovative bodies, such as the UN Permanent Forum on Indigenous Issues, opens up much needed space for such groups. The Forum, established in 2000 by ECOSOC (ECOSOC resolution 2000/22), has a unique structure because, for the first time, states and non-state actors are represented in parity in a permanent UN body. It consists of eight members nominated by governments and elected by ECOSOC and eight members appointed by the president of ECOSOC following broad consultations with indigenous organizations and groups. The election has to take into account the geographical distribution and diversity of indigenous peoples and ensure transparency, representativeness and equal opportunity. Members are individual experts in their personal capacity elected for a period of three years, while governments, NGOs in consultative status with ECOSOC, and organizations of indigenous peoples may participate as observers. The Forum shall 'serve as an advisory body to the Council with a mandate to discuss indigenous issues within the mandate of the Council relating to economic and social development, culture, the environment, education, health and human rights' (ECOSOC resolution 2000/22) and will meet annually for ten working days. Despite criticism voiced by representatives of indigenous peoples with regard to its name, which avoids the very words 'people' or 'peoples', and some concerns over its structure and mandate (Carey and Wiessner, 2001), it is an important step towards formal institutional participation of hitherto unrepresented and marginalized parts of the world's population.

It also shows how inter-governmental bodies and NGOs are linked, and how the challenges and limits of one are the challenges and limits of the other. Bringing other (as yet) unrepresented and unorganized groups into the framework of international human rights protection in a way that they can effectively participate is another challenge. While NGOs cannot claim to represent such groups, they serve, as Laurie Wiseberg has noted, an often ignored but immensely important function, namely to 'keep the political system open' (Wiseberg, 2003: 364). Indeed, the participation of NGOs in international institutions gives an (imperfect) idea of what a democratic and inclusive international order might mean.

# 8  CONCLUSION

Global human rights institutions are part of the 'cycle of enthusiasm and despair' (Steiner and Alston, 2000: 369) which characterizes the move to and from international institutions since the beginning of the twentieth century. The preceding chapters have demonstrated the diversity of global human rights institutions which, together with regional human rights institutions, make up our global human rights infrastructure. They have also identified the functions, limits, potential, shortcomings, failures and achievements of global human rights institutions. Let us, in a set of concluding remarks, return to the questions with which we started our inquiry: Are global human rights institutions effective remedies or shallow rituals? Can we discern how such institutions should be designed so as to make success likely, and find out which design constrains effectiveness? And, finally, what do global human rights institutions do *with* the idea of human rights, and what do they do *to* the idea of human rights?

## Coherent multilateralism and proliferation

First, we have briefly to recapitulate our understanding of a 'global human rights institution'. The designation of human rights as a cross-cutting issue in the 1997 UN reform programme, which initiated the process of mainstreaming human rights, rested on the acknowledgement that human rights concerns are often closely intertwined with economic turmoil, political instability or armed conflict. Calls for a more 'coherent multilateralism' (Leary, 2001) which would allow tackling such global challenges imply that most international problems are not simply 'economic' or 'social' in nature (which would justify their allocation to an international institution with the corresponding doorplate) but multi-dimensional. If human rights are indeed a cross-cutting issue and are at the core of such coherent multilateralism, then, strictly speaking, there is no such thing as a human rights institution. Rather, human rights are the concern of all global institutions. Indeed, a large part of this book was devoted to demonstrating that human rights matter beyond UN human rights bodies – in specialized agencies, funds and programmes, in the Security Council and in international courts. We have encountered both the success of mainstreaming human rights in institutions such as UNICEF and UNDP and the obstacles for this process which prevail in so-called non-political institutions, such as the World Bank, IMF and WTO, and in technical institutions, such as the ITU. The latter examples reflect the difficulties of mainstreaming human rights as much as they highlight its necessity. The challenge in considering human rights as the point of reference for many policies, programmes and actions of global institutions is to make sure that the human rights referred to are not lofty goals or self-defined principles, but the international legal framework which has developed over the past half century. If this can be secured, then such 'institutionalizing' of human rights is to their advantage, as it allows them to be dispersed, in a formalized and consistent way, in the management of a range of global concerns. It is also to the advantage of the institutions entrusted with managing such concerns, as it allows for tackling the root causes of problems in a more holistic way.

As for human rights institutions in the proper sense, the challenge is a different one: a host of global institutions is today endowed with channelling the call to 'do something' (to end hunger, stop genocide, secure food and halt torture). The preceding chapters have shown the proliferation of committees, councils, forums and working groups, not to mention the growth of human rights NGOs. It was not only concern over human rights which prompted this development, as Henry Steiner reminds us: 'neither basic principles nor a master plan but rather contingent compromises over time responsive to the positions of the great powers and of regional or ideological blocs of countries, all as supplemented by a gradual increase in powers of international organisations through their internal development, explain our present institutional arrangements' (Steiner, 2003: 761). The sprawl of institutions forces them to compete for resources, allows for contradictory approaches, and often makes the search for coordination, consistence and coherence seem like an end in itself. Yet, given that a global master plan for a human rights infrastructure will never be realized, it seems that such diversity is still more an asset than an aberration (Donnelly, 2006: 109), because it offers multiple channels of influence: where once individuals stood alone in facing governmental oppression, today there are a multitude of formalized avenues for redress and assistance in global human rights institutions.

## Institutions matter

But do such institutions still matter in an international order which is increasingly being shaped by informal sub-national networks of decision-makers, where formal decision-making in international forums is replaced by new modes of governance? Much can be said in favour of these new transformative forces, but equally much would be lost if international institutions were to disapper from the global institutional landscape. What would go missing is

> the counterweight of formal politics, the type of politics that insists on rules relating to voting and decision-making, that knows an *ultra-vires* decision when it sees one, and insists that the ends do not always justify the means, precisely because, ultimately, we cannot agree on the ends and thus end up imposing our ideals, or at least our superior techniques, to others. [. . .] Only through [. . .] formalized procedures can we prevent might from becoming right; only through such a formalized style of politics can we make sure that power is exercised through legal channels rather than nakedly. (Klabbers, 2002: 341–3)

We have explored in some detail the downsides and negative consequences of institutionalizing human rights. Yet, the fragility on which new networks and movements rest their claims of representation questions whether they can remedy the power inequalities or 'politicization' of international institutions. It seems, rather, that they may replicate the power configurations of inter-governmental institutions in a different form, but without the legal channels to which Klabbers referred. Just as we must not return to the bilateral and multilateral power configurations which preceded the rise of global institutions, we cannot (yet) put our trust in forms of governance which dispense with such institutions. Taking a pragmatic view, this makes global human rights institutions, like other institutions, not the ultimately desirable format for realizing human rights but the best one that is presently available.

# Sovereignty and community

'Men and nations', Inis Claude once said, 'want the benefits of inter-national organization, but they also want to retain the privileges of sovereignty, which are inseparable from international disorganization' (Claude, 1984: 39). Global human rights institutions mirror this tension between sovereignty and community in an exemplary way. Like other international institutions, they are constrained by a legal system which rests on the sovereignty of territorial states, yet they are mandated to translate fundamental community norms into practice. In doing so, they help to push open the door towards a more community-oriented international order. Quite remarkably, in international human rights law states agree to substantial intrusions into their sovereignty. Once the UN Charter was understood by many to proclaim that human rights are domestic affairs of states with which international bodies must not meddle. Today, a number of mechanisms do precisely this as a matter of course. Henry Steiner rightly reminds us, again, that, 'however limited and inadequate those arrangements [. . .] appear, we should keep in mind how radical and politically implausible they would have seemed when the human rights movement got underway' (Steiner, 2003: 761).

A significant number of states now routinely cooperate with a mul-titude of working groups, committees and rapporteurs, accept indi-vidual complaints procedures, and allow for inquiries, inspections and on-site visits to take place. The latest innovation, the optional protocol to UN CAT – which legally obliges states to open the doors of their places of detention for international experts and allows those experts to go public with their findings – is a striking example of this develop-ment. While only a decade or two ago it was claimed that human rights were matters of domestic jurisdiction in which international institu-tions should have no influence, today even states which remain hostile towards any form of international scrutiny of their human rights situ-ation have to resort to more sophisticated arguments to defend their position. Global human rights institutions may take huge credit for this particular change of tune in the global discourse on human rights. Their function as a forum for settling disputes, often under the eyes of civil society groups and the public, forces them to rely on arguments rather than simply to reject any possible intrusion on the basis of sovereignty. Such intrusion into what were once domestic matters is also becoming routine rather than being an exception. The ILO's effec-tive monitoring system has long been an example in this regard. Now, the UN Human Rights Council's system of universal periodic review may put an end to the selective form of scrutiny which the discredited Commission on Human Rights used to apply

One must not overlook, however, that global human rights institutions remain subsidiary means for the protection of human rights, and their proliferation must not deflect from the continuing primary responsibility of states to guarantee such rights. Treaty bodies become active once local remedies are exhausted, international courts supplement rather than replace domestic jurisdiction, and technical cooperation programmes are brought in only when states so request. Even where international institutions compensate for the lack of domestic bodies and procedures and behave much like autonomous actors, indeed like governments in all but name (e.g., in post-conflict peace-building or transitional administrations), they are not meant to stay permanently but merely to assist states in regaining their authority. Still, if anywhere in the field of international matters one finds an example of what it may mean to put community concerns before national interests, it is in the field of human rights, and global human rights institutions are the most visible expressions of such an approach.

We have, in the preceding chapters, repeatedly expressed this tension between sovereignty and community as one between dependence and autonomy. As we have seen, most human rights institutions are firmly in the hands of governments. Suggestions back in the 1940s to allow for a design which would have given them greater independence were too bold. And, indeed, in formulating community norms it seems only realistic to let governments decide what obligations they, as the primary subjects of international law, are willing to accept. On the other hand, we have also seen how global human rights institutions accrue independence, either by design (such as the UN treaty bodies and special rapporteurs, or international courts) or by asserting moral authority in matters of human rights in the face of an ambiguous mandate (such as the UN High Commissioner for Human Rights).

Constructivist theories on how international bureaucracies exercise different forms of authority, which in turn enables them to set themselves apart from states and achieve a certain degree of autonomy, are confirmed by the examples of global human rights institutions we have encountered. Indeed, they invoke different forms of authority when standing up to their masters, the states, as predicted by theorists such as Barnett and Finnemore (discussed in chapter 2). Special rapporteurs rely on the expert knowledge they bring or acquire in the course of exercising their mandate. The UN High Commissioner for Human Rights, as the leader of the global human rights movement, speaks to states not so much from higher legal as from higher moral ground. And authority which stems from a rational-legal framework is invoked when, e.g., an international body such as the UN Human Rights Council concludes on the basis of procedural rules that a country has violated international human rights norms. Such evidence supports the view that at least some global human rights institutions can, provided their design matches their function, assert themselves as autonomous actors which operate and develop along their human rights mandate, even when this goes against the preferences of states.

## The pitfalls of bureaucracy

When we proceed with the conclusion we have reached so far, namely that global human rights institutions matter as the best presently available format for realizing human rights, that their proliferation is more a benefit than a danger, and that they can play a meaningful role in putting community interests before national interests, then we should not forget to mention the drawbacks of organizing human rights in such a bureaucratic set-up. The pathologies of international bureaucracies have become obvious in the preceding chapters: insensitivity to situations, alienation of stakeholders, insulation from reality, and self-referential dwelling in perpetual reform, to mention but a few. The Commission on Human Rights compiled lengthy lists of human rights violations with the only purpose of shelving them and engaged in the repetitive, ritualized adoption of resolutions which found little resonance, ECOSOC was busily concerned with cutting back human rights activities on bureaucratic grounds, rules of procedure were invoked not to allow for speedy progress but to prevent discussions on the human rights situation in countries such as China, and so on.

Furthermore, the interlinked processes of legalization, professionalization and bureaucratization shape a distinct understanding of human rights which is often remote from everyday experiences and assumptions, and herein lies considerable danger. Global human rights institutions have the potential to alienate and to jeopardize the idea of human rights as tools for individual empowerment. Should this keep us from entrusting such institutions with managing human rights? Only if such negative consequences are so intrinsic that they cannot be overcome. This, however, does not seem to be the case: the move from headquarters to the field, as undertaken by the High Commissioner for Human Rights, is a welcome corrective, as is the use of new on-site inquiry procedures under UN CAT which bring treaty bodies out of UN headquarters. Transparency and access to human rights bodies have been recognized as areas of reform, and strengthening procedures which deliver visible results to victims of human rights violations, such as individual complaints procedures, can reverse the view of global human rights institutions as remote und unresponsive. Human rights education and training programmes demonstrate how international norms can, with the help of global human rights institutions, be translated into domestic change, and NGOs have specialized in providing guidance and assistance to access such institutions.

Furthermore, we also found examples of the benefits of entrusting international bureaucracies with human rights matters. They bolster theoretical considerations as to the ways in which international bureaucracies can make a difference. As we have assumed in chapter 2, they do indeed define problems and fix meanings (such as when the Special Rapporteur on the right to housing elaborates on the scope, content and consequences of the human rights to housing). They articulate norms and supervise their implementation (for example, in the form of the 'views' and 'general comments' of treaty bodies) and the they offer stability, durability and predictability in dealing with human rights in a way that cannot be brought about by states alone. There is no simple shortcut to avoid the pitfalls of an expanding human rights bureaucracy, but as in other bureaucracies there are means and tools to balance, in a never-ending effort, the advantages of institutionalization with its drawbacks.

# Adequate design in an inadequate legal order

The interplay between form and function has become visible in the preceding chapters, and we have experienced how design impacts on success and failure. Decisions over this design are inherently political, and the struggle over 'architectural' questions (the size of human rights bodies, their meeting time, geographic composition, etc.) reveals much not only about power inequalities and state interests, but also about diverging views of human rights and of their role in international law and politics. Even hardly noticeable changes in the design, which we have come across (such as the small shift in the ratio between countries with a traditionally positive attitude towards country mandates and those opposed to such mandates in the Human Rights Council, as compared to the Commission on Human Rights), can be influential.

Although the way in which human rights scholarship usually presents human rights bodies, pitting them against each other in terms of membership or functions (governmental versus expert bodies and political versus legal bodies) has left us unsatisfied, some lessons may be learned on the design of human rights institutions. Where community interests are developed and adopted in legal form, it seems only realistic that governments should take the lead, thus reflecting the realities of our international legal order. The Commission on Human Rights and its Sub-Commission, the General Assembly, UNESCO, and others have a rich and successful history in creating such human rights norms that could not have been produced anywhere else other than in global institutions. Yet, as some governmental institutions demonstrate, first and foremost the UN Commission on Human Rights (and now the Human Rights Council), in such an environment it is feasible, necessary and wise to bring in civil society actors.

When it comes to supervising the implementation of those norms, however, governments are ill-suited to scrutinizing their own behaviour, as we have seen. The UN Commission on Human Rights has been the most striking example, while others, such as the ILO with its tripartite structure, fared better. It is in this area where – with the ongoing reform and strengthening of UN treaty bodies and the possible creation of courts and new means for inquiry and inspection – much work still lies ahead. In the third core function of global human rights institutions (next to standard-setting and scrutiny), namely assistance to governments, we have encountered both established practice (such as in the ILO's technical cooperation programmes) and innovative design (with the High Commissioner's move to the field and the creation of new bodies), and we have highlighted the importance of mainstreaming (in the way in which UNDP and UNICEF, for example, translate international commitments into policy, programmes and action).

What is expressed here in terms of design may equally be considered in terms of law: global human rights institutions operate in an imperfect international legal order, which excludes entire groups of actors from participating in decision-making. Bringing those actors into lawmaking and interpretative processes is a challenge ahead. Global human rights institutions have some interesting lessons to teach in this respect. Nowhere is the participation of civil society organizations more prosperous than in this field. Two particular examples may suffice: ILO bodies fill their seats with a two-thirds majority of social partners, leaving a mere one-third for governmental representatives; and the new UN Forum on Indigenous Issues recruits half of its members from indigenous communities, thus balancing the power of states with the concerns of individuals. Such creative design allows institutions not only to integrate non-state actors, but also to accrue a higher degree of independence from governments.

Open as this system may be for non-state actors, the participation of the latter in global human rights institutions is still inadequate, as we have repeatedly shown. There is also no uniform attitude towards NGO participation in such institutions. Some remain diffident or hostile towards NGOs (such as the Third Committee of the General Assembly or the WTO), while others cooperate closely with NGOs, which raises their credibility or effectiveness. Moreover, some institutions recruit their members from a combined academic/NGO background and, as a consequence, may be perceived as both an international institution and as part of the scientific community. Such is the case with the Sub-Commission on the Promotion and Protection of Human Rights (at least with regard to some of its members).

The fragile grounds on which NGOs rest their claim to be representative and the legal constraints they face in accessing global human rights institutions have been highlighted above and need not be repeated here. Still, these institutions are at the forefront of assigning space for the participation of non-governmental actors and often join forces with them in a common attempt to promote and protect human rights, even where this may meet with governmental resistance. The ILO and UN institutions, in particular, demonstrate that such 'democratizing' of international law-making is viable (Alvarez, 2006: 332), and they provide a glimpse into a future of a more democratic and participatory international legal order.

# Power, law and politics

Throughout our analysis we have encountered critique on the credibility and legitimacy of global human rights institutions on the account that they are 'politicized'. Indeed, such institutions do not operate on a level playing field; nor does the matter they manage – human rights – elevate them above the murky waters of politics. Like all institutions, they are characterized by inequalities in power. Powerful states exert influence which may seem disproportionate, and hegemonic states or groups of states shape the form and function of global human rights institutions often with little regard for their human rights mandate. Yet, we have concluded that decrying the 'politicization' of global human rights institutions or wishing to dispossess them of the political is unrealistic and unhelpful. Human rights are essentially political, and the struggle to decide on human rights standards and to implement them is fundamentally political. The creation of a law-versus-policy dichotomy, in which those activists taking the side of human rights position themselves as guardians of law which counters political ideology, has been questioned (Mutua, 2001: 158). A similar position may be taken towards creating such a dichotomy in global human rights institutions.

This relates, first and foremost, but not exclusively, to bodies composed of governmental representatives such as the Human Rights Council. As we have demonstrated, states' decisions over resources and design are 'political' decisions. Consequently, they also impact profoundly on allegedly 'legal' institutions such as UN treaty bodies and international courts. The realization that state power continues to matter within international organizations (Alvarez, 2006: 346), including human rights institutions, must not lead us to seek refuge in utopia but to strive for transparent processes, civil society participation and accountability for misbehaviour. Eliminating pathological developments without eradicating the political character of human rights is the challenge. Some innovations give rise to hope, such as the universal periodic review procedure in the Human Rights Council, which perhaps will help to curtail power inequalities.

And, finally, power and authority, as we have seen in chapter 2, rest not solely on territorial sovereignty, or even necessarily on military or economic might. Human rights are in themselves a persuasive power which can provide a counterweight to traditional forms of power. In an international system which is in flux, struggling to accommodate state interests with ethical values and gradually opening up to non-state actors, states find it not only increasingly hard to ignore this new form of power but, on the contrary, seek to exploit if for their own purposes.

# A regulatory framework for failures

Institutions matter, but not always as desired. The more activities global human rights institutions undertake the more striking their failures become. The risks of delegating authority to international institutions call for the creation of mechanisms to ensure their transparency and accountability (Alvarez, 2006: 344). One need not believe that 'a network of economic, social and political international institutions has been established or repositioned, at the initiative of the first world', which 'constitute[s] a nascent global state whose function is to realize the interests of transnational capital and powerful states in the international system to the disadvantage of the third world states and peoples' (Chimni, 2004: 1–2), to see that entrusting international institutions with ever more functions needs to correspond with a regulatory framework.

An idealist view of global human rights institutions is out of place. They are not necessarily always beneficial on two grounds: first, as discussed above, their nature as bureaucracies may entail negative consequences; and, second, when they fail, there is as yet no framework available to remedy such failures. The critique of being unaccountable, which is levelled against international institutions in general, is particularly apposite for human rights institutions, as respect for fundamental rights such as the rule of law, non-discrimination, due process, fair trial, participation, and gender equality should be a matter of routine for institutions which were, after all, set up to promote precisely these values. Understanding and regulating the accountability of international institutions, both governmental and non-governmental, is a challenge ahead, and we have repeatedly alluded to the means and consequences of such regulatory frameworks in the previous chapters. If global human rights institutions are to continue to matter, they must not only overcome the pitfalls of bureaucracy, strive for creative design to balance the drawbacks of an inadequate international order, and respond to the political nature of human rights, but also develop such a regulatory framework to address their failures.

In creating such a framework, however, one needs to be careful not to fall into the trap set up by those who, under the pretext of enhancing the accountability of global human rights institutions, seek in effect to curtail their autonomy. In the reform of such UN human rights institutions which have achieved a considerable degree of autonomy (first and foremost treaty bodies and special procedures), calls for 'streamlining' and 'rationalizing' their work are little more than attempts to subject them to governmental control. We have, for example, dissected the lack of an extensive regulatory mechanism for UN special rapporteurs as one of the components of their success. The necessary search for holding human rights institutions to account for their failures must not trample such valuable creations underfoot.

## Persuasion and coercion

With the exception of the Security Council, global human rights institutions have to rely on persuasion rather than coercion when they seek to influence states to introduce change on the domestic level. Notwithstanding the legal nature of human rights obligations, whatever power global human rights institutions have rests on persuasion. Treaty bodies' 'views' are mere recommendations; in their reports special rapporteurs 'draw attention' to facts and 'recommend' action to states; the Human Rights Council 'urges' states to accede to its requests, etc. The output which global human rights institutions produce is 'soft law'. Even international courts fare no better: the ICJ's requests for interim measures are not bolstered by any form of international enforcement, and the ICC has to wait for states to deliver accused criminals to the court room. Creative suggestions as a way out, such as the establishment of a 'UN constabulary force' (Mendlovitz and Fousek, 2001) with mixed peace-keeping and police functions to prevent, in particular, future cases of genocide, provide safe havens and arrest alleged perpetrators, have not taken hold in the international debate.

Desirable and necessary as it is to give international human rights institutions stronger enforcement means, the way in which such institutions can, even today, apply their persuasive power to induce change should not be underrated. The application of soft forms of compliance to enforce social norms is characteristic of today's international legal order (Shelton, 2006: 319), and global human rights institutions are very much in line with this. Observers concede that states, far from routinely ignoring or dismissing such resolutions and recommendations, use them in their international relations, as do NGOs and other participants in international affairs (Alvarez, 2006: 329). In pouring out a constant flow of such 'soft-law' texts, global human rights institutions are a major contributor to this process. Some criteria may be discerned which can make global human rights institutions more successful in applying these soft forms of pressure (Donnelly, 2006: 108): their application must be non-selective, consistent, and backed by some larger form of political organization. The ILO may be an example in the way it consistently follows up recommendations, takes on board non-state participants in this follow-up, links it with technical assistance, and involves high political bodies if necessary. Other institutions have yet to match the ILO's approach.

## Process and output

When considering the output of global human rights institutions it is also worth noting that what constitutes success and failure may well lie in the eye of the beholder. The human rights diplomat will be delighted to have brought an issue onto the agenda of a global human rights institution for discussion, while the human rights activist will despair that no decision was taken on the issue. What is, in human rights terms, a success for the World Bank may seem futile to an NGO. What human rights activists may consider an inherent structural deficit of an international body may precisely reflect the will of member states, because they have set up an institution designed to be weak. Furthermore, the dichotomy of international institutions as actors and arenas calls for a sophisticated critique: is failure attributable to an autonomous act of the institution or did member states instrumentalize it? The question whether the deviation from an institution's original purpose is a success or a failure may equally divide observers, as is the case with the World Bank's cautious acceptance of human rights as being within its remit.

More importantly, it is not only the output of global human rights institutions which matters; process matters just as much. Participation in global institutions 'builds habits and attitudes that facilitate and foster cooperation' (Bennett and Oliver, 2002: 447). The participatory nature of most global human rights institutions, the way in which they disseminate 'information' on human rights (standards, interpretations, national experiences, best practices, etc.), and the associated processes of socialization and learning of various stakeholders are as important as the results of such processes (Smith, 2006: 291–4). Such socializing factors can be observed in a number of processes, for example, the way in which states had to argue their case rather than simply assert a position in negotiating resolutions in the Commission on Human Rights; the confrontations between international expert and national civil servants in treaty bodies' discussions of state reports, which aim at shaping a uniform understanding of human rights norms; and the changes induced in international bureaucracies when human rights are being mainstreamed into these institutions.

## From vision to reality

Global human rights institutions reflect the move from vision to reality, and this is the most substantial contribution they make to the idea of human rights. They allow the move from the acknowledgment of values to their realization on the international level: agreeing on community norms, casting them in legal form, and inventing tools, mechanisms and instruments. Where, for example, there was once a claim to work under humane conditions, today there is the tripartite ILO structure which allows workers' organizations to participate in the drafting and supervision of international legal obligations on working conditions. When once war lords could look forward to spending their old age in luxury, today they may have to board a chartered plane to The Hague, as was the experience of Thomas Lubanga Dyilo, the first person to be tried before the ICC. And where, not long ago, 'concern' and 'understanding' for the needs of disabled persons was voiced by governments on the international level, since its adoption on 13 December 2006 there has been a legally binding international document, the UN Convention on the Rights of Persons with Disabilities, which assigns entitlements and duties. Who else but global human rights institutions can bring this about?

Global human rights institutions can transform ideas into law, and law into change, in a way that is less haphazard and unpredictable than the actions of states. We have described the many functions they fulfil as an agora; as agenda-setting and decision-making bodies; in standard-setting, interpreting and adjudicating norms; in implementing these norms, monitoring compliance and assisting governments; in operational activities; in seeking to remedy and prevent human rights violations; in substituting domestic processes; and in fostering social change. These may be tedious technical activities, guided by rules of procedure and driven by bureaucratic demands. We have considered the downsides of such a legalistic, institutional approach and how it may narrow our full engagement with the broader idea and vision of human rights. The output of global human rights institutions may often be scant and their power may rest solely on persuasion. Yet, they realize, in a practical manner, what would otherwise remain a philosophical, moral, religious or political discourse, and as such would be even more remote from meeting the demands of those whose dignity is being trampled upon.

The spread of international institutions seems to be founded on the logic that what begins as a utopian aspiration for improving the world either peters out or ends as institutional accomplishment (Kennedy, 1987: 985). What once was utopian has indeed become practice: global human rights institutions meddle with national administrations, poke into ballot boxes, drag mass murderers before tribunals, sponsor judicial education, draft labour laws and rummage around prison cells. They represent a practical, hard-nosed approach to spelling out community norms, shaping their content, realizing them on the ground and deterring deviant behaviour. There may be little glamour in such an approach, which transforms fundamental values into tasks, projects and programmes, ties them down to norms, codes and guidelines, and squeezes them into procedures and mechanisms. Administering and managing human rights, dispersing them into diverse institutional formats and diffusing them in an ever wider array of governmental and human activities may be unexciting and uninspiring and be accompanied by deficiencies and failures common to bureaucracies. This, however, is what it means to pursue a utopian aspiration in a tight political and normative framework, and this is what global human rights institutions do. After all, the road from vision to reality is called pragmatism.

# REFERENCES

Abbott, Kenneth W., and Duncan Snidal 2001: Why states act through formal international organizations. In Paul Diehl (ed.), *The Politics of Global Governance: International Organizations in an Interdependent World*. Boulder, CO: Lynne Rienner, 9–43.

Abi-Saab, Georges 1999: International criminal tribunals and the development of international humanitarian and human rights law. In Emile Yakpo and Tahar Boumedra (eds), *Liber Amicorum Judge Mohammed Bedjaoui*. The Hague: Kluwer, 649–58.

Abraham, Meghna 2006: *A New Chapter for Human Rights: A Handbook on Issues of Transition from the Commission on Human Rights to the Human Rights Council*. Geneva: International Service for Human Rights and Friedrich Ebert Stiftung.

Ainetter, Christine 2002: International human rights law: the relevance of gender. In Wolfgang Benedek, Esther M. Kisaakye and Gerd Oberleitner (eds), *The Human Rights of Women: International Instruments and African Experiences*. London: Zed Books, 3–29.

Alger, Chadwick 2003: Evolving roles of NGOs in member state decision-making in the UN system. *Journal of Human Rights* 2(3), 407–24.

Allott, Philip 1990: *Eunomia: New Order for a New World*. Oxford: Oxford University Press.

Alston, Philip 1992: The Commission on Human Rights. In Philip Alston (ed.), *The United Nations and Human Rights: A Critical Appraisal*. Oxford: Clarendon Press, 126–210.

Alston, Philip 1997: Neither fish nor foul: the role of the High Commissioner for Human Rights. *European Journal of International Law* 8(2), 321–36.

Alston, Philip 2000: Beyond 'them' and 'us': putting treaty body reform into perspective. In Philip Alston and James Crawford (eds), *The Future of UN Human Rights Treaty Monitoring*. Cambridge: Cambridge University Press, 501–26.

Alston, Philip 2001: The historical origins of the concept of 'general comments' in human rights law. In Laurence Boisson de Chazournes and Vera Gowlland-Debbas (eds), *The International Legal System in Quest of Equity and Universality: Liber Amicorum Georges Abi-Saab*. The Hague: Nijhoff, 763–76.

Alston, Philip 2005: The 'not-a-cat' syndrome: can the international human rights regime accommodate non-state actors? In Philip Alston (ed.), *Non-State Actors and Human Rights*. Oxford: Oxford University Press, 3–36.

Alvarez, José E. 2005: *International Organizations as Law-Makers*. Oxford: Oxford University Press.

Alvarez, José E. 2006: International organizations: now and then. *American Journal of International Law* 100(2), 324–47.

Amnesty International 2002: *2003 Commission on Human Rights: A Time for Deep Reflection*. London: Amnesty International [IOR 41/025/2002].

Amnesty International 2005: *United Nations Special Procedures: Building on a Cornerstone of Human Rights*. London: Amnesty International [IOR 40/017/2005].

Annan, Kofi 1999: Two concepts of sovereignty. *The Economist*, 18 September.

Archer, Clive 2001: *International Organizations*. London: Routledge.

Baehr, Peter R. 1998: Mobilization of the conscience of mankind: conditions and effectiveness of human rights NGOs. In Erik Denters and Nico Schrijver (eds), *Reflections on International Law from the Low Countries: In Honour of Paul de Waart*. The Hague: Nijhoff, 135–55.

Bailey, Sidney D. 1992: The Security Council. In Philip Alston (ed.), *The United Nations and Human Rights: A Critical Appraisal*. Oxford: Clarendon Press, 304–36.

Bailey, Sidney D. 1994: *The UN Security Council and Human Rights*. Basingstoke: Macmillan.

Barnett, Michael, and Martha Finnemore 1999: The politics, power and pathologies of international organizations. *International Organization* 53(4), 699–732.

Barnett, Michael, and Martha Finnemore 2004: *Rules for the World: International Organizations in Global Politics*. Ithaca, NY: Cornell University Press.

Bayefsky, Anne 2001: *The UN Human Rights Treaty System: Universality at the Crossroads*. Ardsley, NY: Transnational.

Benedek, Wolfgang 1999: Developing the constitutional order of the WTO – the role of NGOs. In Wolfgang Benedek, Hubert Isak and Renate Kicker (eds), *Development and Developing International and European Law: Essays in Honour of Konrad Ginther*. Frankfurt: Peter Lang, 228–50.

Benedek, Wolfgang 2007: The World Trade Organization and human rights. In Wolfgang Benedek, Koen de Feyter and Fabrizio Marrella (eds), *Economic Globalisation and Human Rights*. Cambridge: Cambridge University Press, 228–49.

Bennett, A. LeRoy, and James K. Oliver 2002: *International Organizations: Principles and Issues*. London: Pearson.

Boekle, Henning 1995: Western states, the UN Commission on Human Rights, and the '1235'-procedure: the question of bias revisited. *Netherlands Quarterly of Human Rights* 13, 367–402.

Boisson de Chazournes, Laurence 2001: Access to justice: the World Bank Inspection Panel. In Gudmundur Alfredsson, Jonas Grimheden, Bertrand Ramcharan and Alfred de Zayas (eds), *International Human Rights Monitoring Mechanisms: Essays in Honour of Jakob Th. Möller*. The Hague: Nijhoff, 513–20.

Boli, John, and George M. Thomas 1997: World culture in the world polity: a century of international non-governmental organization. *American Sociological Review* 62, 171–90.

Bollé, Patrick 1998: Supervising labour standards and human rights: the case of forced labour in Myanmar (Burma). *International Labour Review* 137(2), 391–409.

Bossuyt, Marc 1985: The development of special procedures of the United Nations Commission on Human Rights. *Human Rights Law Journal* 6(2–4), 179–210.

Bossuyt, Marc 2006: The new Human Rights Council: a first appraisal. *Netherlands Quarterly of Human Rights* 24(4), 551–5.

Boyle, Kevin 2003: The United Nations High Commissioner for Human Rights and the Commissioner for Human Rights of the Council of Europe. In Richard Bourne (ed.), *A Strengthened Human Rights Mechanism for the Commonwealth*. London: Commonwealth Policy Study Unit, 23–40.

Breen, Claire 2005: Rationalising the work of UN human rights bodies or reducing the input of NGOs? The changing role of human rights NGOs at the United Nations. *Non-State Actors and International Law* 5(2), 101–26.

Brett, Rachel 2001: Role of NGOs – an overview. In Gudmundur Alfredsson, Jonas Grimheden, Bertrand Ramcharan and Alfred de Zayas (eds), *International Human Rights Monitoring Mechanisms: Essays in Honour of Jakob Th. Möller*. The Hague: Nijhoff, 845–54.

Brodnig, Gernot 2005: *The World Bank and Human Rights: Mission Impossible?* Carr Center for Human Rights Policy Working Paper T-01-05, http://www.ksg.harvard.edu/cchrp/Web%20Working%20Papers/Brodnig HR&WorldBank.pdf.

Buergenthal, Thomas 2001: The U.N. Human Rights Committee. *Max Planck Yearbook of United Nations Law* 5, 341–98.

Canada 2006: *Human Rights Peer Review Mechanism*, non-paper version #2, http://www.eyeontheun.org/assets/attachments/documents/hr_peer_review_mechanism_canada.pdf.

Carey, John, and Siegfried Wiessner 2001: A new United Nations subsidiary organ: the Permanent Forum on Indigenous Issues. *ASIL Insights*, http://www.asil.org/insights/insigh67.htm.

Cassese, Antonio 1992: The General Assembly: historical perspective 1945–1989. In Philip Alston (ed.), *The United Nations and Human Rights: A Critical Appraisal*. Oxford: Clarendon Press, 25–54.

Charlesworth, Hillary, and Christine Chinkin 2000: *The Boundaries of International law: A Feminist Analysis*. Manchester: Manchester University Press.

Charnovitz, Steve 1997: Two centuries of participation: NGOs and international governance. *Michigan Journal of International Law* 8, 183–286.

Charnovitz, Steve 2000: The International Labour Organization in its second century. *Max Planck Yearbook of United Nations Law* 4, 147–84.

Charnovitz, Steve 2006: Non-governmental organizations and international law. *American Journal of International Law* 100(2), 348–72.

Chimni, B. S. 2004: International institutions today: an imperial global state in the making. *European Journal of International Law* 15(1), 1–37.

Chinkin, Christine 1998: The role of non-governmental organisations in standard setting, monitoring and implementation of human rights. In Joseph J. Norton, Mads Andenas and Mary Footer (eds), *The Changing World of International Law in the Twenty-First Century*. The Hague: Kluwer, 45–66.

Chinkin, Christine 2000: Human rights and the politics of representation: is there a role for international law? In Michael Byers (ed.), *The Role of International Law in International Politics*. Oxford: Oxford University Press, 131–47.

Chinkin, Christine 2001: Women's International Tribunal on Japanese Military Sexual Slavery. *American Journal of International Law* 95, 335–40.

Clapham, Andrew 1994: Creating the High Commissioner for Human Rights: the outside story. *European Journal of International Law* 5, 556–68.

Clapham, Andrew 2006: *Human Rights Obligations of Non-State Actors*. Oxford: Oxford University Press.

Clark, Dana L. 2002: The World Bank and human rights: the need for greater accountability. *Harvard Human Rights Journal* 15, 205–26.

Claude, Inis L. 1984: *Swords into Ploughshares: The Problems and Progress of International Organization*. 4th edn, New York: Random House.

Cohen, Roberta 2005: The Guiding Principles on Internal Displacement: an innovation in standard setting. *Global Governance* 10(4), 459–80.

Cohn, Marjorie 2001: The World Trade Organization: elevating property interests above human rights. *Georgia Journal of International and Comparative Law* 29(3), 427–40.

Commission on Global Governance 1995: *Our Global Neighbourhood*. Oxford: Oxford University Press.

Cook, Helena 1993: The role of the special procedures in the protection of human rights: the way forward after Vienna. *Review of the International Commission of Jurists* 50, 31–55.

Coomans, Fons 1999: UNESCO and human rights. In Raija Hanski and Markku Suksi (eds), *An Introduction to the International Protection of*

*Human Rights.* Turku/Abö: Institute for Human Rights, Abö Akademi University, 219–30.

Cottier, Thomas, Joost Pauwelyn and Elisabeth Bürgi 2005: Linking trade regulation and human rights in international law: an overview. In Thomas Cottier, Joost Pauwelyn and Elisabeth Bürgi Bonanomi (eds), *Human Rights and International Trade.* Oxford: Oxford University Press, 1–26.

Cox, Laura 1999: The International Labour Organisation and fundamental rights at work. *European Human Rights Law Review* (5), 451–8.

Crawford, James 2000: The UN human rights treaty system: a system in crisis? In Philip Alston and James Crawford (eds), *The Future of UN Human Rights Treaty Monitoring.* Cambridge: Cambridge University Press, 1–12.

Daes, Erica-Irene A. 2001: A United Nations permanent forum for the world's indigenous peoples – a global imperative. In Gudmundur Alfredsson, Jonas Grimheden, Bertrand Ramcharan and Alfred de Zayas (eds), *International Human Rights Monitoring Mechanisms: Essays in Honour of Jakob Th. Möller.* The Hague: Nijhoff, 371–9.

Danino, Robert 2004: *The Legal Aspects of the World Bank's Work on Human Rights,* http://siteresources.worldbank.org/INTLAWJUSTICE/214576113960430696/20817164/HumanRightsNewYork030104.pdf.

Dao, H. T. 1993: The reform of the human rights institutions in the International Labour Organisation. In La Laguna University (ed.), *The Reform of International Institutions for the Protection of Human Rights.* Brussels: Bruylant, 141–60.

Darrow, Mac 2003: *Between Light and Shadow: The World Bank, the International Monetary Fund and International Human Rights Law.* Oxford: Hart.

Das, Kamleshwar 2001: The early days. In Gudmundur Alfredsson, Jonas Grimheden, Bertrand Ramcharan and Alfred de Zayas (eds), *International Human Rights Monitoring Mechanisms: Essays in Honour of Jakob Th. Möller.* The Hague: Nijhoff, 15–7.

de Zayas, Alfred 2001: The examination of individual complaints by the United Nations Human Rights Committee under the Optional Protocol to the International Covenant on Civil and Political Rights. In Gudmundur Alfredsson, Jonas Grimheden, Bertrand Ramcharan and Alfred de Zayas (eds), *International Human Rights Monitoring Mechanisms: Essays in Honour of Jakob Th. Möller.* The Hague: Nijhoff, 67–121.

Dimitrijevic, Vojin 2001: State reports. In Gudmundur Alfredsson, Jonas Grimheden, Bertrand Ramcharan and Alfred de Zayas (eds), *International Human Rights Monitoring Mechanisms: Essays in Honour of Jakob Th. Möller.* The Hague: Nijhoff, 185–200.

Dommen, Caroline 2005: The WTO, international trade and human rights. In Michael Windfuhr (ed.), *Beyond the Nation State: Human Rights in Times of Globalization.* Uppsala: Global Publications Foundation, 52–74.

Dommen, Caroline 2006: Safeguarding the legitimacy of the multilateral trading system: the role of human rights law. In Frederick M. Abbott, Christine Breining-Kaufmann and Thomas Cottier (eds), *International*

*Trade and Human Rights: Foundations and Conceptual Issues*. Ann Arbor: University of Michigan Press, 121–32.

Donnelly, Jack 1984: International human rights: a regime analysis. *International Organization* 40(3), 599–642.

Donnelly, Jack 2003: *Universal Human Rights in Theory and Practice*. Ithaca, NY: Cornell University Press.

Donnelly, Jack 2006: *International Human Rights*. Boulder, CO: Westview Press.

Duxbury, Alison 2000: Saving lives in the International Court of Justice: the use of provisional measures to protect human rights. *California Western International Law Journal* 31(1), 141–76.

Eide, Asbjorn 1992: The Sub-Commission on Prevention of Discrimination and Protection of Minorities. In Philip Alston (ed.), *The United Nations and Human Rights: A Critical Appraisal*. Oxford: Clarendon Press, 211–64.

Eide, Asbjorn 2001a: The role of the Sub-Commission on Promotion and Protection of Human Rights and its working groups in the prevention of conflicts. *International Journal on Minority and Group Rights* 8(1), 25–9.

Eide, Asbjorn 2001b: Minorities at the United Nations: from standard-setting to the Working Group on Minorities. In Gudmundur Alfredsson, Jonas Grimheden, Bertrand Ramcharan and Alfred de Zayas (eds), *International Human Rights Monitoring Mechanisms: Essays in Honour of Jakob Th. Möller*. The Hague: Nijhoff, 381–90.

Ermacora, Felix 1993: The reform of the human rights institutions of the United Nations. In La Laguna University (ed.), *The Reform of International Institutions for the Protection of Human Rights*. Brussels: Bruylant, 133–42.

Evatt, Elizabeth 2000: Ensuring effective supervisory procedures: the need for resources. In Philip Alston and James Crawford (eds), *The Future of UN Human Rights Treaty Monitoring*. Cambridge: Cambridge University Press, 461–79.

Flinterman, Cees 1999: Extra-conventional standard-setting and implementation in the field of human rights. In Raija Hanski and Markku Suksi (eds), *An Introduction to the International Protection of Human Rights*. Turku/Abô: Institute for Human Rights, Abô Akademi University, 143–50.

Flood, Patrick 1998: *The Effectiveness of UN Human Rights Institutions*. Westport, CT: Praeger.

Forsythe, David P. 2006: *Human Rights in International Relations*. 2nd edn, Cambridge: Cambridge University Press.

Fowler, Alan 1997: *Striking a Balance: A Guide to Enhancing the Effectiveness of Non-Governmental Organizations in International Development*. London: Earthscan.

Franck, Thomas M. 1984: Is there a double standard in the United Nations? *American Journal of International Law* 78, 811–33.

Freeman, Anthony G. 2005: ILO: a case study in mainstreaming human rights. In Michael Windfuhr (ed.), *Beyond the Nation State: Human Rights in Times of Globalization*. Uppsala: Global Publications Foundation, 96–138.

Freeman, Michael 2002: *Human Rights*. Cambridge: Polity.

Gaer, Felice D. 2003: Implementing international human rights norms: UN human rights treaty bodies and NGOs. *Journal of Human Rights* 2(3), 339–57.

Gallagher, Anne 1999a: Human rights in the wider United Nations system. In Raija Hanski and Markku Suksi (eds), *An Introduction to the International Protection of Human Rights*. Turku/Abồ: Institute for Human Rights, Abồ Akademi University, 153–67.

Gallagher, Anne 1999b: United Nations human rights field operations. In Raija Hanski and Markku Suksi (eds), *An Introduction to the International Protection of Human Rights*. Turku/Abồ: Institute for Human Rights, Abồ Akademi University, 251–72.

Garland, Ross 2001: The International Court of Justice and human rights in the 1990s – linking peace and justice through the right to life. In Sienho Yee and Wang Tieya (eds), *International Law in the Post-Cold War World: Essays in Memory of Li Haopei*. London: Routledge, 398–408.

Gaudart, Dorothea 2002: Charter-based activities regarding women's rights in the United Nations and specialized agencies. In Wolfgang Benedek, Esther M. Kisaakye and Gerd Oberleitner (eds), *The Human Rights of Women: International Instruments and African Experiences*. London: Zed Books, 50–104.

Gearty, Conor 2006: *Can Human Rights Survive? The Hamlyn Lectures 2005*. Cambridge: Cambridge University Press.

Ghandhi, P. R. 2000: The Human Rights Committee: developments in jurisprudence, practice and procedures. *Indian Journal of International Law* 40(3), 405–54.

Gianviti, François 2001: Economic, social and cultural human rights and the International Monetary Fund. Paper delivered to the UN Committee on Economic, Social and Cultural Rights, UN doc. E/C.12/2001/WP.5.

Gorlick, Brian 2000: Human rights and refugees: enhancing protection through international human rights law. *Journal of Humanitarian Assistance*, http://www.jha.ac/articles/u030.htm.

Grant, Stefanie 2006: Functional distinction or bilingualism? Human rights and trade: the UN human rights system. In Frederick M. Abbott, Christine Breining-Kaufmann and Thomas Cottier (eds), *International Trade and Human Rights: Foundations and Conceptual Issues*. Ann Arbor: University of Michigan Press, 133–44.

Grimheden, Jonas 2001: The International Court of Justice in furthering the justiciability of human rights. In Gudmundur Alfredsson, Jonas Grimheden, Bertrand Ramcharan and Alfred de Zayas (eds), *International Human Rights Monitoring Mechanisms: Essays in Honour of Jakob Th. Möller*. The Hague: Nijhoff, 469–84.

Hannum, Hurst 2004: Implementing human rights: an overview of NGO strategies and available procedures. In Hurst Hannum (ed.), *Guide to International Human Rights Practice*. Ardsley, NY: Transnational, 19–39.

Hegarty, Angela 1999: Non-governmental organisations: the key to change. In Angela Hegarty and Siobhan Leonard (eds), *Human Rights: An Agenda for the 21st Century*. London: Cavendish, 267–85.

Heintze, Hans-Joachim 2004: On the relationship between human rights law protection and international humanitarian law. *International Review of the Red Cross* 86(856), 789–813.

Higgins, Rosalyn 1997: Interim measures for the protection of human rights. In Jonathan I. Charney, Donald K. Anton and Mary Ellen O'Connell (eds), *Politics, Values and Functions: International Law in the 21st Century: Essays in Honour of Professor Louis Henkin*. The Hague: Nijhoff, 87–103.

Higgins, Rosalyn 1998: The International Court of Justice and human rights. In Karel Wellens (ed.), *International Law: Theory and Practice*. The Hague: Kluwer, 691–705.

Higgins, Rosalyn 2002: The International Court of Justice and human rights. In Frances Butler (ed.), *Human Rights Protection: Methods and Effectiveness*. London: Kluwer, 163–85.

Hobbins, A. J. 2001: Humphrey and the High Commissioner: the genesis of the Office of the UN High Commissioner for Human Rights. *Journal of the History of International Law* 3(1), 38–74.

Horta, Korinna 2002: Rhetoric and reality: human rights and the World Bank. *Harvard Human Rights Journal* 15, 227–43.

Howland, Todd 2004: UN human rights field presence as proactive instrument of peace and social change. Lessons from Angola. *Human Rights Quarterly* 26(1), 1–28.

Humphrey, John P. 1984: *Human Rights and the United Nations: A Great Adventure*. Dobbs Ferry, NY: Transnational.

Hurlock, William L. 1997: The International Court of Justice: effectively providing a long overdue remedy for ending state-sponsored genocide (Bosnia-Herzegovina v. Yugoslavia). *American University Journal of Transnational Law and Policy* 12(2), 299–328.

ICISS (International Commission on Intervention and State Sovereignty) 2001: *The Responsibility to Protect*, http://www.iciss.ca/pdf/Commission-Report.pdf.

ILO (International Labour Office) 1976: *The Impact of International Labour Conventions and Recommendations*. Geneva: International Labour Office.

International Commission of Jurists 2005: *Reforming the United Nations Human Rights System: A Chance for the United Nations to Fulfil its Promise*. Geneva: International Commission of Jurists.

International Federation for Human Rights 2005: *Understanding Global Trade and Human Rights*. Geneva: International Federation for Human Rights.

Iwamoto, Yoshiyuki Lee 2002: The protection of human life through provisional measures indicated by the International Court of Justice. *Leiden Journal of International Law* 15(2), 345–66.

Ize-Charrin, Maria Francisca 2001: 1503: a serious procedure. In Gudmundur Alfredsson, Jonas Grimheden, Bertrand Ramcharan and Alfred de Zayas (eds), *International Human Rights Monitoring Mechanisms: Essays in Honour of Jakob Th. Möller*. The Hague: Nijhoff, 293–310.

Jenks, Wilfred C. 1960: *Human Rights and International Labour Standards*. London: Stevens.

Joachim, Jutta 2003: Framing issues and seizing opportunities: the UN, NGOs, and women's rights. *International Studies Quarterly* 47, 247–74.

Kälin, Walter, and Cecilia Jimenez 2003: Reform of the UN Commission on Human Rights. Study commissioned by the Swiss Ministry of Foreign Affairs. Bern: University of Bern.

Kedzia, Zdzislaw 2003: United Nations mechanisms to promote and protect human rights. In Janusz Symonides (ed.), *Human Rights: International Protection, Monitoring, Enforcement*. Aldershot: Ashgate, 3–90.

Kellerson, Hillary 1998: The ILO declaration of 1998 on fundamental principles and rights: a challenge for the future. *International Labour Review* 137(2), 223–7.

Kennedy, David 1987: The move to institutions. *Cardozo Law Review* 8(5), 841–988.

Kennedy, David 2002: The international human rights movement: part of the problem? *Harvard Human Rights Journal* 15, 101–25.

Kent, Ann E. 1999: *China, the United Nations, and Human Rights: The Limits of Compliance*. Philadelphia: University of Pennsylvania Press.

Kirkpatrick, Jeane 2003: UN human rights panel needs some entry standards. *International Herald Tribune*, 14 May.

Klabbers, Jan 2002: *An Introduction to International Institutional Law*. Cambridge: Cambridge University Press.

Krasner, Stephan 1983: *International Regimes*. Ithaca, NY: Cornell University Press.

Lang, Winfried 1994: Regimes and organizations in the labyrinth of international institutions. In Konrad Ginther, Gerhard Hafner, Winfried Lang, Hanspeter Neuhold and Lilly Sucharipa-Behrmann (eds), *Völkerrecht zwischen normativem Anspruch und politischer Realität: Festschrift für Karl Zemanek zum 65. Geburtstag*. Berlin: Duncker & Humblot, 275–89.

Leary, Virginia A. 1992: Lessons from the experience of the ILO. In Philip Alston (ed.), *The United Nations and Human Rights: A Critical Appraisal*. Oxford: Clarendon Press, 580–619.

Leary, Virginia A. 2001: International institutions: towards coherent multilateralism. In Laurence Boisson de Chazournes and Vera Gowlland-Debbas (eds), *The International Legal System in Quest of Equity and Universality: Liber Amicorum Georges Abi-Saab*. The Hague: Nijhoff, 823–9.

Lebakine, Guennadi 2003: Some reflections on the rules and procedures followed by the Sub-Commission for the Promotion and Protection of Human Rights. In Morten Bergsmo (ed.), *Human Rights and Criminal Justice for the Downtrodden: Essays in Honour of Asbjorn Eide*. Leiden: Nijhoff, 655–63.

Lempinen, Miko 2001: *Challenges Facing the System of Special Procedures of the United Nations Commission on Human Rights*. Turku/Abö: Institute for Human Rights, Abö Akademi University.

Leuprecht, Peter 2005: Brave new digital world? Reflections on the World Summit on the Information Society. *Revue québécoise de droit international* 18(1), 41–56.

Lewis-Anthony, Sian, and Martin Scheinin 2004: Treaty-based procedures for making human rights complaints within the UN system. In Hurst Hannum (ed.), *Guide to International Human Rights Practice*. Ardsley, NY: Transnational, 43–63.

Lindblom, Anne-Karin 2006: *Non-Governmental Organisations in International Law*. Cambridge: Cambridge University Press.

Lubell, Noam 2005: Challenges in applying human rights law to armed conflict. *International Review of the Red Cross* 87(860), 737–54.

McGoldrick, Dominick 1994: *The Human Rights Committee: Its Role in the Development of the International Covenant on Civil and Political Rights*. Oxford: Clarendon Press.

Machel, Graça 1996: *The Impact of Armed Conflict on Children*. New York: United Nations, UN doc. A/51/306.

Malone, David 1998: *Decision-Making in the UN Security Council: The Case of Haiti, 1990–1997*. Oxford: Clarendon Press.

Marceau, Gabrielle 2002: WTO dispute settlement and human rights. *European Human Rights Law Review* 13(4), 753–814.

Marceau, Gabrielle 2006: The WTO dispute settlement and human rights. In Frederick M. Abbott, Christine Breining-Kaufmann and Thomas Cottier (eds), *International Trade and Human Rights: Foundations and Conceptual Issues*. Ann Arbor: University of Michigan Press, 181–260.

Marks, Stephen P. 2004: The complaint procedure of the United Nations Educational, Scientific and Cultural Organization. In Hurst Hannum (ed.), *Guide to International Human Rights Practice*. Ardsley, NY: Transnational, 107–23.

Martin, Ian 2001: The High Commissioner's field operations. In Gudmundur Alfredsson, Jonas Grimheden, Bertrand Ramcharan and Alfred de Zayas (eds), *International Human Rights Monitoring Mechanisms: Essays in Honour of Jakob Th. Möller*. The Hague: Nijhoff, 403–14.

Mavrommatis, Andreas 2001: The first ten years of the Human Rights Committee. In Gudmundur Alfredsson, Jonas Grimheden, Bertrand Ramcharan and Alfred de Zayas (eds), *International Human Rights Monitoring Mechanisms: Essays in Honour of Jakob Th. Möller*. The Hague: Nijhoff, 147–52.

Mégret, Frédéric, and Florian Hoffmann 2003: The UN as human rights violator? Some reflections on the United Nations changing human rights responsibilities. *Human Rights Quarterly* 25, 314–42.

Mendez, Juan E. 2000: International human rights law, international humanitarian law, and international criminal law and procedure: new relationships. In Dinah Shelton (ed.), *International Crimes, Peace, and Human Rights: The*

*Role of the International Criminal Court.* Ardsley, NY: Transnational, 65–74.

Mendlovitz, Saul, and John Fousek 2001: A UN constabulary to enforce the law on genocide and crimes against humanity. In Laurence Boisson de Chazournes and Vera Gowlland-Debbas (eds), *The International Legal System in Quest of Equity and Universality: Liber Amicorum Georges Abi-Saab.* The Hague: Nijhoff, 449–61.

Mertus, Julie 2005: *United Nations and Human Rights.* London: Routledge.

Mokhiber, Craig C. 2001: The United Nations programme of technical cooperation in the field of human rights. In Gudmundur Alfredsson, Jonas Grimheden, Bertrand Ramcharan and Alfred de Zayas (eds), *International Human Rights Monitoring Mechanisms: Essays in Honour of Jakob Th. Möller.* The Hague: Nijhoff, 415–27.

Moore, Gerald 2005: FAO: towards a right to food approach? In Michael Windfuhr (ed.), *Beyond the Nation State: Human Rights in Times of Globalization.* Uppsala: Global Publications Foundation, 139–54.

Mosoti, Victor 2005: Institutional cooperation and norm creation in international organizations. In Thomas Cottier, Joost Pauwelyn and Elisabeth Bürgi Bonanomi (eds), *Human Rights and International Trade.* Oxford: Oxford University Press, 165–79.

Mukherjee, Bhaswati 2001: United Nations High Commissioner for Human Rights: challenges and opportunities. In Gudmundur Alfredsson, Jonas Grimheden, Bertrand Ramcharan and Alfred de Zayas (eds), *International Human Rights Monitoring Mechanisms: Essays in Honour of Jakob Th. Möller.* The Hague: Nijhoff, 391–402.

Mutua, Makau 2001: Human rights international NGOs: a critical evaluation. In Claude E. Welch Jr. (ed.), *NGOs and Human Rights: Promise and Performance.* Philadadelphia: University of Pennsylvania Press, 149–63.

Nowak, Manfred 1991: Country-oriented human rights protection by the UN Commission on Human Rights and its Sub-Commission. *Netherlands Yearbook of International Law* 22, 39–90.

Nowak, Manfred 2003: *Introduction to the International Human Rights Regime.* Leiden: Nijhoff.

Nowak, Manfred 2006: From the Human Rights Commission to the new Council. In Jessica Almqvist and Felipe Gómez Isa (eds), *The Human Rights Council: Challenges and Opportunities.* Madrid: Fundación para las Relaciones Internacionales y el Diálogo Exterior, 19–29.

Nygren-Krug, Helena 2005: *Integrating Human Rights in Health: Human Rights in the Context of Public Health.* Bulletin of Medicus Mundi Switzerland, no. 96.

Oberleitner, Gerd 1998: *Menschenrechtsschutz und Staatenberichte.* Frankfurt: Peter Lang.

Oberleitner, Gerd 2005: Human security: a challenge to international law? *Global Governance* 11(2), 185–203.

Oberleitner, Gerd 2007: Das UN Menschenrechtsystem und die Informations-gesellschaft. In Wolfgang Benedek and Catrin Pekari (eds), *Menschenrechte in der Informationsgesellschaft.* Stuttgart: Richard Boorberg, 53–76.

O'Byrne, Darren 2003: *Human Rights: An Introduction.* London: Longman.

O'Donovan, Declan 1992: The Economic and Social Council. In Philip Alston (ed.), *The United Nations and Human Rights: A Critical Appraisal.* Oxford: Clarendon Press, 105–25.

Oestreich, Joel E. 2004: The human rights responsibilities of the World Bank: a business paradigm. *Global Social Policy* 4(1), 55–76.

O'Flaherty, Michael 1993: *Human Rights and the UN: Practice before the Treaty Bodies.* London: Sweet & Maxwell.

Olivera, Oscar 2004: *Cochabamba!: Water War in Bolivia.* Cambridge, MA: South End Press.

Oloka-Onyango, J., and Deepika Udagama 2001: *Globalization and its Impact on the Full Enjoyment of Human Rights: Progress Report,* UN doc. E/CN.4/Sub.2/2001/10.

Ovett, Davinia 2007: Making trade policies more accountable and human rights-consistent: an NGO perspective of using human rights instruments in the case of access to medicines. In Wolfgang Benedek, Koen de Feyter and Fabrizio Marrella (eds), *Economic Globalisation and Human Rights.* Cambridge: Cambridge University Press, 271–302.

Pace, John P. 1998: The development of human rights law in the United Nations: its control and monitoring machinery. *International Social Science Journal* 50(158), 499–511.

Partsch, Karl Josef, and Klaus Hüfner 2003: UNESCO procedures for the protection of human rights. In Janusz Symonides (ed.), *Human Rights: International Protection, Monitoring, Enforcement.* Paris: UNESCO, 111–32.

Pauwelyn, Joost 2005: Human rights in WTO dispute settlement. In Thomas Cottier, Joost Pauwelyn and Elisabeth Bürgi Bonanomi (eds), *Human Rights and International Trade.* Oxford: Oxford University Press, 205–31.

Pennegard, A. M. Bolin 2001: Overview over human rights – the regime of the UN. In Gudmundur Alfredsson, Jonas Grimheden, Bertrand Ramcharan and Alfred de Zayas (eds), *International Human Rights Monitoring Mechanisms: Essays in Honour of Jakob Th. Möller.* The Hague: Nijhoff, 19–66.

Pereira Leite, Sérgio 2001: Human rights and the IMF. *Finance and Development* 38(4); http://www.imf.org/external/pubs/ft/fandd/2001/12/leite.htm.

Petersmann, Ernst-Ulrich 2001: *Time for Integrating Human Rights into the Law of Worldwide Organizations: Lessons from European Integration Law for Global Integration Law.* Jean Monnet Working Paper 7. New York: Harvard Law School.

Petersmann, Ernst-Ulrich 2003: Human rights in the law of the World Trade Organization. *Journal of World Trade* 37(2), 241–81.

Provost, René 2002: *International Human Rights and Humanitarian Law*. Cambridge: Cambridge University Press.

Quinn, John 1992: The General Assembly into the 1990s. In Philip Alston (ed.), *The United Nations and Human Rights: A Critical Appraisal*. Oxford: Clarendon Press, 55–106.

Rahmani-Ocora, Ladan 2006: Giving the emperor real clothes: the UN Human Rights Council. *Global Governance* 12(1), 15–20.

Ramcharan, Bertrand 2002a: *Human Rights and Human Security*. The Hague: Kluwer.

Ramcharan, Bertrand 2002b: *The Security Council and the Protection of Human Rights*. The Hague: Nijhoff.

Ramcharan, Bertrand 2002c: *The United Nations High Commissioner for Human Rights: The Challenges of Protection*. The Hague: Nijhoff.

Reanda, Laura 1992: The Commission on the Status of Women. In Philip Alston (ed.), *The United Nations and Human Rights: A Critical Appraisal*. Oxford: Clarendon Press, 265–303.

Rechenberg, Hermann H.-K. 1997: Non-governmental organisations. In Rudolf Bernhardt (ed.), *Encyclopedia of Public International Law*. Amsterdam: Elsevier, 612–19.

Rehman, Javaid 2003: *International Human Rights Law: A Practical Approach*. London: Longman.

Ricca, Michele 2002: Human rights and the UN special rapporteurs' system: tendencies in reporting on conflict areas. *Humanitäres Völkerrecht* 15(3), 165–74.

Rice, Andrew E., and Cyril Ritchie 1995: Relationships between international non-governmental organizations and the United Nations. *Transnational Associations* 47(5), 254–65.

Rieter, Eva 1998: Interim measures by the world court to suspend the execution of an individual: the Breard case. *Netherlands Quarterly of Human Rights* 16(4), 475–94.

Risse, Thomas, Steven C. Ropp and Kathryn Sikkink 1999: *The Power of Human Rights: International Norms and Domestic Change*. Cambridge: Cambridge University Press.

Rodley, Nigel 2001: Urgent action. In Gudmundur Alfredsson, Jonas Grimheden, Bertrand Ramcharan and Alfred de Zayas (eds), *International Human Rights Monitoring Mechanisms: Essays in Honour of Jakob Th. Möller*. The Hague: Nijhoff, 279–83.

Rodley, Nigel 2002: The evolution of United Nations' charter-based machinery for the protection of human rights. In Frances Butler (ed.), *Human Rights Protection: Methods and Effectiveness*. London: Kluwer, 188–96.

Rodley, Nigel 2003: United Nations human rights treaty bodies and special procedures of the Commission on Human Rights – complementarity or competition? *Human Rights Quarterly* 25, 882–908.

Ron, James, Harold Ramos and Kathleen Rodgers 2005: Transnational information politics: NGO human rights reporting, 1985–2000. *International Studies Quarterly* 49(3), 557–88.

Roth, Kenneth 2005: The UN reform agenda and human rights. In Paul Heinbecker and Patricia Goff (eds), *Irrelevant or Indispensable? The United Nations in the Twenty-First Century.* Waterloo, Ont.: Wilfried Laurier University Press, 131–9.

Rudolf, Beate 2000: The thematic rapporteurs and working groups of the United Nations Commission on Human Rights. *Max Planck Yearbook of United Nations Law* 4, 289–329.

Samson, Klaus, and Kenneth Schindler 1999: The standard-setting and supervisory system of the International Labour Organisation. In Raija Hanski and Markku Suksi (eds), *An Introduction to the International Protection of Human Rights.* Turku/Åbö: Institute for Human Rights, Åbö Akademi University, 185–218.

Santos Pais, Marta 1999: *A Human Rights Conceptual Framework for UNICEF.* Florence: United Nations Children's Fund, http://www.unicef-icdc.org/publications/pdf/essay9.pdf.

Schabas, William 2003: Criminal responsibility for violations of human rights. In Janusz Symonides (ed.), *Human Rights: Protection, Monitoring, Enforcement.* Paris: UNESCO, 281–302.

Schmidt, Markus G. 1999: The Office of the United Nations High Commissioner for Human Rights. In Raija Hanski and Markku Suksi (eds), *An Introduction to the International Protection of Human Rights.* Turku/Åbö: Institute for Human Rights, Åbö Akademi University, 169–84.

Schmidt, Markus G. 2000: Servicing and financing human rights supervision. In Philip Alston and James Crawford (eds), *The Future of UN Human Rights Treaty Monitoring.* Cambridge: Cambridge University Press, 481–98.

Schmidt, Markus G. 2001: Follow-up procedures to individual complaints and periodic state reporting mechanisms. In Gudmundur Alfredsson, Jonas Grimheden, Bertrand Ramcharan and Alfred de Zayas (eds), *International Human Rights Monitoring Mechanisms: Essays in Honour of Jakob Th. Möller.* The Hague: Nijhoff, 201–15.

Schmitz, Hans Peter, and Kathryn Sikkink 2002: International human rights. In Walter Carlsnaes, Thomas Risse and Beth A. Simmons (eds), *Handbook of International Relations.* London: Sage, 517–37.

Shelton, Dinah 2006: Normative hierarchy in international law. *American Journal of International Law* 100(2), 291–323.

Simmons, Beth A., and Lisa L. Martin 2002: International organizations and institutions. In Walter Carlsnaes, Thomas Risse and Beth A. Simmons (eds), *Handbook of International Relations.* London: Sage, 192–211.

Skogly, Sigrun 1999: The position of the World Bank and the International Monetary Fund in the human rights field. In Raija Hanski and Markku Suksi (eds), *An Introduction to the International Protection of Human Rights.* Turku/Åbö: Institute for Human Rights, Åbö Akademi University, 231–50.

Skogly, Sigrun 2003: The human rights obligations of the World Bank and IMF. In Willem van Genugten, Paul Hunt and Susan Mathews (eds), *The*

*World Bank, IMF and Human Rights.* Nijmegen: Wolf Legal Publishers, 45–78.

Skogly, Sigrun 2005: The Bretton Woods institutions – have human rights come in from the cold? In Michael Windfuhr (ed.), *Beyond the Nation State: Human Rights in Times of Globalization.* Uppsala: Global Publications Foundation, 155–66.

Slim, Hugo 2002: *By What Authority? The Legitimacy and Accountability of Non-Governmental Organisations.* Geneva: International Council on Human Rights Policy.

Smith, Courtney B. 2006: *Politics and Process at the United Nations.* Boulder, CO: Lynne Rienner.

Soerensen, Bent 2001: CAT and Articles 20 and 22. In Gudmundur Alfredsson, Jonas Grimheden, Bertrand Ramcharan and Alfred de Zayas (eds), *International Human Rights Monitoring Mechanisms: Essays in Honour of Jakob Th. Möller.* The Hague: Nijhoff, 167–83.

Steiner, Henry 1998: Securing human rights. *Harvard Magazine*, September–October, http://www.harvardmag.com/so98/world3.html.

Steiner, Henry 2003: International protection of human rights. In Malcolm D. Evans (ed.), *International Law.* Oxford: Oxford University Press, 755–87.

Steiner, Henry, and Philip Alston 2000: *International Human Rights in Context: Law, Politics, Morals.* Oxford: Oxford University Press.

Strohal, Christian 1993: The United Nations responses to human rights violations. In Kathleen Mahoney and Paul Mahoney (eds), *Human Rights in the Twenty-First Century: A Global Challenge.* Dordrecht: Nijhoff, 347–60.

Strohal, Christian 1999: The development of the international human rights system by the United Nations. In Franz Cede and Lilly Sucharipa-Behrmann (eds), *The United Nations: Law and Practice.* The Hague: Kluwer, 157–76.

Sucharipa, Ernst, and Engelbert Theuermann 1997: The new United Nations and human rights: the human rights perspective in the integrated follow-up to United Nations conferences and in the UN reform process. *Austrian Review of International and European Law* 2, 239–59.

Sunga, Lyal S. 2001: The special procedures of the UN Commission on Human Rights: should they be scrapped? In Gudmundur Alfredsson, Jonas Grimheden, Bertrand Ramcharan and Alfred de Zayas (eds), *International Human Rights Monitoring Mechanisms: Essays in Honour of Jakob Th. Möller.* The Hague: Nijhoff, 233–77.

Swepston, Lee 2001: The International Labour Organization and human rights access to the ILO. In Gudmundur Alfredsson, Jonas Grimheden, Bertrand Ramcharan and Alfred de Zayas (eds), *International Human Rights Monitoring Mechanisms: Essays in Honour of Jakob Th. Möller.* The Hague: Nijhoff, 485–503.

Swepston, Lee 2003: The International Labour Organization's system of human rights protection. In Janusz Symonides (ed.), *Human Rights: International Protection, Monitoring, Enforcement.* Aldershot: Ashgate, 91–109.

Symonides, Janusz 2001a: UNESCO. In Gudmundur Alfredsson, Jonas Grimheden, Bertrand Ramcharan and Alfred de Zayas (eds), *International*

*Human Rights Monitoring Mechanisms: Essays in Honour of Jakob Th. Möller.* The Hague: Nijhoff, 505–20.

Symonides, Janusz 2001b: UNESCO's contribution to the progressive development of human rights. *Max Planck Yearbook of United Nations Law* 5, 307–40.

Szasz, Paul C. 2001: General law-making processes. In Edith Brown Weiss (ed.), *Paul Szasz: Selected Essays on Understanding International Institutions and Legislative Process.* Ardsley, NY: Transnational, 21–57.

Thakur, Ramesh 2001: Human rights: Amnesty International and the United Nations. In Paul Diehl (ed.), *The Politics of Global Governance: International Organizations in an Interdependent World.* Boulder, CO: Lynne Rienner, 365–87.

Thompson, Cecilia 2003: The United Nations Sub-Commission Working Group on Minorities: what protection for minority rights? In Morten Bergsmo (ed.), *Human Rights and Criminal Justice for the Downtrodden: Essays in Honour of Asbjorn Eide.* Leiden: Nijhoff, 513–36.

Tistounet, Eric 2000: The problem of overlapping among different treaty bodies. In Philip Alston and James Crawford (eds), *The Future of UN Human Rights Treaty Monitoring.* Cambridge: Cambridge University Press, 383–401.

Tolley, Howard, Jr. 1987: *The U.N. Commission on Human Rights.* Boulder, CO: Westview Press.

Tomasevski, Katarina 1993: The reform of the place of human rights in the World Health Organisation. In La Laguna University (ed.), *The Reform of International Institutions for the Protection of Human Rights.* Brussels: Bruylant, 185–212.

Tomuschat, Christian 2003: *Human Rights Between Idealism and Realism.* Oxford: Oxford University Press.

Trechsel, Stefan 2003: A world court for human rights? *Northwestern University Journal of International Human Rights* 1(3), http://www.law.northwestern.edu/journals/JIHR/v1/3.

UN (United Nations) 1992: *An Agenda for Peace.* Report of the United Nations Secretary-General, UN doc. A/47/277.

UN (United Nations) 1997: *Renewing the United Nations: A Programme for Reform.* Report of the United Nations Secretary-General, UN doc. A/51/950.

UN (United Nations) 2000: Report of the panel on United Nations peace operations, UN doc. A/55/305.

UN (United Nations) 2002: *Strengthening of the United Nations: An Agenda for Further Change.* Report of the United Nations Secretary-General, UN doc. A/57/387.

UN (United Nations) 2004: *A More Secure World: Our Shared Responsibility.* Report of the United Nations High-Level Panel on Threats, Challenges and Change, UN doc. A/59/565.

UN (United Nations) 2005: *In Larger Freedom.* Report of the United Nations Secretary-General, UN doc. A/59/565.

UNDP (United Nations Development Programme) 1998: *Integrating Human Rights with Sustainable Development*, http://www.undp.org/governance/docs/HR_Pub_policy5.htm.

UNDP (United Nations Development Programme) 2005: *Human Rights in UNDP: A Practice Note*, http://www.undp.org/governance/docs/HRPN_English.pdf.

UNHCR (United Nations High Commissioner for Refugees) 1997: *UNHCR and Human Rights: A Policy Paper*, http://www.unhcr.org/cgi-bin/texis/vtx/home/opendoc.pdf?tbl=RSDLEGAL&id=3ae6b332c.

UNHCR (United Nations High Commissioner for Refugees) 2003: *An Agenda for Protection* (3rd edn), http://www.unhcr.org/protect/PROTECTION/3e637b194.pdf.

UN High Commissioner for Human Rights (n.d.): *Complaints Procedure.* Fact Sheet No. 7/Rev.1, http://www.ohchr.org/english/about/publications/docs/fs7.htm

UN High Commissioner for Human Rights 2005a: *Human Rights and World Trade Agreements*, http://www.ohchr.org/english/about/publications/docs/WTO.pdf.

UN High Commissioner for Human Rights 2005b: *The OHCHR Plan of Action: Protection and Empowerment*, UN doc. 1/59/2005/Add.3.

UN High Commissioner for Human Rights 2005c: *HIV/AIDS: Stand up for Human Rights*, http://whqlibdoc.who.int/publications/2003/9241591145.pdf.

UN High Commissioner for Human Rights 2006: *High Commissioner's Strategic Management Plan 2006–2007*, http://www.ohchr.org/english/about/docs/strategic.pdf.

Valticos, Nicolas 1994: Once more about the ILO system of supervision: in what respect is it still a model? In Niels Blokker and Sam Muller (eds), *Towards More Effective Supervision by International Organizations.* Dordrecht: Nijhoff, 99–113.

Valticos, Nicolas 1998: International labour standards and human rights: approaching the year 2000. *International Labour Review* 137(2), 135–47.

van Boven, Theo 2003: 'Political' and 'legal' control mechanisms revisited. In Morten Bergsmo (eds), *Human Rights and Criminal Justice for the Downtrodden: Essays in Honour of Asbjorn Eide.* Leiden: Nijhoff, 539–53.

Vidar, Margret 2001: Approaching FAO. In Gudmundur Alfredsson, Jonas Grimheden, Bertrand Ramcharan and Alfred de Zayas (eds), *International Human Rights Monitoring Mechanisms: Essays in Honour of Jakob Th. Möller.* The Hague: Nijhoff, 521–4.

Walker, Simon 2005: Mainstreaming human rights in the WTO – making headway? In Michael Windfuhr (ed.), *Beyond the Nation State: Human Rights in Times of Globalization.* Uppsala: Global Publications Foundation, 75–95.

Weiss, T., E. Forsythe and R. Coate 1997: *The United Nations and Changing World Politics.* Oxford: Westview Press.

Weiss, Thomas G., and Leon Gordenker 1996: *NGOs, the UN, and Global Governance*. Boulder, CO: Lynne Rienner.

Welch, Claude E., Jr. 2001a: Introduction. In Claude E. Welch Jr. (ed.), *NGOs and Human Rights: Promise and Performance*. Philadelphia: University of Pennsylvania Press, 1–22.

Welch, Claude E., Jr. 2001b: Conclusion. In Claude E. Welch Jr. (ed.), *NGOs and Human Rights: Promise and Performance*. Philadelphia: University of Pennsylvania Press, 261–80.

Weschler, Joanna 2004: Human rights. In David M. Malone (ed.), *The UN Security Council: From the Cold War to the 21st Century*. Boulder, CO: Lynne Rienner, 55–68.

White, Nigel 1997: Accountability and democracy within the United Nations: a legal perspective. *International Relations* 13(6), 1–18.

White, Nigel 2002: *The United Nations System: Toward International Justice*. Boulder, CO: Lynne Rienner.

White, Nigel 2005: *The Law of International Organisations*. 2nd edn, Manchester: Manchester University Press.

WHO (World Health Organization) 2005: *Working Paper on Health and Human Rights Activities within WHO*, http://www.who.int/hhr/activities/Mapping%20HHRactivities%20in%20WHO%20_for%20website%2012%20Sept%202005.pdf.

Wiseberg, Laurie 2003: The role of non-governmental organisations (NGOs) for the protection and enforcement of human rights. In Janusz Symonides (ed.), *Human Rights: Protection, Monitoring, Enforcement*. Paris: UNESCO, 347–72.

Wolfensohn, James D. 2005: *Note from the President of the World Bank to the Development Committee, 12 April 2005*, http://siteresources.worldbank.org/DEVCOMMINT/Documentation/20446310/DC2005-0005(E)-PresNote.pdf.

Wolfrum, Rüdiger 1999: The Committee on the Elimination of Racial Discrimination. *Max Planck Yearbook of United Nations Law* 3, 489–519.

Wörgetter, Aloisia 1999: Gender issues in the United Nations. In Franz Cede and Lilly Sucharipa-Behrmann (eds), *The United Nations: Law and Practice*. The Hague: Kluwer, 177–93.

Yearbook of International Organizations 2004, http://www.uia.org/statistics/organizations/types-2004.pdf.

Young, Kirsten A. 2002: *The Law and Process of the U.N. Human Rights Committee*. Ardsley, NY: Transnational.

## Court Cases

Permanent Court of International Justice, *Questions Relating to Settlers of German Origin in Poland*: Advisory Opinion No. 6 (PCIJ, Ser. B., No. 5, 1923).

Permanent Court of International Justice, *Rights of Minorities in Upper Silesia (Minority Schools)*: Judgment No. 12 (PCIJ, Ser. A., No. 15, 1928).

Permanent Court of International Justice, *Treatment of Polish Nationals and Other Persons of Polish Origin or Speech in the Danzig Territory*: Advisory Opinion No. 23 (PCIJ, Ser. A./B., No. 44, 1932).

Permanent Court of International Justice, *Minority Schools in Albania*: Advisory Opinion No. 26 (PCIJ, Ser. A./B., No. 64, 1935).

International Court of Justice, *Reservations to the Convention on the Prevention and Punishment of the Crime of Genocide*, Advisory Opinion, ICJ Reports 1951, 15.

International Court of Justice, *Barcelona Traction, Light and Power Company, Limited*, Judgment, ICJ Reports 1970, 3.

International Court of Justice, *Legal Consequences for States of the Continued Presence of South Africa in Namibia (South West Africa) notwithstanding Security Council Resolution 276 (1970)*, Advisory Opinion, ICJ Reports 1971, 16.

International Court of Justice, *United States Diplomatic and Consular Staff in Tehran* (United States of America v. Iran), Provisional Measures, ICJ Reports 1979, 7.

International Court of Justice, *Military and Paramilitary Activities in and against Nicaragua* (Nicaragua v. United States of America), Provisional Measures, ICJ Reports 1984, 169.

International Court of Justice, *Applicability of Article VI, Section 22, of the Convention on the Privileges and Immunities of the United Nations*, Advisory Opinion, ICJ Reports 1989, 177.

International Court of Justice, *Legality of the Use by a State of Nuclear Weapons in Armed Conflict*, Advisory Opinion, ICJ Reports 1996, 66 and *Legality of the Threat or Use of Nuclear Weapons*, Advisory Opinion, ICJ Reports 1996, 226.

International Court of Justice, *Difference Relating to Immunity from Legal Process of a Special Rapporteur of the Commission on Human Rights*, Advisory Opinion, ICJ Reports 1999, 62.

International Court of Justice, *LaGrand* (Germany v. United States of America), Judgment, 2001, not yet published, http://www.icj-cij.org/.

International Court of Justice, *Arrest Warrant of 11 April 2000* (Democratic Republic of the Congo v. Belgium), Judgment, 2002, not yet published, http://www.icj-cij.org/.

International Court of Justice, *Avena and other Mexican Nationals* (Mexico v. United States of America), Judgment, 2004, not yet published, http://www.icj-cij.org/.

International Court of Justice, *Legal Consequences of the Construction of a Wall in the Occupied Palestinian Territory*, Advisory Opinion, 2004, not yet published, http://www.icj-cij.org/.

International Court of Justice, *Armed Activities on the Territory of the Congo* (Democratic Republic of the Congo v. Rwanda), Judgment, 2006, not yet published, http://www.icj-cij.org/.

International Court of Justice, *Application of the Convention on the Prevention and Punishment of Genocide* (Bosnia and Herzegovina v. Serbia and Montenegro), Judgment, 2006, not yet published, http://www.icj-cij.org/.

# INDEX